Munster, Indiana
A Centennial History

Proceeds from the sale of this book will benefit the

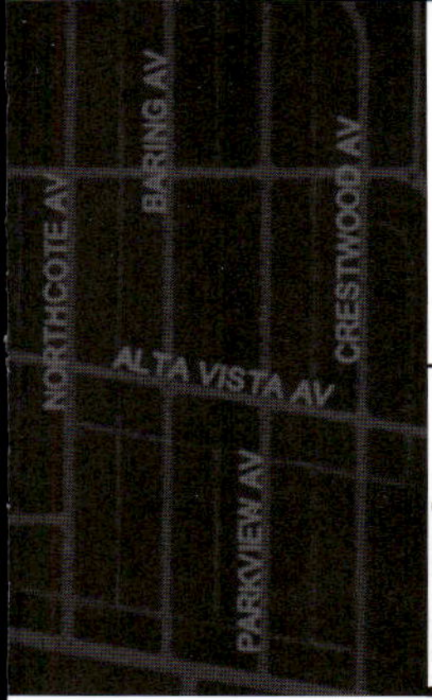

Munster, Indiana
A Centennial History

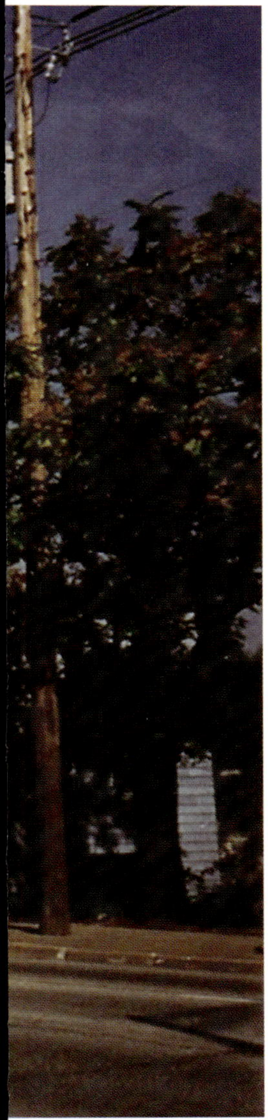

by
Lance Trusty

Illustrations and Captions Collected and Prepared
by
Kenneth J. Schoon

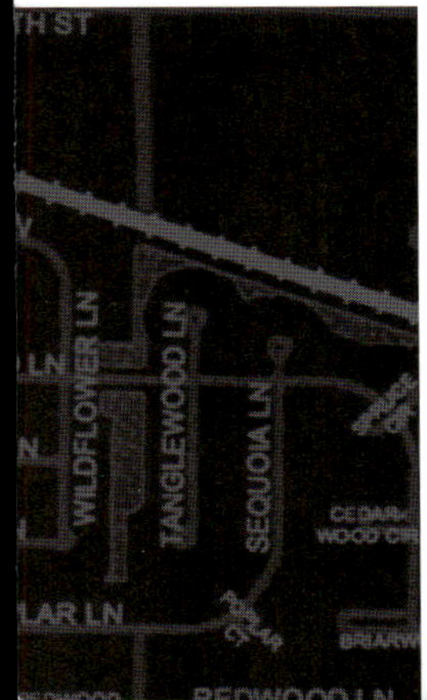

Dedication: To Jan, the power behind the drone.

Copyright © 2006 by the Munster Civic Foundation
1005 Ridge Road
Munster, IN 46321

All rights reserved, including the right to reproduce this work in any form whatsoever without permission in writing from the publisher, except for brief passages in connection with a review. For information, please write:

The Donning Company Publishers
184 Business Park Drive, Suite 206
Virginia Beach, VA 23462

Steve Mull, *General Manager*
Barbara B. Buchanan, *Office Manager*
Richard A. Horwege, *Senior Editor*
Stephanie Danko, *Graphic Designer*
Mellanie Denny, *Imaging Artist*
Debbie Dowell, *Project Research Coordinator*
Scott Rule, *Director of Marketing*
Tonya Hannick, *Marketing Coordinator*

G. Bradley Martin, *Project Director*

Library of Congress Cataloging-in-Publication Data
Trusty, Lance.
 Munster, Indiana : a centennial history / by Lance Trusty ; illustrations and captions collected and prepared by Kenneth J. Schoon.
   p.   cm.
 Includes bibliographical references and index.
   ISBN 978-1-57864-386-8 (hardcover : alk. paper)
 1. Munster (Ind.)—History. 2. Munster (Ind.)—History—Pictorial works. I. Schoon, Kenneth J. II. Title.
  F534.M93T77 2006
  977.2'99—dc22
                                    2006034063

Printed in the USA by Walsworth Publishing Company

War bonds parade proceeded down Ridge Road. (MHS photo)

Title page: Ridge Road showing the Klootwyk General Store.

Contents page: "Viet Nam" at the Community Veterans Memorial.

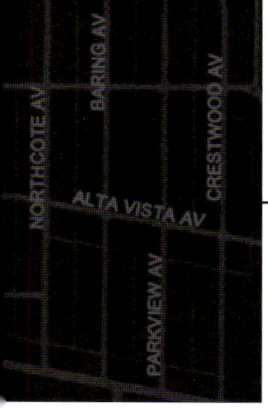

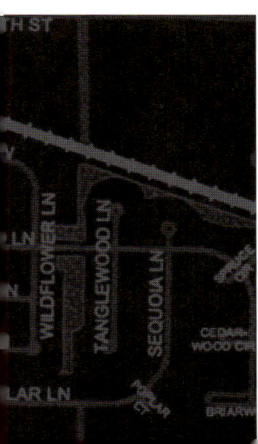

Table of Contents

Acknowledgements	8
CHAPTER I	
Munster Today	10
CHAPTER II	
The Land	22
CHAPTER III	
The Struggle for the Land	26
CHAPTER IV	
Settlement Time	32
CHAPTER V	
The Wooden Shoe Years, 1850–1907	42
CHAPTER VI	
The New Town	60
CHAPTER VII	
From War to War, 1917–1941	80
CHAPTER VIII	
War and Peace, 1941–1950	102
CHAPTER IX	
The Busy 1950s	118
CHAPTER X	
The Fast-Growing 1960s	134
CHAPTER XI	
And Still More Expansion, 1970–1980	150
CHAPTER XII	
Modern Suburb, 1980–2000	164
CHAPTER XIII	
Munster Institutions	182
Bibliography	216
Index	218
About the Authors	224

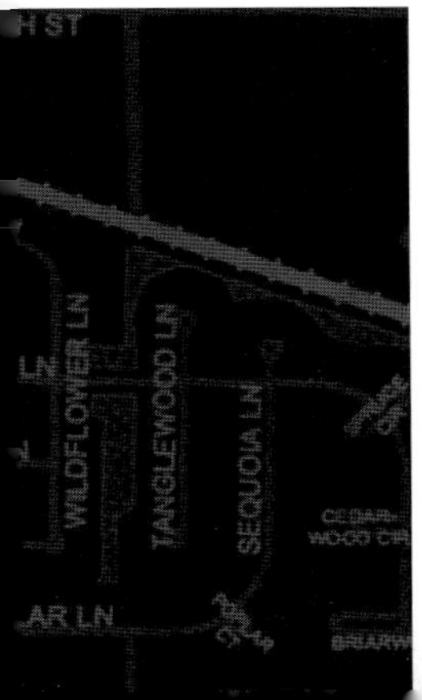

Acknowledgments

THIS HAS BEEN A REWARDING TASK. I HAVE BEEN HELPED BY MANY. DIANE Hansen, a stellar graduate student in History at Purdue University Calumet with the brains and creativity of an Einstein and the ability to dig things up that might shame a badger, was essential in finding and verifying information, and was very nice about putting up with the author's foibles. Much of the basic research was done over the years by students in my seminars at Purdue. You know who you are: you did well. Ken Schoon read my manuscript with a keen eye, and helped me avoid many boners. I am grateful to the Munster Centennial Committee and the Munster Civic Foundation for their support. Mary Alice Martin and Frank Darrington provided the names of those who died in World War II and Vietnam. Tom DeGuilio and Bob O'Shaughnessy bailed me out of several holes I dug by myself. And kudos to Margaret S. "Peg" Schoon, a master indexer.

I grudgingly accept responsibility for all errors. Happy Centennial!

Lance Trusty

Many thanks to all those who donated photographs and helped with photograph identification: Robert Boyle, Larry Brechner, Zbigniew Bzdak, Calumet Regional Archives, Robert Cashman, Citizen's Financial Bank, Community Foundation, Rhonda Damjanovich, Frank Darrington and Galaxy Arts, Daughters of the American Revolution, First Reformed Church of Lansing, James Ghrist, Don and Nancy Johnson, Emil and Ruby Dufala, Helen Engstrom, Ronald Feldner, John Friend, Gary Public Library, Bill Hasse, Sue Hendrickson, Indiana Historical Society, Steve and Kathy Kennedy, Diane Kitchell, Fred Klooster, LaPorte County Historical Society, Betty Leibert Lukoshus, Barbara Meeker, Sylvester Meeter, Larry Mickow Jr. and the Northwest Indiana Symphony Orchestra, Margaret Morris, Munster Chamber of Commerce, Munster Christian Reformed Church, Munster Fire Department, Munster High School Athletic Department, Munster Historical Society (MHS), Munster Lions Club, Munster Parks and Recreation, Munster Police Department, Ted Muta Advertising, Paula Nellans, Herman Paepke, Shirl Pawlowski, People's Bank, PepsiAmericas, Ashley Porta, Gloria Rudzinski, Debbie and Shirley Schmueser, School Town of Munster, Lois Schoon, Pearl Schoon, David and JoAnne Shafer, George Shinken, Russell Snyder, South Holland Historical Society, Mark Stanek, Three Floyds, Tim Swan, the *Munster Times*, John and Sally Trent, Robert Trusty, Edward Verklan, Westminster Presbyterian Church, Carmen White, and Martha Wilke. Photos without credits were taken by me.

Ken Schoon

Ridge Garden Center

CHAPTER 1

Munster Today

THE TOWN OF MUNSTER, INDIANA, CELEBRATED its centennial in 2007. It occupied 7.6 square miles of the earth's surface, unchanged since the town was incorporated in 1907. Its official 2000 population count was 21,511, and three years later was estimated at 22,135, and probably passed 23,000 as the town celebrated its centennial. Half were Indiana natives. Eight percent of the town's residents had been born abroad, about evenly divided between European and Asian origins. Five percent had Dutch ancestors; one in five, German, one in five, Polish. Fourteen percent described themselves as Irish.

The town enjoyed many assets. Its median income in 2000 was $63,243; three thousand families earned over $60,000 in a year. Income distribution was fairly even, clustered around $50,000; few were very rich, even fewer, in poverty. The educational level of the population was remarkable. Four in ten held a bachelor's degree, and 16 percent had earned either a graduate or a professional degree. Employment statistics were equally remarkable. In 2000, one in four worked in health, education, or social services. Sixteen percent worked in manufacturing, 11 percent in retailing. Unemployment was minimal, except among teenagers in fear of finding a summer job.

Munster Centennial Poster, commissioned in honor of the Munster 2007 Centennial was designed and painted by Mitch Markovitz.

While retaining its middle class and family-centered outlook, Munster was becoming more culturally diverse. The black population remained below the state average, while the Hispanic percentage was above that mark. Munster folk were getting along in years; the average age was well above the Indiana norm. The crime rate was about half the national average. Murders were rare, assaults and robberies slightly more common. Burglary, auto thefts, and larceny levels were hardly "big city" style, but seemed endemic. Munster, Indiana, wasn't exactly a young person's idea of heaven, but it certainly suited most residents.

Munster, though almost "full," was still a growing community. Between 1996 and 2004, over 700 single-family homes had been built at a steady pace, although 1996, when 120 new homes were completed, was particularly busy. Between 2000 and 2006, over 1,000 homes were built. The average cost of a new home rose in those years from $227,000 to well over $300,000. The average value of an existing home was over $160,000 in 2000. Nearly all new homes were built in the far south side; almost none were built north of Forty-fifth Street.

Over eight thousand "residential units" were occupied in 2000. Half carried a mortgage. The mansion age had arrived: by 2007, there were dozens of million-dollar-plus homes in town, and perhaps a hundred homes valued at a half million to one million. Nearly two thousand homes were in the $200,000–$500,000 range. Munster had far fewer renters—seven hundred in 2000—than most Indiana towns, but town homes and condos were a growing part of the new housing stock.

Town Government

Town Councilors were still "civic volunteers" and paid $11,000 per year, up from $5,200 in the 1980s. Voters seemed more interested in good town services than partisanship. Cooperation among town officials continued, with little reference to political parties, except at election time. The primaries revealed an odd contradiction for a purportedly Republican town: more Democrats than Republicans were registered. But many voters crossed over in November, because the personal qualities of the candidates were more important than party affiliation. Those who held offices revealed no sharp party lines, and no hard-edged competing ideologies.

Munster Centennial Logo, designed by Ted Muta.

The Nancy and Michael Harrigan House at 1547 Ridge Road, one of the houses featured in the Munster Flower Garden Series, a collection of paintings of Munster gardens by Kim Johnson Belange and Mike Daumer.

In 2002 the Town Council was divided evenly on party lines, which pleased few. The solution was reasonable and practical: redistrict to five wards. The 2000 census already required a realignment of wards, and it seemed easier to make five, to end tie votes on the Council.

The question was placed on a referendum in November 2002, with cool support from existing Councilors. It passed with a narrow 51–49 percent margin. Democrats generally voted yes, Republicans, no. Things weren't quite as civic leader Sid Rothstein observed, with a wink, "It's still the town of integrity. We have no faults."

In 2004 Councilors began a practice of mingling with citizens before formal meetings, to answer questions and share information. That muted complaints over an established practice that required citizens to wait until all official business had been transacted before being heard. It was a sensible and democratic solution.

A statewide property tax dustup paralyzed town budgets for years after 2001. The "chaos" made planning impossible. Budgets covered essentials, and a number of smaller projects were completed. Schoon Ditch was again cleaned out. Several new traffic signals were installed, sewers were improved and storm/sewer separation continued. Three small parks were opened in 2001. Calumet Avenue was widened and given turn lanes, while other street projects were shelved for lack of financial certainty. The old Public Works Building on Fisher was demolished in 2001, and a new building replaced it in 2002. A new pumping station was installed at River Bend.

The prospect of a railroad underpass at Forty-fifth Street and Calumet tantalized everyone. As many as fifty trains a day passed by, and made rush hour—yes, Munster now had rush hours—contemplation time. Many had moved to Munster to escape just that. But by 2000 there was housing on both sides of the tracks, and plenty of traffic. But the project would cost around $50 million. Real money! Studies were underway, but Washington was cool to writing a check for construction costs.

The ancient bugaboo of amalgamation revived in 2003, when the mayor of East Chicago proposed a union of all North Township communities. That brought a "collective sigh" from Munster residents. Another, and valuable, old custom: the town still followed the 1938 Master Plan, with updates. The town budget, over $25 million in 2003, was delivered in a three-hundred-page book.

Privatization affected town government in several ways. Ambulance service was "outplaced." A Solid Waste Committee studied trash removal, and concluded that it, too, could be privatized. The Council agreed, and signed a contract in 2002 with Illiana of Crown Point. Six members of the town crew were absorbed into other posts, and eight were terminated. The outcome made little visible difference to ordinary citizens, but some good town jobs disappeared.

By 2006 the town had twenty-two large and small parks, and one more, Centennial Park, in the works. In 2003 Ridgeway Park was renamed in honor of Patrolman Robert S. Grove.

Munster High School Band at the Independence Day Parade, July 4, 2006.

Sounds at Sunset is a series of six concerts each summer held at the Gazebo at Heritage Park. Is there a nicer way to spend a Sunday evening?

Munster's annual Blues, Jazz, and Fine Arts Festival is the largest Blues/Jazz Festival Southeast of Chicago.

Prom night at Heritage Park. The Gazebo near the corner of Ridge and Columbia has become a popular place for weddings and celebratory photographs. (Photo courtesy of Ashley Porta)

Few major new residential developments were initiated after 2000, while established ones continued to fill out. One major project was on White Oak south of Forty-fifth Street, on conjoined sites owned by Parks and Recreation, the Civic Foundation, the School Town, and Mercantile National Bank. The plan was to build seventy larger homes on thirty acres. ATG's Wildwood Condominium project on Forty-fifth Street was approved in 2002. Other than the Lansing Country Club Golf Course, Munster now had little open land to build on.

Munster had become an exceptional suburb in another sense: many residents actually worked in town. More typical was the mass commuter syndrome to the core city. "Drive to work" times reported in the 2000 census suggested that perhaps five thousand residents worked in or near town. Deep analysis might conclude that many who worked in Munster industries commuted from elsewhere.

The largest retailing event in town after 2000 was the reconstruction of the Calumet Shopping Center. The entire Montgomery Ward Company foundered in 2001, and all its stores were closed. For two years the anchor store at the south end of the Calumet Shopping Center stood empty. Smaller stores in the mall limped along. Target's negotiations with the town and with property owners produced tax abatement, and the company decided to build a store on site. The entire south end of the mall was demolished; in its place emerged a $4 million, 123,000 square foot "big box." Target's new store opened in July 2004, with almost two hundred employees.

In 2005 Munster had thirty-two large and small industrial concerns, providing 16 percent of all the jobs in town. Some were quite large: the largest, *Northwest Indiana Times,* employed around 500. PepsiAmericas employed 325, Munster Steel and Star Case, 60 each, Rockwell Automation, 75, and Town and Country Industries, 51. The remainder was small, employing between 1 and 50. By any standard it was a remarkably strong and varied industrial base for any small town.

Munster's medical establishment had evolved into a major humanitarian and economic center. Far and away its largest element was Community Hospital. One job in four in town was either medical or educational. In 2006, several hospitals, twenty-six clinics, many office groups, associations, and medical centers provided services. At least four hundred medical professionals, fifty-eight dentists, and four veterinarians either lived or practiced in town.

Target, the new anchor of the Calumet Shopping Center.

PepsiAmericas' colorful silos facing Calumet Avenue advertise a longtime, community-minded Munster business. (PepsiAmericas photo)

Munster never developed a true downtown, but few minded that, since hundreds of small businesses were in operation after 2000. A second shopping area had emerged along the east end of Forty-fifth Street. In 2006, by one count, there were 173 retail and service stores, mostly groceries, banks, hardware stores, and the like, but few "destination" stores. Avid shoppers bent on chasing down the really good stuff still drove to Southlake Mall or Chicago.

All those new places made it easy to spend money. In 2005 Milne Supply expanded onto a two-acre site with a new retail store, warehouse, and an eight-unit retail mall. Hampton Inn and Suites opened in 2005, the first motel built in town in a half century. Bank branches and even headquarters proliferated. Citizens Financial Bank came to town in 1973 with a new branch on Forty-fifth Street, bought First Federal Savings in 1983, and moved its corporate headquarters to the existing building on Ridge Road in 1994. A large new building beside the Peoples Bank branch on Columbia Avenue became corporate headquarters in 2000. Locally owned Centier Bank opened a branch in 2000 on White Oak at Forty-fifth. Even Illinois banks came to town, including one from Hegewisch.

A variety of restaurants, ranging from chain and fast food places to locally owned, upscale dining spots prospered. Giovanni's and Café Elise, which had opened in 1998, continued to thrive. No one starved for lack of good pizza. Schoop's evolved into the Mother House of a chain of clones in five states. The Munster Walgreens on Forty-fifth Street was replaced by a stand-alone store on Calumet Avenue near the hospital. Walgreens' former store became an Ace Hardware.

Oddly enough, after Munster carefully separated business, residences, and industry for years, a modern idea of blending things became a virtue in the form of the Planned Unit Development, or PUD. The town fathers agreed to rezone eighteen acres north of the Lake Business Center on Calumet for "mixed" retail and residential use. On the western end of the tract, Cambridge Court, an extended circle of nineteen two-story condos, was sandwiched between Fisher and the Lake Business Center. The new Hampton Inn was built at the east end, along with the new Walgreens and Charlie's Ale House.

Citizens Financial Bank has had its corporate offices in this building at 707 Ridge Road since February of 1994. (Citizens Financial photo)

Peoples Bank Corporate Center was constructed in 2003 to hold its corporate headquarters. Designed by architect Robert Priesol to match the 1985 Munster Branch Office next door, its construction created a handsome two-acre campus on Fran-Lin Parkway at Columbia.

Community Hospital, the center of Munster's medical community and the town's largest employer. (MHS photo donated by Community Hospital)

Munster Chamber of Commerce Board in 2006: Front: Belinda Lopez and Elizabeth DeBolt; Second row: Karen Maravilla, Nancy Trimboli, Dianne Kowalski, and Charles Gessert; back row: Craig Harrell, Melanie Dunajeski, Donald Erminger, Executive Director Rhonda Damianovich, President Michael McIntyre, and James Foster. (Chamber photo)

The Center for Visual and Performing Arts is home to the Munster Chamber of Commerce, South Shore Arts, Theatre at the Center, Muncab (Cable TV), Villa Catering, and the Northwest Indiana Symphony Orchestra and Chorus. (CVPA photo)

John Higley and Janie Wilson, played the lead rolls in *The King and I*. (Photo by Larry Brechner)

The King and I was a community theatre production performed in June 2006, at Munster High School as a benefit for the Samaritan Counseling Center. Here Anna teaches the royal Siamese children. (Photo by Larry Brechner)

Finian's Rainbow, produced in 1997, is one of many musicals produced at the Theatre at the Center, which uses local and professional actors. (Photo by Larry Brechner)

18 • MUNSTER, INDIANA: A CENTENNIAL HISTORY

In 2006 Munster was home to five public and two parochial schools. The School Town operated one high school, one middle school, and three elementary schools, and employed almost two hundred teachers. The student-teacher ratio was 17:1. Enrollment was 3,782 in 2000 and 4,221 in 2005. Academic excellence was visible: in the 1990s, nearly all graduates pursued some form of post–high school education, many with National Merit and other Scholarships.

The cost of a school modernization plan proposed at the end of 2000 was projected at a startling $45 million, and passed with little public opposition. That was a surprising outcome after a major high school updating had cost about the same amount just a few years earlier. The central question was whether to rebuild or replace Elliott and Eads Schools. A careful study found that remodeling would cost almost as much as building entirely new structures, and yield less desirable results.

Architect Dan Szany was commissioned to design one building suitable for both elementary schools. The result was a pair of seventy-two-thousand-square-foot structures with a large central corridor and four diamond-shaped pods containing classrooms. Noisy stuff—music room, gym, and multipurpose room—was sequestered at one end of the building, away from academic space. The design was made with security and safety in mind: the office was given a clear view of all four entrances. Cameras were mounted on walls. Provision was made for distance learning.

The new buildings cost almost $10 million apiece; the total expenditure was $25 million. The general contractor was Gil Behling and Son of Hammond. The new Eads School opened in 2003. The old Eads School became, at least temporarily, an Early Child Development Center, and housed the West Lake Special

---

Fiddler on the Roof was produced at Munster High School in May of 2000 and directed by Dr. Tim Bartlett. Here, Tevye (Brandon Sweeney), his family, and the whole village of Anatevka sing "The Sabbath Prayer" at sundown. (Photo by Larry Brechner)

The New Eads Elementary School opened in 2003.

Education Preschool and some classes. Long-term, it would either be demolished or become a community center. Elliott School was demolished; in its place in 2005 emerged a new, state-of-the art Elliott School.

Frank Hammond School enrollment had blossomed from seven hundred in 1991 to nearly a thousand in 2004. Hammond School was remodeled, expanded, and updated in 2003. In 2004 Wilbur Wright Middle School added a twenty-three-thousand-square-foot gym, nine classrooms, and more office space. The original bus barn in back was demolished to make room for construction of the new wing. A new bus barn was built on Indiana Parkway in the industrial park on fifteen acres at a cost of $3.2 million.

No plans were afoot for any major projects in 2006. The Munster public schools had finally reached equilibrium. All schools held Four Star and Blue Ribbon ratings. In 2006 just over fifteen hundred students attended Munster High School, which remained a remarkable capstone to the system. MHS was nationally ranked in several categories, its students placed well above average in ISTEP (Indiana Statewide Testing for Educational Programs) scores, and nearly all continued their educations.

Munster's elementary schools offered advanced curricula and facilities, including a Title I program, programs for math and reading, a school psychologist, resource teachers for those with disabilities, aides for special education students, and tutorial services.

Those who argued that public education had failed needed to look at Munster schools.

The two parochial schools continued to thrive. St. Thomas More School was the largest in the diocese, with 567 students. St. Paul's Lutheran School educated over 400 in grades K–8.

Towns, like people, have a life cycle. By its hundredth birthday, Munster had completed its transformation from farm village to suburb. In 2006 it was a mature residential community, with some characteristics of a small city. Munster remained a residential community above all, but with a nice salting and peppering of retail businesses and clean industries. The town still enjoys freedom from abrasive political factionalism. Fine people serve on boards and commissions. Citizens were pleased with their honest and efficient small government and municipal services that might be the envy of any community. Nice homes, great schools, excellent parks, and interesting and rewarding employment all added up to a remarkable quality of life. But things weren't always that way.

Elected Town officials, 2006: Back row: John Edington, David Nellans, Michael Mellon; front row, Clerk-Treasurer David Shafer, Helen Brown, and Rob Mangus. (Town Council photo.)

The Polish Pilgrimage is an annual event in which up to five thousand Catholics, most of them of Polish descent, walk from the South Side of Chicago to Merrillville. On the way these pilgrims stay for the night at Munster's Carmelite Monastery on Ridge Road. That night, monastery grounds are transformed into a huge campground and a place of prayer and singing. Here pilgrims ascend on their knees to the Thirteenth Station of the Cross. (Photo by Zbigniew Bzdak)

CHAPTER I MUNSTER TODAY • 21

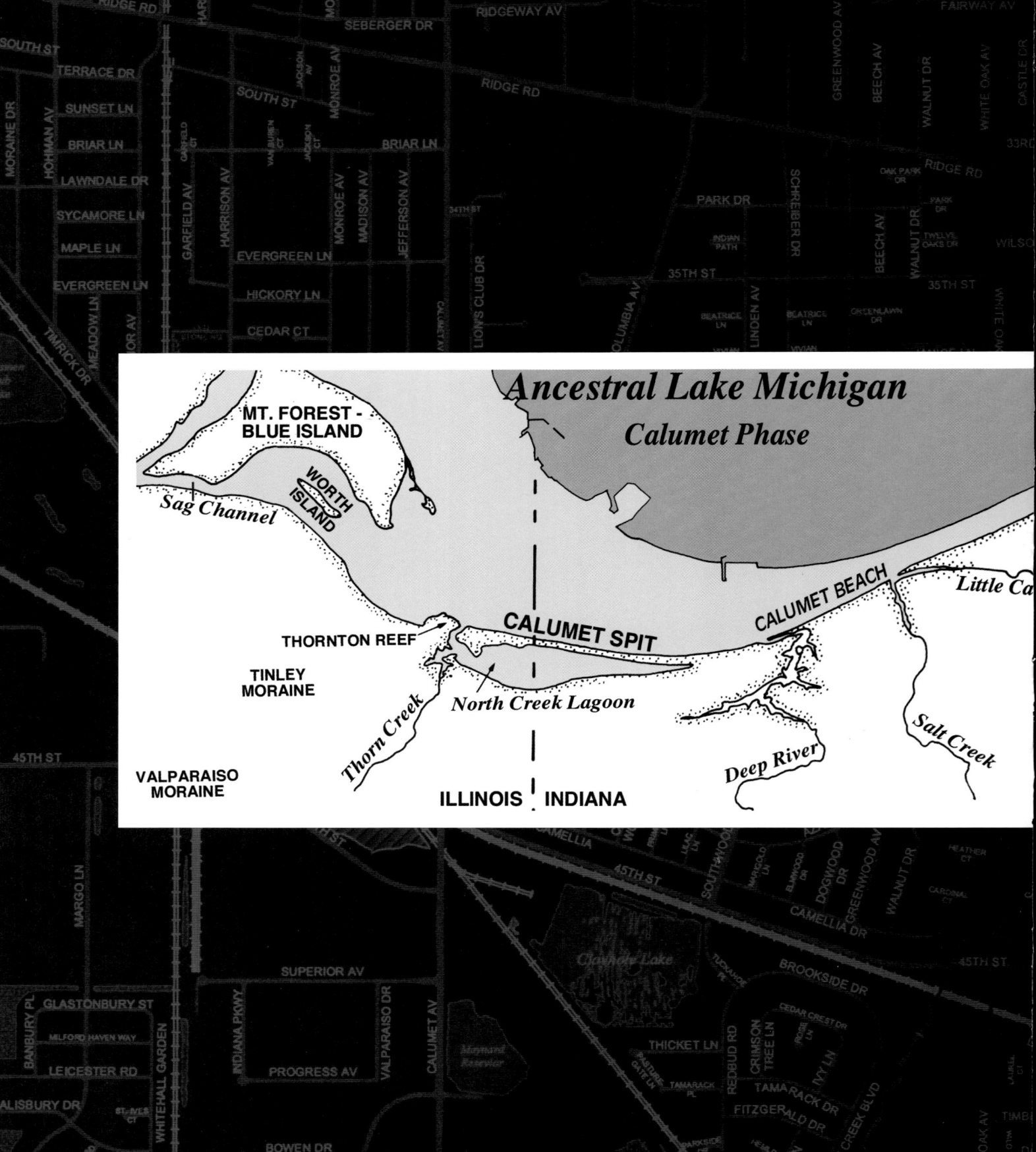

CHAPTER II

The Land

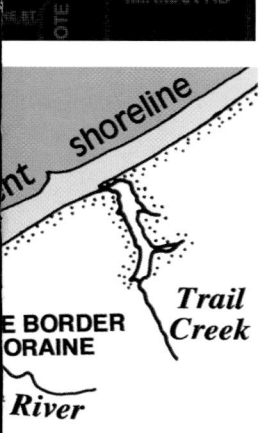

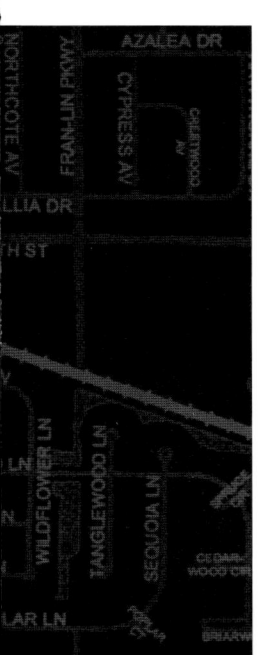

FEW PLACES IN THE MIDWEST SEEMED LESS suitable for human habitation than the site of the future Town of Munster, Indiana. Much of its north side was the flood plain of a sluggish, unpredictable little stream. To the south, a broad marsh offered sanctuary to insects, wildfowl, and smaller mammals. Midtown, a sandy ridge ran east-to-west. In time, the busy hands and machines of man would convert those wetlands into one of the Midwest's more attractive suburban towns.

Munster is part of the Calumet Region, which parallels the southern shore of Lake Michigan from Illinois to Michigan City in Indiana. Its southern boundary is a low, glacial headland. The Region's dominant natural features were shallow, meandering streams, mostly destined to carry some variation of the name Calumet; dunes; oak openings and pine islands; and swamps. Except for one band of rich soil in mid-county, the area offered little of interest to farmers, or anyone else.

About 11,500 years ago, during Lake Michigan's Calumet Phase, the waves and currents of the lake built up a sand peninsula or "spit." Today Ridge Road is built upon that old sandy feature. (Adapted from Chrzastowski and Thompson, 1992)

That landscape was geologically new. In the Paleozoic Era, the area lay under an ancient sea and, later, lush swamps. Glaciers later buried that terrain under thick deposits of rock and soil. The Wisconsin Glacier, the last of those moving sheets of ice, first scoured the landscape, then, only twelve to fourteen thousand years ago, as the climate warmed, melted away to the north. In its wake lay the Great Lakes and the Calumet.

As that last glacier paused some fifteen miles south of the present Lake Michigan, it deposited a "stillstand" known to geologists as the Valparaiso Moraine. Topped with rich soil, it follows the southern shore of Lake Michigan, arcing northeasterly from Illinois through Crown Point and Valparaiso and on into Michigan. Seventeen miles wide in Lake County, the Valparaiso Moraine is a modest continental divide. Waters to its north flow eastward through the Great Lakes and on to the Atlantic Ocean. To its south the Kankakee River flows toward the Mississippi.

The Great Lakes were the most visible product of the glaciers. Lake Michigan was originally about sixty feet above current lake level, and drained westward toward the Mississippi. Over the centuries, the Great Lakes opened different paths to the seas, and surface levels dropped time and again. Route 30 in Dyer follows the shoreline of the Glenwood Stage, Lake Chicago's first and highest level. A second shoreline, the Calumet Stage, emerged around 11,000 B.C. about thirty-five feet above modern Lake Michigan. The shoreline of a third stage, the Tolleston, today is followed by 169th Street in Hammond. Finally, about two hundred years ago, Lake Michigan reached its present level.

Munster's sandy Ridge was the shoreline of the Calumet stage. The rest of the town is former lake bottom nestled between the Ridge and the Glenwood and the Tolleston shorelines. The unpredictable Little Calumet River and Cady Marsh were also by-products of the lake's retreats.

Humans changed these watery entities to suit themselves. Late in the nineteenth century Aaron Norton Hart cut through the Ridge and drained Plum Creek into the Little Calumet. Cady Marsh dried up into farmland, and, later, homesites. A second project that shaped Munster was completed as recently as 1926. Until then the Little Calumet grew *Big* several times a year. Chicago magnate Randall Burns, the owner of some twelve hundred acres of Calumet Region swampland, sliced a mile-long channel through the lakefront dunes, drained the Little Calumet into Lake Michigan, and dried up another marshland. Quite impossible under today's environmental standards, that bold project partially tamed the unruly Little Cal, earned Burns a handsome profit, and fattened the tax rolls. And so Munster became—usually—dry, and eminently habitable.

North of Ridge Road from about Tapper Avenue eastward is a steep slope or "scarp." It is believed that Lake Michigan waters eroded the slope after the Calumet Phase was over. (Photo published by State Geologist Willis Blatchley in 1897)

Geologic map of the Munster area that shows the three ancient shorelines of Lake Michigan.

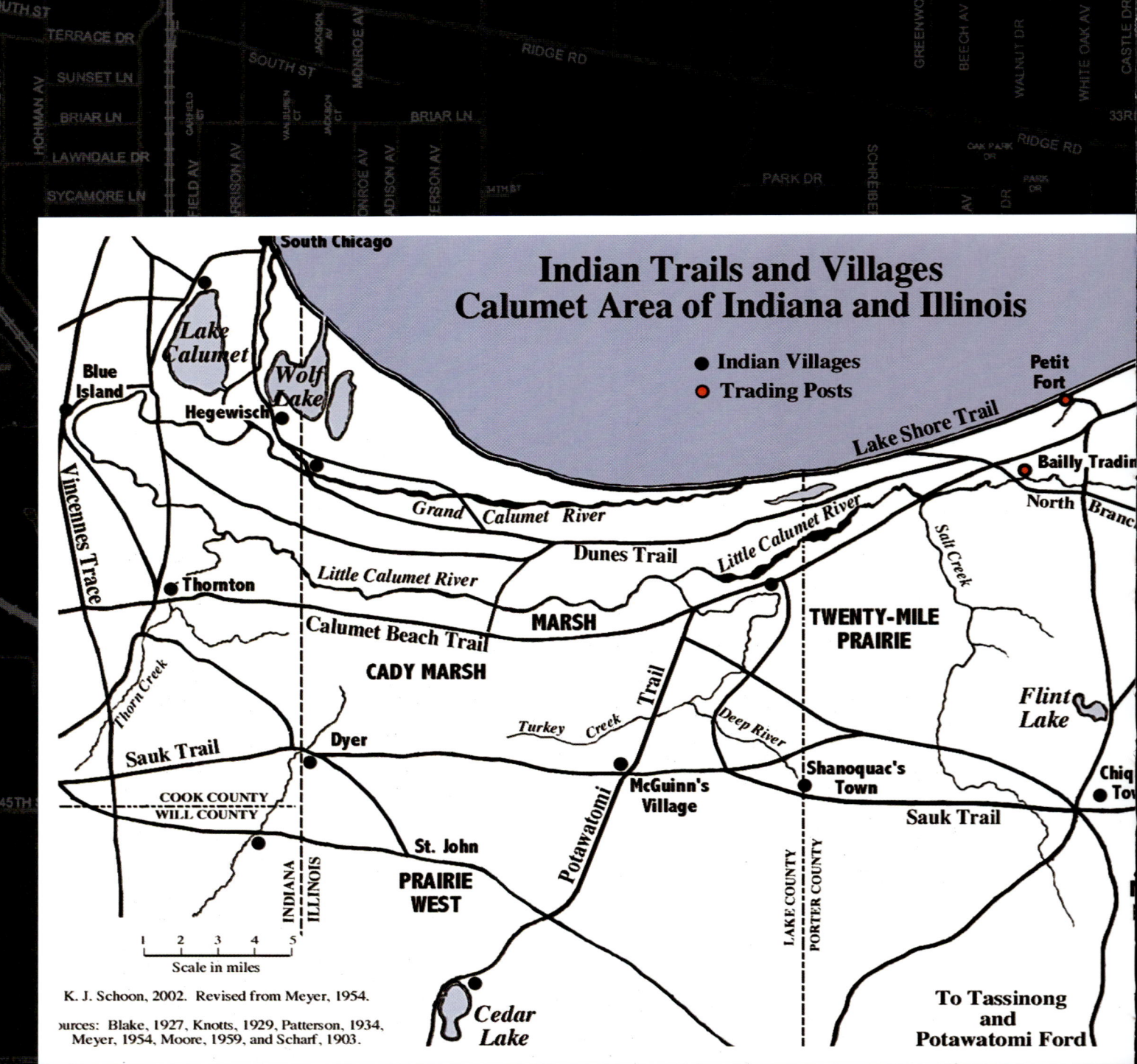

CHAPTER III

A Struggle for the Land

THE FUTURE STATE OF INDIANA MIGHT WELL have ended up in Spanish, French, or British hands, or, just possibly, remained in the possession of Native Americans. European wars that started one way and often ended otherwise determined the eventual outcome. But nothing was inherently in the cards.

The First Settlers

Archaeologists know little about the first humans in the New World. Around fifteen—or more—thousand years ago the misnamed "Indians" crossed over a land bridge from Siberia to Alaska, and fanned out over the Americas. Scholars trace their transformation from "Archaic" wandering hunters into more settled "Woodland Indians." Some of the later peoples are known as "Mound Builders."

By A.D. 1000 the bow and arrow had made them the terror of the animals. Now the tribesmen raised corn, beans, and squashes, made fine pots, and worked stone and copper. When the Europeans arrived, the more advanced Mississippian culture was living in villages and large towns, cultivating extensive field crops, and making excellent ceramics.

Indian trails afforded early settlers the best routes through the region. Ridge Road still follows the old Calumet Beach Trail.

The Potawatomi, "Keepers of the Council Fire," are closely identified with the Calumet. They lived far to the East when Champlain met them in 1616. Originally a tribe of some 3–4,000 people with close ties to the Ottawa and Ojibway or Chippewa, they were forest-oriented Algonquians. The Potawatomi built comfortable lodges, farmed, trapped, hunted, fished, and gathered wild berries, rice, and nuts. Governed by councils of elders, they practiced polygamy and an animist religion. Explorers and traders found them a good-humored, affable people.

But under pressure from the Iroquois and other tribes, the Potawatomi migrated westward. In 1714, after meeting fierce plains Indians, they moved eastward, and settled in former Miami lands around southern Lake Michigan. For better or worse, they welcomed, rather than fought, Western explorers, traders, and then settlers. Business-minded fellows, the Potawatomi prospered as middlemen in the western fur trades.

In the Midwest the Potawatomi were divided into over thirty clans. Six of their hundred villages were in the Calumet. Two of the larger ones were along the future state line, in Dyer, and along the Grand Calumet River. One of their many trails followed the Ridge. They summered in villages and wintered in small groups along the Kankakee.

Nice people, awful politicians: between 1750 and 1815 they allied themselves with the losers in every war: other tribes, the Spanish, and the French in the French and Indian War. Next they helped the British in the Revolution, and—a final mistake—joined the British in the War of 1812.

Afterward, the Potawatomi faced a fast-expanding and unforgiving United States. The Potawatomi were compelled to sign land-cession "treaties," and live on a federal dole until they were sent westward. Their Trails of Tears ended in Missouri, Kansas, where many still dwell, and Oklahoma. Little evidence of the Potawatomi is visible in the modern Calumet, but buried beneath the sandy Ridge in Munster are bones, potsherds, spearpoints, and arrowheads aplenty.

Under Four Flags

The Seven Years or French and Indian War placed the heartland of North America in the balance. Great Britain's thirteen North American colonies held thinly supported claims to the West. Spain claimed—however weakly—the Midwest, by right of prior discovery. Mighty France, long established in both Canada and Louisiana, argued that those same lands were hers. French claims to Indiana were supported by a few wilderness forts—at Ouiatenon, near Lafayette, Kekionga (Fort Wayne, later), Post Vincennes, Petite Fort on the lakeshore, and Fort St. Joseph—and a few trade routes linking Quebec with Louisiana. Not unreasonably, the Indian nations thought the land was theirs, by right of ancient settlement.

This stone axe was found in the sand by John Haimbaugh as workers were excavating near his parents' home on Greenwood Avenue.

Indian points collected by Neil Tanis on his farm south of Ridge Road west of Calumet Avenue.

Shabonna, an Ottawa and Potawatomi chief, was best known as the "Peace Chief." He visited several of the early inns and so it is likely that he was a guest at the Gibson Inn or Brass Tavern. Shabonna continued to dress in leggings and moccasins even after his daughters had adopted European dress. (Gary Public Library photo)

The Brits won game, set, and match in the French and Indian War. French claims to North America were terminated. Canada and the Ohio Country came under the British flag. Louisiana and the far west went to Spain, which did little more than occupy New Orleans and St. Louis, and maintain trades along the lower Mississippi.

Mother Britain's hard line with the tribes sent many into rebellion and forced the Crown to close the West to American settlers. Even so, Virginia retained her ancient claim to the lands that would one day become Indiana. Explorers and traders streamed into the Ohio Country after 1765, and westbound farmers simply ignored the Crown.

The American Revolution changed everything. The rebellious colonies insisted on their titles to the West, and dueled with the British for Indian support. The Indians held little love for either side, but clearly understood what was happening. Their tribal fragmentation and ancient rivalries made it impossible for them to influence the outcome.

The conduct of that war in the Midwest was heroic enough, but, given the stakes, small potatoes. George Rogers Clark's tiny force of Virginians picked off several British outposts in the Indiana-Illinois country, including Post Vincennes. But Detroit, the base of British power in the Upper Midwest, was never threatened, and, despite his victories, Clark *held* little territory. The peace treaty with Great Britain acknowledged the independence of the new United States and American title to the territory between the Appalachians and the Mississippi. Still in Indian hands, Indiana-to-be was now part of a new nation.

A New Republic, 1783–1816

Despite ongoing disputes and a second war with Great Britain, the Old Northwest remained part of the United States, if only because of an irresistible population movement. The new republic cemented its relations with the West with two landmark laws. The Ordinance of 1785 arranged the transfer of land from the central government to the people. In 1789 the brilliant Northwest Ordinance provided for admission to the union of Indiana and her sister territories as states, fully equal to the "Old Thirteen."

Ohio was the first of the northwestern territories to enter the union, in 1803. Indiana followed in 1816. Statehood had little immediate effect on northern Indiana, as most migrants clustered in the southern part of the state. Over the next quarter century, Indian removals continued, and the settlement line moved northward. Northern Indiana was the last part of the Hoosier State to develop. The Calumet Region was surprisingly late in attracting settlers, considering its proximity to the rising city of Chicago.

Jean-Baptiste Franquelin's map of 1688 shows the Theakiki (Kankakee) and a portion of the Calumet River. Franquelin was the first cartographer to place Chicago on a map. (Wisconsin Historical Society)

CHAPTER IV

Settlement Time

IN 1822 FUR-TRADER JOSEPH BAILLY PLANTED THE first American settlement in the Calumet Region. Ten years later a few other hardy souls found the mid-county areas attractive, and a little farming center emerged around Crown Point. Porter County and Lake County were separated from LaPorte County and incorporated in 1836 and 1837. But several barriers kept "Indiana's Last Frontier" unsettled before the middle of the nineteenth century. Much of the land south of Lake County was closely held by investors who were awaiting higher prices. And those who did cross that barrier faced the impassable Kankakee Marshes.

Moreover, before the railroad era many emigrants came west by steamer, docked at Chicago, and proceeded west. Overland travelers usually detoured southward around the Black Swamp of northwestern Ohio. Most of Indiana and even Illinois were settled long before migrants put roots down in Lake County, Indiana.

Log cabin at the Bailly Homestead before reconstruction. (Calumet Regional Archives)

Eventually the Chicago-Detroit Road passed through the region along the lakefront. Several planned town sites—Baillytown, Liverpool, City West—never got off the paper. As late as 1850, Crown Point, the only settlement of note in Lake County, was a quiet little county seat. A few villages with little general stores with a post office in one corner were planted here and there in the northern parts of the county.

But no train track between the East and Chicago could avoid Lake County, and in 1852 the Windy City was finally linked to the East. Long-sighted Chicago investors like realtor Aaron Hart, civil engineer George M. Roberts, Jacob Forsythe, and George Tolle bought huge tracts of Calumet "waste" land for very little money.

Settlers finally trickled in. The 1850 census reported ninety-seven residents in all of North Township (later, Whiting, East Chicago, Hammond, Munster, and Highland). Some cut wood for Chicago builders and the railroads, while others were hardscrabble trappers and traders. A few hostelries catered to stagecoach passengers. Ernest and Caroline Hohmann operated an inn and a toll bridge near the future downtown Hammond. Settlement drew nearer to Munster in 1847 when Joseph Humpfer made a farm on the north bank of the "Little Cal" in an area called Saxony. Four years later Joseph Hess opened a restaurant at West Point (later called Hessville) beside the new tracks of the Michigan Central. North Township was booming.

The First Munster Folk

The first settlers of Munster are difficult to identify because the censuses of those early years identified settlers only as residents of North Township. Plain folk, with few worldly goods, they left little evidence of their lives. Most travelers studied the mosquito-laden wetlands on either side of the sandy ridge, and continued their westward journey. Many of those who did give the place a try soon moved on.

By 1850 Ridge Road was a one-wagon-wide dirt trail on the north side of a low crest that ran between Lake Station and the "Highlands" to the east and Oak Glen (later called Lansing), just over the Illinois state boundary, to the west. Local residents had built the road by plowing up the sides, pushing the loose dirt to the center, and then leveling the surface with drags. Eventually it became part of a longer route connecting Michigan and Chicago.

Called the "Old Pike" until later in the century, Ridge Road was "one step beyond an Indian trail, sandy, and full of stumps." A terror in winter, often impassable after an ice storm when bent branches crossed over the roadway, it was hub-deep in mud in the spring and after a heavy rain. Even so, as the years passed, traffic along the Ridge became a "steady" progression of farm carts, horses, and buggies.

Records disagree about the location of the area's first north-south road, but it probably was the "Old Highway," a dirt pathway that carried travelers to and from Hammond-to-be and Chicago. Later called Columbia Avenue, it passed through a fenced field just south of the Ridge. In 1837 David Gibson built an inn for thirsty travelers and locals at the southeast corner of the intersection of the Old Pike and the Old Highway. Little is known about the Gibson inn, except that it was the first building in Munster.

Log cabin at the Bailly Homestead before reconstruction. (Calumet Regional Archives)

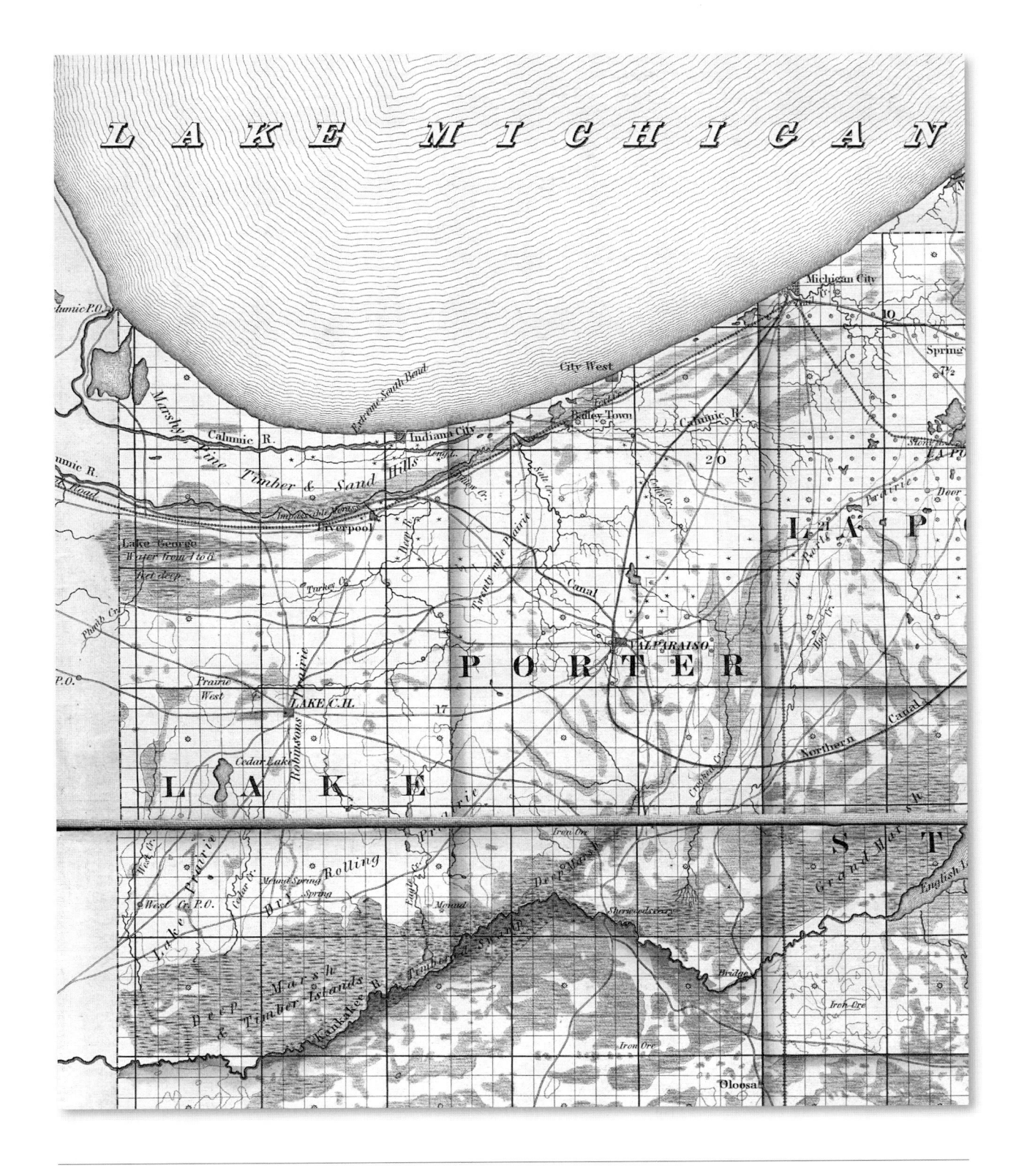

This 1838 map of Indiana by J. H. Colton clearly shows the stagecoach route (Ridge Road) south of the Little Calumet River as well as the low wetlands both north and south of the Ridge. (Indiana Historical Society photo)

New Yorker Allan H. Brass (1818–1892), his wife Julia (1818–1907), and her extended family came to the Ridge from Illinois in 1845. Brass purchased and demolished Gibson's primitive inn, and built the Brass Tavern, a plain, flat-roofed, two-story building with six bedrooms, a taproom, dining room, and a sitting room. An open porch at buggy-step height ran the length of the house; vines later softened its squarish lines. Brass and his family lived downstairs. Cast-iron stoves provided heat; water was drawn from a wellhouse in back.

Julia's mother, Lucy Watkins; her brother, Oliver S. Watkins; and his wife, Sarah, did the cooking, cleaning, washing, and woodcutting at the Brass Tavern. Allan Brass caught gold fever in 1850, and joined the California Gold Rush. He returned some years later, poorer but wiser, and resumed innkeeping, and prospered. The Brass Tavern housed a telegraph—the first Internet—after 1860, which no doubt helped business. In 1864 Brass sold the tavern and two hundred acres for a handsome $5,000, and returned to Illinois.

The Brass's daughter, Cecilia, was born in New York; a son, Oliver, was born in Illinois; and Olive was born in Munster. Allan's wife, Julia Watkins Brass (1818–1907), was the daughter of a Revolutionary War veteran, Oliver Watkins. After Allan's passing Julia moved to Crown Point, and is buried there in Maplewood Cemetery with Allan, their daughter, and their son-in-law. The Crown Point DAR chapter is named in her honor. She was honored by the DAR in 1927 with a bronze plate attached to the old hitching post in front of the tavern site, and, after it fell victim to an automobile bumper in 1953, by a granite boulder.

This drawing of the Brass Tavern by Edward M. Verklan was based on early twentieth-century photographs of the building.

Julia Watkins Brass was hostess and manager for several years of the Brass Tavern. This photo was taken years later and published in 1901 by the Daughters of the American Revolution.

Pork   Pheasant
Quail   Prairie Chicken
Buckwheat Cakes with Maple Syrup
Potatoes

Bread and Butter   Honey
Coffee   Tea   Milk

D.A.R. monument noting the location of the Brass Tavern was rededicated in grand fashion. (MHS photo)

This stagecoach ran, among other routes, between Valparaiso and LaPorte. (LaPorte County Historical Society Museum)

Stagecoach Inn menu. Price for meals at the nearby Oak Hill Tavern was twenty-five cents; for lodging, fifty cents. Gary historian J. W. Lester noted that menus and rates were fairly standard at the many inns in Northwest Indiana.

CHAPTER IV SETTLEMENT TIME • 37

Ira C. Dibble, another early settler, bought land from the state (which had received title to 1.2 million acres of "swamp and other overflowed lands" from Washington in 1850). In 1855 Dibble sold acreage between the Ridge and the river to Harvey and Phoebe Wilson (Wilson Street bears their name), who built the first family home in Munster on the site. Their son, Chauncey, who later died in the Civil War, married and had five children. One Dibble plot was sold to Charles Wicker, whose family name survives in Wicker Park. Another early Munster speculator was Benjamin Hopkins, who also bought land from the state and later sold it to the busy Mr. Dibble. Dibble, a widower, eventually moved to a house located where the Carmelite Monastery stands in 2006.

Johann Friedrich Stahlbaum (1825–1899), later known as John Stallbohm, and Wilhelmina Magdalena Dorothea Boettcher Stallbohm (died 1901) were immigrants from Schwerin, Germany. They bought the Brass Tavern and two hundred acres along the Ridge in 1864. A year later, according to local recollections, the first local news of the assassination of Abraham Lincoln came over the wire to the inn. Later known as the "Green House" or "Stallbohm's Corner," it had room for as many as a dozen travelers arriving by buggy, horseback, farm cart, and on foot. John's homemade currant wine was widely admired.

By the 1890s new roads and routes had bypassed Stallbohm's country inn, and he closed his doors. The family farmed, raising potatoes, corn, hay, and oats, and lived there until 1909, when it was consumed by fire. Townspeople were able to save much of the furniture, and even the piano. The present building on the site, now housing the Munster History Museum, was built immediately afterward by their neighbors, the Kooy brothers.

The Wilson/Benoit House was the home of Chauncy and Julia Ann Wilson in the mid-1800s. Chauncy was a justice of the peace and the area's first schoolteacher. (MHS photo donated by Norma Benoit)

Johann Stallbohm. (MHS photo)

Members of the Stallbohm family in front of the Brass Tavern/Stallbohm Inn. (MHS photo)

Johann and Wilhelmina Stallbohm and children Caroline, Charles, and Ernest (who died young). (MHS photo)

Wilhelmina Stallbohm. (MHS photo)

Tending livestock on the Stallbohm farm. (MHS photo)

CHAPTER IV SETTLEMENT TIME • 39

Daughter Caroline was the most interesting member of the family. Born in Germany, she arrived in America as a two-year-old in 1857, and lived until 1914. Caroline was a plain-looking, independent soul, not fond of farm life. She obtained an education "of sorts," according to her niece, Helen Kaske Bieker, and became a kindergarten teacher in Evanston.

Hired as a nanny at the age of twenty by the family of William Demarest Lloyd, the parent of one of her students, Caroline soon became his personal secretary. Lloyd was an editorial writer for the *Chicago Tribune,* the son-in-law of one of the paper's owners, and a nationally recognized reformer. Among his books was *Wealth Against Commonwealth* (1894), a popular, hard-hitting attack on plutocracy.

Caroline, a spinster, lived with the family in Winnetka, Illinois, met and corresponded (as "Fraulein" Stallbohm) with many leaders of the day, among them Ida Tarbell and Helen Keller, and was a friend of Jane Addams. She also traveled abroad with the Lloyds. Years later, local Girl Scouts found a trunk under the porch of the Kaske House. Inside were bundles of letters to Lloyd and Caroline from well-known reformers. Purdue University Calumet has archived and preserved them on behalf of the Munster Historical Society, and has published a guide to their contents.

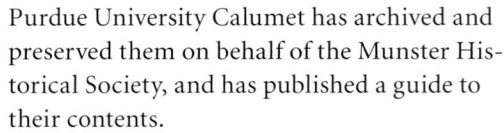

The Stallbohm descendants lived in Munster for many years. Caroline's more prosaic brother Charles, a farmer, lived in a still-standing house on the eastern edge of the property. Another Stallbohm daughter, Wilhelmina, married Hugo F. Kaske in 1884, moved to Minnesota, then returned to Munster in 1905. Hugo farmed and served over the years as a justice of the peace, town clerk, and on several town committees.

Their daughter Helen married Lawrence Bieker, an engineer at Graver Tank and a Town Board member. She taught at Hammond Tech and the University of Chicago and was active with the Save the Dunes Council and other community groups. Helen lived on the family property until her passing in 1988. She sold thirty-two acres to the town in 1969 and the remaining eleven acres with the homestead and barn, with a life right, in 1986. The old Stallbohm property became a museum, two town parks, a middle school, and a school administrative center.

Caroline Stallbohm. (MHS photo)

Wilhelmina Stallbohm/Hugo Kaske wedding, 1884. (MHS photo)

Wilhelmina Stallbohm Kaske was born in 1856 in the old Brass Tavern. Her published essay, "Early Days in Munster" gives us some of the best information about life in the early days. (MHS photo)

Judge Hugo F. Kaske, one of early Munster's most valuable citizens. (MHS photo)

Lawrence Bieker as a young man. (MHS photo)

Helen Kaske Bieker carried on the family tradition of civic involvement. When she died her house and property came under the care of the Munster Parks Department. (MHS photo)

Carl Sandburg, an occasional visitor to the Stallbohm/Kaske family. (MHS photo)

MUNSTER GENERAL STORE
DRY GOODS SEED
CIGARS TOBACCO
019/300
1/97

CHAPTER V

The Wooden Shoe Years
1850–1907

THE POST-NAPOLEONIC ERA WAS GENERALLY peaceful, but difficult for many Netherlanders. That busy land of traders and small farmers was industrializing, side-by-side with an agricultural revolution. Population pressures increased. Poverty, unemployment, rising taxes, and rising land prices squeezed many. In the late 1840s crop failures and famine made life miserable, especially for small farmers.

Religious traditionalists, mostly in the lower economic groups, were also afflicted by intramural and theological differences. Splinter groups, secessionists, and sects roiled the *Netherlands Hervormde Kerk*, the Dutch National Reformed Church. Dissenters were harassed by the government. An *aufscheiding* (separation) from the state church in 1834 affected many. The "American fever" was rising, and would affect all religious groups into the twentieth century. One church historian called emigration a product of "corruption in life as well as in doctrine." In fact, most of the Dutch who migrated to America came more for economic than theological reasons.

The Munster General Store in 1870 on Ridge Road (Drawing by Edward M. Verklan)

Good soil and the chance to own a really big farm, by Dutch standards, attracted Dutch folk to the Midwest. "Wooden Shoe" settlements emerged in High Prairie (later, Roseland), Low Prairie (South Holland), and in southwestern Michigan. And in a little-noticed eastward migration, a few Dutch-Americans settled along a fertile Ridge east of the Illinois border in Indiana.

It was a remarkably "quiet" migration, mostly of small farmers. They arrived in family groups of two, and even three generations, and they certainly intended to stay. Why not? Here was a country where a poor man might own a hundred acres! They brought no grand sense of mission, no plans for cities on a hill, and no missionary purpose. Their assets were decency, a farmer's basic literacy, and plain old grit.

Peter Jabaay, late of Strijen, a farm village nine miles south of Rotterdam, was the first "Wooden Shoe" to settle on the Ridge, and was probably the first Netherlander in Lake County. Jabaay, who later married Aartje VerSteeg, settled in Roseland in 1854. But a year later he moved to a farm along the Little Calumet between present-day Jackson Street and Hohman Avenue. Young Jabaay's enthusiastic letters to home soon attracted family and friends. They sailed from Rotterdam to New York City aboard the good ship *Mississippi*, arrived on the fifth day of July 1855, made their way to the Midwest, and within a month were settled into their new homes.

The passenger list included Peter's parents, Dingeman and Gurtje Jabaay; his brothers, Leendert and Arie; Arie's wife, Sara Dekker Jabaay; and their son, Foppe. The *Mississippi* also carried Antonie and Jannigje Bouman or Bouerman (later, Bowman), their daughter, Nieltje, and her new husband, Eldert Monster (1797–1865). With them were Eldert's three sons from his previous marriage, Jacob, Antonie, and little Pieter, all of four years old.

Eldert Monster was the founder of the American branch of the family (mercifully, they changed the name to Munster around 1860). Illinois land prices drove Eldert and his tribe to an area informally known as "Strattmore," later, Munster. They made a farm on the Ridge about a half block from the site of a future town hall. Antonie died young.

Skaters on the Little Calumet River. (South Holland Historical Society photo)

Aartje and Peter Jabaay. (MHS photo donated by their grandson Peter Jabaay)

Jacob (1845–1924) attended the local school, clerked in a Chicago grocery store and at the advanced age of seventeen, became a construction laborer for the Eastern Illinois Railroad. After a bout with smallpox, Jake and his friend Henry Schrage of Whiting went off to fight for the Union. The two youths marched with General William T. Sherman to the sea in Company K of the Thirtieth Illinois Volunteer Infantry.

After the war Jacob Munster married Hendrike (Henrietta) Van Mynen and together they raised thirteen children. Jacob became a farmer and a storekeeper. The Munster Store was built at the edge of the family farm on the north side of Ridge Road. Munster also served as a postmaster (and so gave the town its name), School Board member, and road supervisor. His little wooden store later became the Munster Cash Grocery, a used car lot building, and Parks Department headquarters. Finally, it was torn down to make room for a Pizza Hut.

Probably also aboard the *Mississippi* in 1855 were Cornelius and Lena Klootwyk and their children, Peter, Nellie, and Cornelius Jr. They bought land from Ira Dibble; in later years son Peter operated a general store on a corner of the family farm, stocked with everything from hairpins to wooden shoes. That well-built store building, still standing at 619 Ridge Road, has served a variety of small businesses.

The Dingeman A. Jabaay home, about 1899, at the corner of Ridge Road and today's Hohman Avenue. Standing in the rear are Ida and Dingeman Jabaay. In front of them are their children and his parents, Gertrude and Arie Jabaay. To the right are Albert and Jennie Flym and their son, Clarence. (MHS photo)

Jacob Munster was a Union soldier in the Civil War. (MHS photo)

CHAPTER V THE WOODEN SHOE YEARS 1850–1907 • 45

Jacob and Henrietta Munster and their twelve children. (MHS photo)

The Munster family homestead. (MHS photo)

Peter and Maaike Klootwyk. Peter (1847–1914) and Maaike (1854–1919) were farmers, shopkeepers, and parents of at least eleven children. (MHS photos donated by James Dekker)

Over time, hundreds of Wooden Shoes moved to the Ridge. Some came eastward from Illinois. The Dutch migration was never large. The 1850 census found only fifty foreign-born Dutch-Americans in all of Indiana; the number reached 450 in 1860; doubled by 1870; and rose to 1,678 at the end of the nineteenth century. But they trickled in steadily, and peaked at around 2,000 in the first third of the twentieth century.

The state line mattered little. After four years in America, Gerrit and Janetje Eenigenburg bought a sandy and well-forested 160 acres (for $.93 per acre) in Oak Glen, in 1853. The Kooy family arrived in Roseland in 1855, and, while they lived temporarily in Pieter DeJong's barn, their son Gerbrand was born. Two years later they moved to Munster, bought land from Peter Jabaay, and their Indiana life was underway.

Gerbrand, who, with his wife, Mary, would raise fourteen children, and his brothers became carpenters and home builders. The sturdy-looking Kaske House was their work. Gerbrand was also recognized as a pretty good water witch (easy work hereabouts), artist, violin-maker, and coffin-builder. In his spare time (?) he was the town house mover.

The 1860 census listed fifty-four residents in seven Dutch-American families with eighteen children, living on eight farms along the Ridge. In addition to those mentioned above, the tally included the Van Bodegraven family: Catherine, Dewitte, Nellie, Peter, and William (two from the Old Country and three from Illinois), and one "Slykens." Living among them were Martin Forman, a Hungarian; Samuel Schultze, a Swiss; German Peter Kraft; the Wilsons; and Ira Dibble. Also in residence were Richard Kimball, late of Maine, and two former Buckeyes, Michael Johnson and Benjamin Hopkins. All were farmers except tavern keeper Allan Brass and family, and carpenter Jacob Kats or Katz.

Ernst G. Schreiber came from Germany to North Township sometime before 1856, via New Orleans. Schreiber exchanged his labor—brush clearing, road grading, and general maintenance for the county—for over two hundred acres in several plots on both sides of the Little Calumet. Members of the family later married into the Stallbohms, moved to the Ridge, built homes, and settled in.

Based on land sales and swaps, Munster-to-be was a bustling place. Parcels were divided, bought, and sold time and again, always at modest prices, compared with south-of-Chicago acreage. For examples: Dibble bought thirty-six acres from Alexander and Ruth McDonald in 1853 for about a dollar an acre, and almost eighty more adjoining acres a year later. The Wilsons bought forty acres from Dibble in 1855; son Chauncey Wilson bought almost ninety acres from Dibble in 1857 for a princely $515. And these are only samples of the land deals that went on, year after year, among those industrious and land-hungry farmers.

Mary and Gerbrand Kooy. A town father in many ways, Gerbrand (1855–1933) built many early homes, found water for wells, assisted in organizing the town in 1907, and helped his wife Mary (1860–1938) raise fourteen children. (MHS photo donated by Marion Postma)

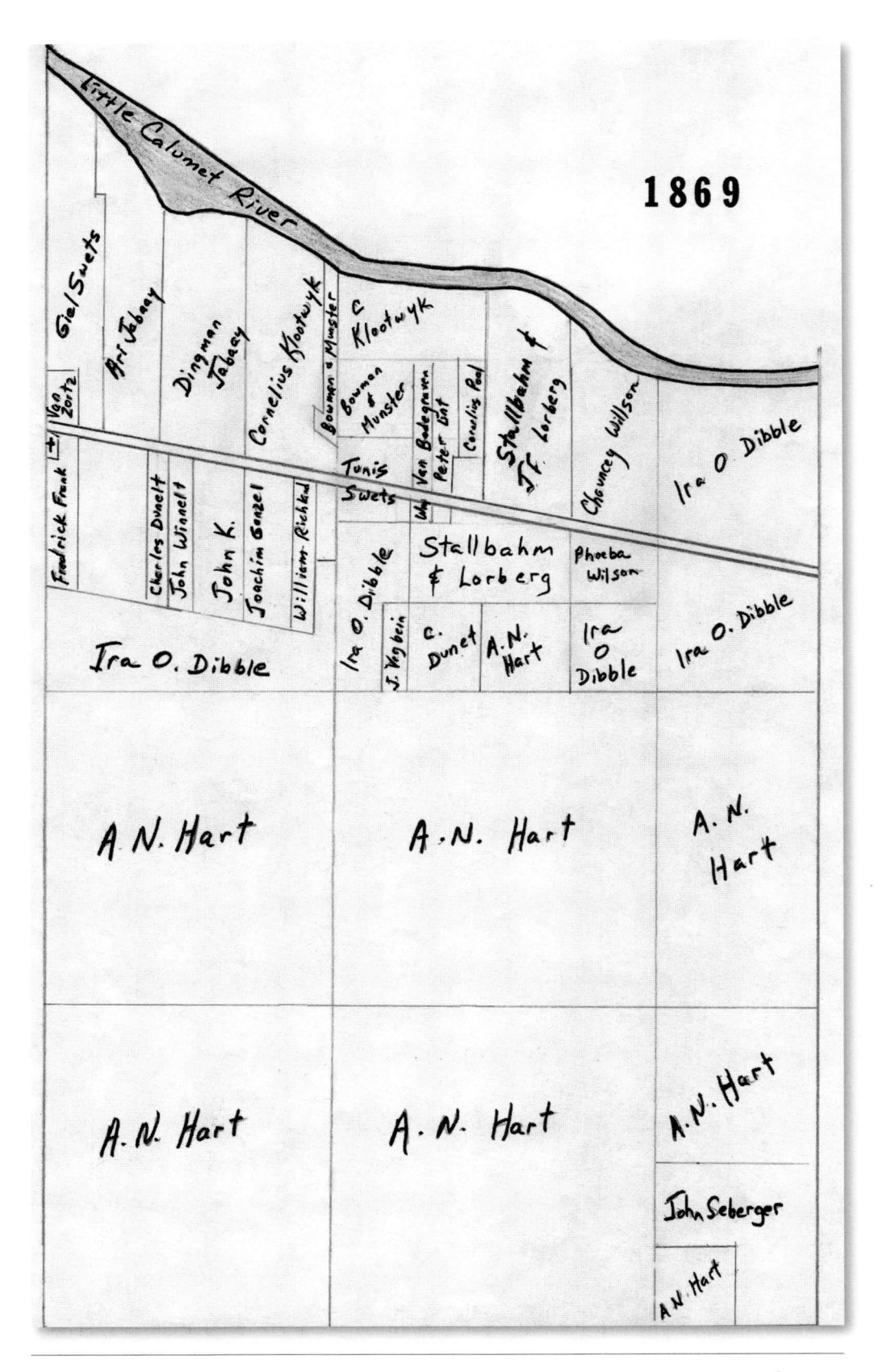

This map showing land ownership in 1869 was compiled from individual section maps by K. J. Schoon.

By 1870, all the "good," land was either being farmed by Dutch-Americans or for sale by Ira Dibble. That meant, in later terms, from thirty-fifth Street northward to the Little Cal plain. Most of the "useless" land to the south was held by Aaron Hart. Of the twenty-seven property owners living along the Ridge, twenty-three were Dutch-Americans. The area's population—swollen by the very large families of the day—was about 125. Giel Swets had crossed the ocean in 1855, but did not settle in the Calumet until 1864. Swets, his wife, and three sons lived near the "Hollander church" between the Ridge and the Little Calumet.

Among the newer families were Stoffel and Martha Vinke, from Gilderland in the Netherlands, the families Lint, Wagener, Van Kirk (via Ohio), and Pool. Hugo Kaske, who would marry a Stallbohm daughter, moved from Hobart in 1872. Two former Prussian families, the Schultzes and Bohns, and one ex-Mecklenburger, Charles Dinewall, dwelt peacefully in what was gradually becoming a multicultural area. New to the nonfarming contingent was Cornelius White, a laborer who probably either worked on someone else's farm or in the local brickyard while he saved money to buy his own homestead.

As late as 1880, the nonfarm group consisted of storekeepers Munster and Klootwyk, Bernard Swets, a "peddler" no doubt hoping to open a store, a few laborers—young fellows mostly—and one railroad worker. The population was about evenly divided between immigrants and native-born Americans.

Among the Dutch were Peter Schoon and thirteen relatives who migrated from Noord-Holland in 1865. They settled in Riverdale, and moved to Munster a few years later. After 1884, the Kikkerts, DeBoers, Vander Walls, Grugers, Jansens, Dekkers, Bakkers, Broertjes—their son John would grow up and marry Dinah Jabaay and raise thirteen children—and others arrived. Walter Krooswyk left the Netherlands, settled in West Pullman, then moved to a thirty-acre farm north of the Ridge. But change was glacial along the Ridge: the incorporation of the town in 1907 was probably the biggest local event before the 1930s.

Life along the Ridge

The Dutch-Americans were market farmers, or perhaps market gardeners, rather than subsistence farmers. Their Munster farms averaged around thirty acres. At first they raised field crops (corn and grain), and cattle. But Roseland and South Holland, where access to fast-rising Chicago was relatively easy, was their model, and most of the Ridge folk soon became "truck" farmers. *Truck* is an older term for a variety of crops raised for sale to city folk. Some continued to raise dairy and beef cattle.

Certainly they understood intensive agriculture, and their fields, long narrow strips running from the Ridge to the river, looked more like gardens. Potatoes and parsnips sold well, as did melons and cabbage. Onions and later onion sets, which wintered well enough in barns, became major cash crops. Homemade cheese and butter were profitable for dairymen. Later, flowers brought a nice seasonal income from both Chicago markets and passers-by. "Off-season," Munster farmers cleared land, spread manure, worked for the railroads or in the smoky brick plant at Maynard, and dug ditches for Aaron Hart. No idle hands hereabouts!

Their first homes were more functional than impressive. They lived in little clapboard structures, often surrounded by sod or banked snow for insulation in winter, rather resembling Dutch laborer's huts. More effort went into hay barns, stables, chicken coops, hog houses, and strong fences to keep the wolves out. Comfortable family homes had to wait.

The Munsters, Klootwyks, and Jabaays were old-fashioned, labor-intensive farmers well into the twentieth century. Gradually more and more "power" tools became available. In 1850 a typical Munster farmer's inventory included "an ax, grub hoe, sledgehammer and wedges, a breaking plow, one s[c]ythe, grain cradle, one wheel Kirby mower, two wheel mower, a Kirby selfrake, a Buckeye mower, a grain flail, a fanning mill, two farm wagons, one light rig, one single buggy, one hay rake, two hay racks, one dog power churn. . . ." Farming was no business for the lazy, and that included Rover.

They brought their crops to market in lumbering one- and two-ton wagons. After crossing a primitive wooden bridge over the Little Calumet at Hohman Avenue, they rumbled on to High Prairie and even Chicago. In summer, Ridge Road was lined with farm stands, outdoor markets, and simple tables loaded with produce and flowers. A few survived until the late twentieth century.

Travelers along the Ridge saw a little "Happy Valley." In 1870 one passerby described Munster as "a bit of old Holland; the spotless Dutch homes, the quaint dress of their occupants, the huge beds of flowers, and the truck gardens which produced luxuriant yields of vegetables for the Chicago market." The immigrants often became citizens "soon after their arrival," but "clung to their national dress, including the wooden shoes." News from the outside world came in English from the *Lake County Times,* and in Dutch from *Grondwet,* a weekly Dutch-language paper published in Holland, Michigan.

An 1895 description: "the Hollander neighborhood, so pleasantly situated on the sandridge road between Lansing and Highland, improves from year to year. It might well be called a village of one street for one mile and a half east of the State Line. It has on this one street two stores, a post office, a church, a railroad stopping place, a school house with two rooms, and very many dwelling houses, nearly all occupied by industrious, prosperous Hollander families."

So Big, Edna Ferber's Pulitzer Prize–winning 1924 novel, provided a clear-eyed look into the daily life of Dutch-Americans. Her fictional truck-farming village was closely

---

The Kooy House at what is today the corner of Jackson Avenue and Ridge Road. (MHS photo donated by Marion Postma)

Johanna Jabaay Neven in front of her home on Neven Drive, now Harrison Street. (MHS photo)

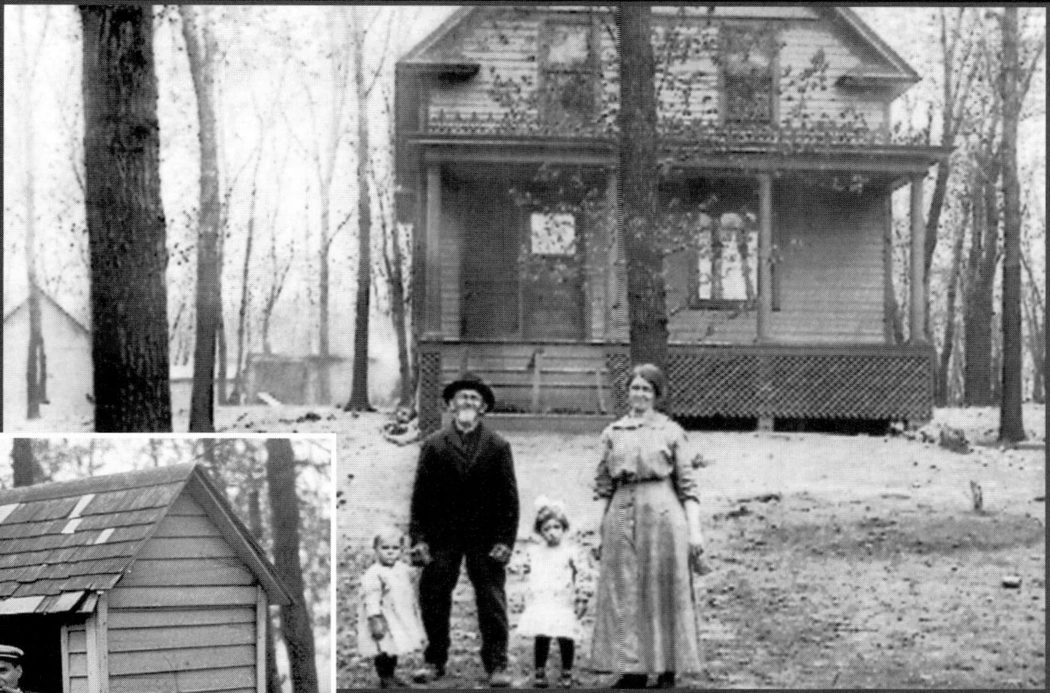
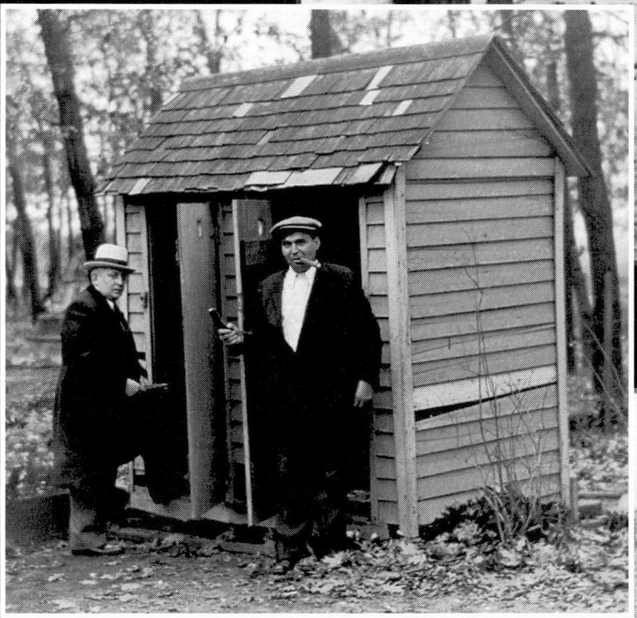
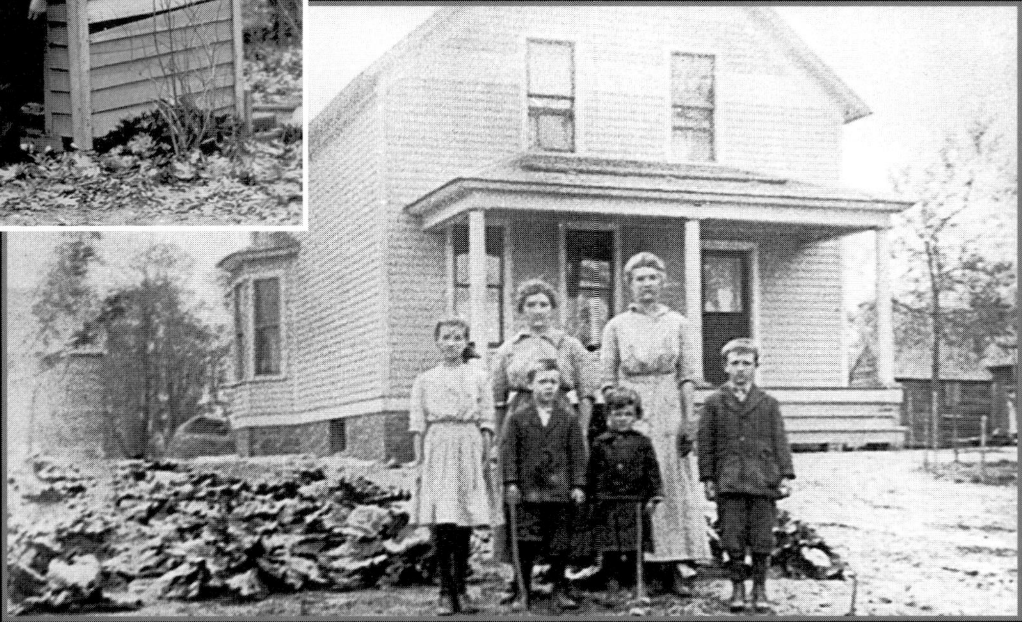

modeled on South Holland, Roseland, or Munster; her cast of hardy characters celebrated the strengths and determination of those long-ago farm folk.

Later in the nineteenth century, the center of town was either Klootwyk's General Store or Jake Munster's Cash Grocery-cum-post office. For some years the area was informally known as Munster because of this tiny operation. The rest of town consisted of the "Dutch" school, the Dutch Reformed Church, two dirt roads, two or three country lanes, and, in 1900, some sixty-four farm homes. Well-tended cinder paths connected homes and stores.

While the name *Munster* appeared on few maps, the village was hardly isolated. Railroad tracks were everywhere after 1850. Later in the century, *Maynard Junction* or *Maynard* did appear on maps. Maynard was a busy little passenger and freight depot for the ancestors of the Grand Trunk Railway and the Pennsylvania Railroad. The Louisville, New Albany and Chicago Railway, later called the Monon, collected freight and passengers at a depot on the Ridge near Harrison Avenue. Chicago was about as accessible then as it was a hundred years later, and with fewer traffic jams.

"Social life," recalled one resident, "was mostly of the visit-the-neighbor type, but we made a gay time of it." Dances were held at the Brass Tavern, and later at the Stallbohm Inn, for all ages. Music was provided by a piano and Mr. Wettering's "large and costly accordion." The Wilson boys, Robert and Charles, and Wilhelmina Stallbohm (Kaske), and Frank and George Van Steenburg formed a dancing club that met twice monthly in various homes. Wilhelmina Stallbohm remembered that "we traveled miles for those dances."

Nineteenth-century Munster was a natural paradise, despite its seasonal clouds of mosquitoes. The woods and marshes were filled with wildlife. Herds of deer made life difficult for corn farmers. Much of marshy southern Munster was covered with wild hay, a favored refuge of small creatures. Timber wolves, once common, were finally hunted out, but foxes, deer, and less-than-welcome skunks remained common. Raccoon pelts were sold for cash or made into coats, and young fellows ran trap lines for mink and muskrat. Rabbits and squirrels were everyday provender.

The Klootwyk General Store was established by Peter and Maaike Klootwyk and later run by their son, John. Standing in front of the building (about 1907) are Peter and Maaike's daughter, Mary, and their grandson, Peter. (MHS photo)

Wildfowl provided sport, food, and cash. Geese, swans, and cranes favored the wetlands and the Little Calumet. Quail, prairie chickens, partridges, plover, and grouse filled many a family pot. Eagles, hawks, and horned owls circled, watching for a meal. Great streams of passenger pigeons flew over the Ridge—as many as three million daily in migration season. One observer remembered that "it looked like one continuous cloud." Some fifty million passed over the Calumet twice each year until market gunners blasted them to extinction.

Money was scarce, but everyday life for the kids in town was rewarding, and fun, too. Munster farm boys held "snake drives" that collected four or five hundred of the scary critters. Harry Eenigenburg, one of those mighty hunters, recalled that they "were big fat fellows too." Fortunately, rattlers were rare. Proper young ladies spent their summer and fall hours gathering huckleberries and cranberries for homemade jams, jellies, and sauces.

Everything changed on October 9, 1871. After a hot, dry summer, the local marshes (and Chicago, and Peshtigo, Wisconsin) caught fire. Hordes of small animals fled over the Ridge, seeking haven by the Little Cal. Black smoke obscured the skies day and night. The bone-dry grasses and trees burned for ten days; smoky peat fires persisted until winter. Farmers saved their homes by plowing firebreaks. After the fires burned out, Munster wildlife was mundane; the more exotic fliers were replaced by robins, sparrows, grackles, and mourning doves.

School Days

The area's first school was opened in 1852 by the North Township Trustee in a one-room schoolhouse on the corner of Ridge Road and present-day Greenwood Avenue. The fourteen-by-sixteen-foot clapboard building had cost $16, including one door, two windows, and a chimney. The interior was plastered, with blackboards "running all around." Everyone from kindergartners to late-blooming adults perched on the same hard, backless benches in ungraded classes; only the teacher had a desk. An iron stove kept winter at bay. Sessions lasted six months. Even so, attendance was irregular; most local folk thought that a basic education was "important," but anything more was considered "excessive," and might spoil a good farmer. Farm work always came first.

The first teacher was Chauncey Wilson. At first classes were held in his home. After he went to war, his wife, Julia Ann, completed his term as teacher, and his daughter, Frances, later taught in the little school. Miss Mary D. Howe presided over classes in the later 1860s. But few schoolmasters stayed very long, because of low wages and unconcerned students. Teachers often boarded with the Stallbohms.

The Jacob Munster family established the Munster General Store in 1870 on Ridge Road. The post office in the store was run by Jacob Munster and the community adopted his name. (Drawing by Edward M. Verklan)

The public school on Calumet Avenue was erected in 1875. (Drawing by Barbara Meeker)

Munster schoolchildren with their teachers on June 4, 1895. (MHS photo)

The county managed the school until 1908, and made some improvements over the years. A brick, three-classroom township school was completed in 1875. In 1914, as a new Munster School was nearing completion, the Town Board purchased the building and lot for $1,500 and used it as Town Hall until 1920. The little first schoolhouse became a family home, and was later dragged to the Stallbohm house to become a toolshed. In 1924 the building, now derelict, was pushed over by the Kaske children.

The Dutch Church

Dutch immigrants of all persuasions were still fundamentalist Calvinists; until the early twentieth century women and men were segregated at services. The Reformed Church majority and the secessionists alike were welcomed by another Dutch Reformed Church (later, the Reformed Church in America), which had functioned in the New World since 1628. Many found that church too "lax," which led to even more rows, factions, and secessions, especially in the Midwest. It was a sad business: ancient disputes among members of the "true" state church, independents, and fundamentalists had followed the emigrants, and now festered among them.

Those issues resurfaced in Oak Glen, Illinois. In 1861, with the approval of the Dutch Reformed Classis in Wisconsin, Gerrit Eenigenburg and a group of former Roselanders and South Hollanders bought a site and built a little one-hundred-seat church. Many of the Munster Dutch attended services there. Others, like the Jabaay family, attended church in South Holland every Sunday morning.

Between 1868 and 1873 either a squabble between supporters of the established church and Dutch-American dissenters, or reluctance to pay for a larger church, or distance caused the secession of most of the Indiana-side group. Jacob and Hendrika Munster remained behind, probably to protect the property. The Lansing church barely survived until 1875, when twenty families reorganized the congregation.

On August 25, 1870, the Indiana group and some Illinoisans, led by Jan Vogel, Gerrit Eenigenburg, and Adam Ooms, established the True Holland Reformed Church, which became the Munster Christian Reformed Church. Services were held in private homes without a minister for some years. Sermons were delivered by a moderator, the Reverend Meinders. Vogel served as the president of the little congregation, Gerrit Eenigenburg, the clerk.

In 1874 thirteen families, among them Dingeman A. Jabaay and his sister, Mrs. John Broertjes, "pioneer Hollanders" of the village, pooled their resources and built a home for the new congregation. A one-acre site on the Ridge at Hohman Avenue was either sold or donated by Stoffel

First Reformed Church of Lansing served the Dutch community of Munster until 1870 when the entire congregation, except the Munsters, seceded. (First Reformed Church photo)

Reverend Dirk Mollema was the first minister in the town of Munster. (Munster Christian Reformed Church photo)

The Holland Christian Reformed Church on Ridge Road at today's Hohman Avenue. (Munster Christian Reformed Church photo)

Vinke. The twenty-four-by-thirty-six-foot wooden building was no grand edifice. It had cost $401.98, plus $17.75 for the tower. A bell from the South Holland church was mounted in the little tower.

The first regular pastor, the Reverend Dirk Mollema, came from Steam Boat, Iowa, in 1879 with the promise of a new parsonage, which was built a year later by Jacob Schoon. Pastor Mollema and his successors got about town on a bicycle until the congregation finally bought him a horse and sulky. *Voorzinger* (singing master) Cornelius Schoon organized a singing school that presented seasonal concerts. John Meeter brought an organ from the South Holland church around 1880; John Eenigenburg and John Ooms were the first organists. About the same time Mike Vander Aa donated a bell, which "called the faithful to the house of God" until the fire of 1952.

A growing congregation required a larger church in 1884, and the next year it was renamed the Holland Christian Reformed Church. Land for an expansion of the church cemetery was purchased from Dirk Schoon around 1895. Continued growth led to the construction of an entirely new and spacious $3,223 wooden church building with a handsome steeple in 1900. The old church became the stable.

By then the church had an active Sunday school and seventy serious-minded members. This was no Sunday-go-to-meeting congregation. Elders often passed judgment on "erring brethren." One member was almost voted out of the church in 1875 because "he did not rule his house well." The Calvinist Sabbath was rigidly enforced: one fellow was chastised for riding a train on Sunday. Wandering cattle prompted a church edict about better fences making better neighbors. In 1884 another member was brought before the consistory for selling a lame horse. Public confession of sins with promised repentance was apparently not a rare event. They were indeed fundamentalists.

Aaron Norton Hart, the "Ditchdigger"

The former *Nederlanders* were tradition-bound folk, contented with their small farms and village, but one fellow had grand plans for the area. Aaron Norton Hart (1816–1883) was born and raised in Akron, Ohio. A Whig and then a Republican, Hart married Martha Reed Dyer (1824–1897) of New Bedford, Massachusetts, in 1844. They had four children, James, Flora, Milton, and Malcolm. Co-owner of Hart and Rice in Philadelphia, he was a successful publisher of pictorial books. He then helped form Chicago realty firm Hart and Biggs sometime after 1855.

But he had his eye on grander opportunities than even those to be found in Chicago. In the mid-1850s Hart began buying "useless" Calumet swampland from the state of Indiana, which was eager to sell. In 1861 Hart purchased much of Cady Marsh and a large pond called Lake George for less than $1.00 an acre. By 1880, at a cost of between $.75 and $1.25 an acre, he had amassed fifteen to twenty thousand "inundated" acres and owned much of the future towns of Schererville, Dyer, and Munster.

Aaron Norton Hart and Martha Dyer Hart once owned most of southern Munster. Aaron died trying to improve his lands. The town of Dyer was given Martha's New England family name. (MHS photo enhanced by Galaxy Arts)

CHAPTER V THE WOODEN SHOE YEARS 1850–1907

In 1861, Hart, clearly a prosperous man, moved his wife, an invalid for many years, and their children to a fifteen-room Colonial-style house at what would one day become Hart and Joliet Streets in downtown Dyer. Hartsdale was a working farm on eight thousand acres along the southern edge of Cady Marsh, although he also platted a town site—never built—for the property. Hart remained busy in the booming Chicago real estate market, while as many as forty hands cut his Indiana hay, maintained some twenty-five miles of fences and ditches, managed his dairy and beef herds, and tended his grain and produce.

The true value of Hart's swampy domain emerged after the tracks of several railroads crossed it, and he turned his enterprising hand to reclamation. Cady Marsh was some thirty feet above the Little Cal. It was almost completely blocked to the west by vegetation and to the north by the Ridge. Hart hired local farmers, among them, Ben and Eldert Munster Jr., to cut drainage ditches (for some reason, they were always called ditches hereabouts, never canals) toward the Ridge and the Little Calumet. They managed yokes of oxen and box scrapers as Hart supervised from aboard his one-horse buggy. By 1883 a deep cut had been made through the Ridge, and the waters of the marsh began flowing northward through Plum Creek into Hart Ditch, and on to the Little Calumet.

Hart was a smart developer, though some locals thought he was a "rustic," a "crank on ditches," and a "ditch nut." Wilhelmina Stallbohm Kaske remembered seeing Hart "dressed in overalls [sensible gear for ditchdiggers, after all] and a plug hat, riding through the town on horseback." On January 12, 1883, while working in half-frozen Plum Creek, poor Hart was instantly killed in a cave-in. Martha Hart completed the "Big Dig," the swamp dried up, and she sold the new farmland for up to sixty dollars an acre. She later moved to Crown Point, where her two-story home still stands on South Street.

This photo of a wagon bridge over Hart Ditch in Calumet beach was published by Willis Blatchley in an 1897 report by the Indiana Geological Survey.

The New Century

As the nineteenth century ended, about fifty Dutch-American families with some 140 children lived along the Ridge in a pleasant little Indiana farm village. Like Dutch-Americans elsewhere, they defined their lives through church, school, family, and, always, work. Beneath that charming exterior was a hard, everyday struggle for existence on a narrow strip of land. The Munster Dutch would endure much hard labor and little prosperity until the 1950s, when a southward migration from the lakefront cities brought suburban developments and handsome prices for their farms.

Their little farmers' town was almost an anomaly in 1900. Little changed for fifty years, Ridge Road was a "pleasant" dirt pathway shaded by handsome oaks and sumacs and lined by a double row of modest but well-built farmhouses. Ridge Road was intersected by the Dyer Road (later Columbia Avenue) and also by busy railroad tracks pointing toward a major city of a million citizens just over the horizon. Nearby, Whiting, East Chicago, and Hammond were rising industrial centers. US Steel had not yet arrived on the Lake Michigan waterfront and no City of Gary yet existed. South of town, Lake County, despite its web of railroad tracks, was still a land of small farms and dirt roads. Quiet villages like Lowell, St. John, and Crown Point, the county seat, had emerged here and there. But Munster's time was coming: the Dutch-Americans of North Township were stirring.

Bridge over Hart Ditch a hundred years later.

30TH PL
RIDGE RD
HARRISON AV
MONROE AV
SEBERGER DR
RIDGEWAY AV
FULLERTON AV
HOWARD
FAIRWAY AV
SOUTH ST
TERRACE DR
SUNSET LN
BRIAR LN
LAWNDALE DR
SYCAMORE LN
MAPLE LN
MORAINE DR
HOHMAN AV
GREENWOOD AV
BEECH AV
WALNUT DR
WHITE OAK AV
CASTLE DR
PARK DR
TIMRICK DR
MEADOW LN
45TH ST
MARGO LN
SUPERIOR AV
GLASTONBURY ST
MILFORD HAVEN WAY
LEICESTER RD
SALISBURY DR
WHITEHALL GARDEN
NORWICH CT
BANBURY PL
INDIANA PKWY
PROGRESS AV
VALPARAISO DR
CALUMET AV
BOWEN DR
SINGLETON DR
BROOKSIDE DR
CEDAR CREST DR
THICKET LN
REDBUD RD
CRIMSON TREE LN
IVY LN
TAMARACK DR
FITZGERALD DR
TWIN CREEK BLVD
POPLAR LN
REDBUD RD

CHAPTER VI

The New Town

INCORPORATING THE TOWN SHOULD HAVE been an easy process. The rapid expansion of the industrial Calumet to the north and the construction of US Steel's mill and the City of Gary in 1906 made it necessary, to preserve the little community's independence, agrarian way of life, and low taxes. Annexation was easy in Indiana, and big cities were notoriously predatory. The City of Hammond had already gobbled up territories to its north and south, and was hungry for more.

Two major landowners, Lucius G. Fisher, president of the Union Paper Bag Company of Chicago, and owner of some nine hundred acres in the area—about a fifth of the proposed town—and Harry S. Brown opposed incorporation. Fisher and Brown were convinced that a new town government would raise their taxes and interfere with their plan to await higher land prices. The citizens proceeded, while Fisher tried to block them. Finally, they assured him that they were a frugal lot, he dropped his objections, and Fisher Street was named in his honor.

On Ridge Road in 1911, John Swart's grocery wagon is about to pass the home of the principal of the Christian School, then the school, and finally, the Christian Reformed Church. (MHS photo)

The guiding hand of the incorporation movement was Cornelius P. Schoon. He had arrived in the New World at the age of one, lived in the Chicago area for some years, and moved to the Ridge in 1886 as a young man. Schoon, who lived a block west of the future town hall on the south side of the Ridge, was a Republican leader, North Township assessor from 1890 to 1905, a farmer, and an auctioneer described as "greatly in demand." Schoon passed on in 1941 at the age of eighty, after a lifetime of service to Munster.

Incorporation was carried out democratically. A public meeting was held in the Munster Public School on June 15, 1907. Most of those present approved incorporation. Gerbrand Kooy, Jacob Munster, and Charles Stallbohm formed a Board of Inspectors, and formally presented the proposition, which passed handily, seventy-six to twenty-eight. Hammond attorney "Colonel" LeGrand T. Meyer drew up papers for formal approval by the Indiana General assembly. On July 1, 1907, the County Commissioners declared the Town of Munster duly incorporated.

The new town occupied 7.5 square miles or 4,736 acres. A 1910 map shows, rather than rural isolation, a farming community with a spider web of railroad tracks crossing its lands. Its public places were few: a pair of small general stores, a church-and-parsonage complex, a schoolhouse, and a post office. It was the home of some five hundred citizens in seventy families, mostly living in modest homes along Ridge Road. A few families lived in Maynard, located at the future intersection of Calumet Avenue and Forty-fifth Street. Nearly all were farmers of Dutch and other western European extraction.

A few years later the place seemed to one historian "a picture lifted bodily out of old Holland itself," and "one of the most industrious prosperous and unique communities in Lake County." The future was visible: a pocket-sized "housing boom" was underway, and "several" houses were nearing completion. In 1915, Oakwood Subdivision, planned for a dozen homes, was platted along Wilson Street.

Governing the New Town

Munster was divided into four wards in 1907, and the first Town Board was elected. Jacob Bakker, Peter Klootwyk, John Devries, and Fred Lange would represent Wards One through Four respectively. Garret W. Jansen became the first treasurer, and Munster's essential man, Cornelius P. Schoon, became the town clerk. August Richter was the first marshal. They took an oath to support the Indiana Constitution and promised to "impartially discharge our duties." Theirs was a simple and frugal government. The Town Board members sat on the boards of just about everything else, including finance. They carefully divided the town treasury among the Bank of Dyer and two Hammond banks.

Lucius Fisher, landowner on the south side of town, worked for lower taxes and expenditures. (MHS photo)

Cornelius P. Schoon, town organizer and the first town clerk. (MHS photo)

In November, they assessed property owners in the new town $.50 per hundred dollars valuation for town operations. At the request of the Town Board, in March 1908, the Lake County Commissioners appointed Hugo Kaske justice of the peace. In August the Board voted to pay themselves $3 per meeting; the treasurer and the clerk were given $125 per annum; the town marshal, $60; and the new town attorney, Colonel LeGrand Meyer, a grander $200 a year. A month later the Board voted to license peddlers at $10 per year, "pack peddlers" at half that rate. The town clerk would receive $.25 per license issued.

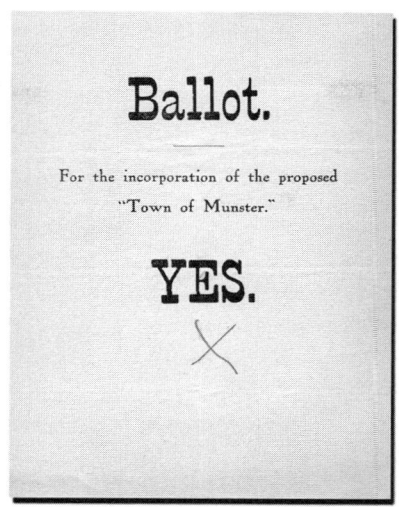

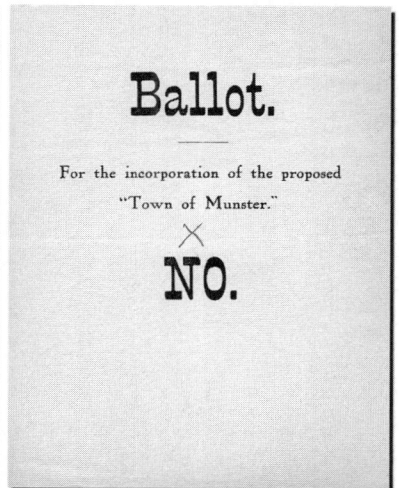

More serious matters cropped up. In 1909 the trustees first refused to issue a liquor license to Fred Lange, then reconsidered, but imposed a stiff, $50 fee for the privilege. Some thought that rather hard on the "poor saloon men," referring first to Lange and, later, Bart McKee, who purchased Lange's Columbia Avenue saloon in 1910.

Relations with the railroads were bumpy. The Grand Trunk Railway Depot at Maynard must have been a rather flimsy structure; it blew over one night in November 1907, and the Monon Depot on Ridge Road burned in 1918. Maynard residents complained that Monon passenger service was "next to useless." Even when the train had stopped—and no one knew exactly where or when it might stop—the doors often remained locked.

Munster declared "war" on the Pennsylvania Railroad after thirty "Italian section men," clearly under orders, ripped up Munster's plank crossing over the Pennsy tracks. Town Attorney LeGrand Meyer earned his handsome salary that day. In the "Battle of the Panhandle," Meyer and one Hammond policeman armed with a musket marched to the scene of the crime, arrested them all, and charged them with obstructing a public highway. The prisoners, no doubt amazed by these events, were taken to the Monon tracks, put on the next train north, and sent to the Hammond jail. Munster was a tough town!

The automobile revolution was underway even before the town was organized. Almost shocked by automobility, those founders could hardly fathom that in twenty years there would be an airport on the west side of town. Munster's first "automobilers" were Jacob Kooy and Peter Klootwyk, who bought their wheels in 1909. But complaints were already rising about "speed demons," noisy motorcycles, lumbering trucks, and "automobiles on the Munster road with covered numbers."

In 1909 someone counted almost two hundred autos passing Stallbohm's Corner in one hour. "When the roads are clear a good run is sport," said one observer, "but the farmers cannot see the fun of the run when they are continually losing chickens." Speeders were warned to "slacken their speed," or "something will be done." In May 1909, the Town Board imposed an eight-mile-an-hour speed limit.

Ballots used for the vote on incorporation. (MHS photo)

Garrett Jansen, Munster's first treasurer, second town marshal, and the station agent for the Monon Depot. (MHS photo donated by Marion Postma)

CHAPTER VI THE NEW TOWN • 63

John DeVries and two of his children at his home down by the river. (MHS photo)

Dingeman A. Jabaay was a member of the Town Board off and on for twenty-eight years from 1908 to 1943. (MHS photo donated by Martin Jabaay)

Fred Lange Half Way House south of "town" at Maynard Junction. Lange served on the first Town Board when it was established in 1907. (MHS photo)

Major Calumet Area Rail Lines in 1910. (K. J. Schoon, 2003)

Garrett and Mary Jansen family: Standing are John, Sarah, Harry, Maggie, Peter, Minnie, and William. Seated are Ada, Mary, Garrett, and Peachie. Train tickets were sold in the Jansen kitchen since the house was located just west of the tracks. (MHS photo donated by Marion Postma)

Hugo Kaske and friends in front of the Brass Tavern/Stallbohm Inn—about 1909.

CHAPTER VI THE NEW TOWN • 65

Still, accidents were everyday occurrences. The *Lake County Times* printed frequent reports of collisions and rollovers, trucks hitting pedestrians, and motorcycles—already a popular mode of getting around among daredevils—hitting cars, trees, and trucks. In 1909 farmer Peter Molenaar Jr. "came out of the marsh with a load of hay," was hit by an automobile that "seemed to want to take the Dyer road," and was overturned. In 1912 a motorcyclist flew twenty feet through the air at Stallbohm's Corner. The town marshal was instructed to "observe" automobiles on Ridge Road in 1915. A 1916 newspaper article on Munster referred to "the first accident of the day." Modern times were changing a once quiet farm town.

As traffic multiplied in numbers and weight the flimsy bridge over Hart Ditch became a problem. A new bridge that "one may drive across without fear of going through the planks" was built in 1908 (while frustrated drivers complained about the detour). Only five years later another, even stronger bridge was needed, and built.

By 1910 Ridge Road, reputedly the busiest road in Northwest Indiana, was "cut to shreds" by hordes of "local and foreign" autos and trucks. On summer weekends up to seven hundred Sunday drivers toured the town. In 1913 the town widened, leveled, graveled, and reoiled Ridge Road. Afterward, some complained that the stones were dangerous for bicyclists. It was a never-ending process: only four years later Ridge Road again needed rebuilding.

Road projects became common. "Maynard Road" was rebuilt by unemployed men paid from the township poor fund. A southward extension of Hohman Avenue from the river to Ridge Road was completed in 1910. In 1914, following a joint public meeting with Dyer townspeople, Munster extended Columbia Avenue or "the south road" toward the Dyer town line, despite the cost of moving some houses out of the right of way. The ever-testy Mr. Fisher objected to a highway over his property that might interfere with a planned factory. Munster again proceeded according to plan.

On the more positive side, Munster folk got about rather handily by 1915. An hourly bus shuttled up and down the Ridge between Griffith and Hammond. The Lion Store in Downtown Hammond ran a free shoppers' bus along the Ridge three times a week in 1913. A bakery wagon delivered freshly baked pies and other goodies to Munster daily after 1915.

Modern utilities were also on the way. A first attempt at installing phone lines in 1907 failed. Three years later, the town granted a fifty-year franchise to the Telepost Company of New Jersey to run wires "for the purpose of transmitting intelligence." Little came of that concession, either. But in 1915, the town fathers franchised the Chicago Telephone Company, which went right to work. People could choose between one-, two-, and much more entertaining four-party lines for their crank telephones.

In 1912 Northern Indiana Gas and Electric asked the Town Board if Munster wanted electricity. A public meeting in the schoolhouse loudly opposed the idea ("too costly, unnecessary, only one bidder"), but the Board still awarded the franchise. Three years later crews of power company workers arrived to cut and trim trees, erect poles, string wires, and, finally, attach "60 candlepower" streetlights.

James Munster DeYoung in his World War I uniform and on a favorite means of transportation for young men in the early twentieth century. (MHS photo)

Tree-huggers complained that the appearance of the Ridge had been ruined, but the town "got over it," and eventually signed up for "the electricity." Peter Klootwyk's son John ran wires to his store, bought a "fine refrigerator," and opened an ice cream parlor. In 1918 Jacob Kooy presented his wife with "something every woman wants," an electric washing machine.

The Trustees faced a problem in 1914 when a Hammond church sought to establish a cemetery on Ridge Road. Ordinance No. 24, Munster's first zoning law, banned "cemeteries, saloons or other noxious businesses" from a half-mile-wide residential district centered on Ridge Road. Strong zoning codes followed that precedent. If Munster never quite developed a classic "downtown," it did avoid becoming a "slurb" with mixed business-and-residential developments and here-and-there strip malls.

Town government remained economical. The budget for 1920 for salaries, stationery, fuel, janitor service, and "misc" was $2,860. Assessed valuations continued to rise, and tax levies totaled $.28 per hundred, divided into $.12 each for the general fund and "streets and alleys," and street lighting, $.04 per hundred.

Government was generally quiet, polite, and effective. Charles Chick, Joseph Douthett, and C. P. Schoon were election inspectors. Schoon also chaired the Munster branch of the Republican Party; Judge Kaske was the secretary. Meetings were held in the schoolhouse. Local political parties, including the Citizens, Independent, and Peoples Parties fielded slates of Dutchmen, spiced up with the occasional German-American.

The 1911 election was typical: a record turnout endorsed the Citizens "Ticket." Peter Kikkert and C. P. Schoon won with 73 and 77 votes, respectively, over Independent

Munster Town Hall drawn in 1982 by Barbara Meeker.

candidates John J. Kraay (57 votes) and Peter Klootwyk (54 votes). G. W. Jansen was named town marshal by 89 votes. Popular fellow! Folks must have been satisfied: the following year voter registration declined to 113.

Town government gradually outgrew its home. The Town Board had planned to enlarge Town Hall, the former public school building. Voters opposed spending more than two thousand dollars on the entire project, and the bids for the work were rejected by a chastened Town Board. The Board was determined to "dispose of the town hall question," but was stymied by the voters. Finally, in early 1920, the Board sold Town Hall to "Mr. Lenz," who sold the various fixtures and tore it down.

The Town Board immediately advertised for bids for a new brick, two-story Town Hall. With a borrowed $30,000, a new Town Hall was built on the same site as the old one, on the northeast corner of Ridge and Calumet. The existing site was too small, so the town offered Jacob Munster $25 for an adjoining acre. Munster—a farmer and School Board member, road supervisor, and a health officer—was also a tough bargainer, and held out for $30. In 2006 the building housed a Mexican restaurant and a dentist's office.

Construction was carried out over the winter of 1920–21. The Board first met in its handsome new facility in June 1921. A public dedication followed a week later, with speeches from Judge V. S. Reiter and Town Attorney Meyer, who expounded on both the town's past and tax increases. Surely a hard way to sell history! A serenade by the town band and refreshments followed those more solemn events.

The new Town Hall was quite an improvement, if only because it had central heating and electricity. Town offices occupied the first floor. The upstairs was the original multipurpose room. The Town Board met there, Judge Kaske presided over traffic court there, and for many years it was a community center for public and private meetings, plays, dances, and card parties. A kitchen helped with luncheons and munchies. It was a good investment, after all.

A Farmer's Village

The organization of the town had little effect on daily life. Fending off annexations and keeping taxes low were fine, but raising and marketing crops was serious business. Munster farmers turned their hands to a wide variety of crops. The Ridge remained a truck farming center, but field crops were grown to the south. Cabbage, pickling onions, and cucumbers were always profitable. A "sauerkraut" or "pickle factory" operated for years in Highland near Kennedy Avenue. Operated at different times by Clark, Herman Meeter, and Libby, McNeill and Libby, the plant purchased cabbages from local farmers, but eventually moved to Chicago Heights. Cabbage also went to market from railroad sidings in Maynard and Lansing.

Town Hall cornerstone.

Onions did well, although in 1909 Mr. Koster's onion pickers—apparently a traveling crew—went on strike for more work. Onion buyers came to town from "all sources." In January 1909, they offered a penny a pound. During a very rainy August in 1915 local farmers knocked onion crates together and hurriedly harvested their crops before they rotted in the fields. Some cabbage growers switched to sugar beets, which seemed a likely crop. Potatoes were also a good crop. Peter Molenaar sold Otto Knoerzer's OK Champion Potato Diggers faster than the factory in Hammond could make them.

Wheat and corn were the major crops in the south side of town. As many as forty mowing machines brought in the hay. In 1908, the *Times* reported that "if the grain turns out as good as the hay, horses will not be the luxury to keep that they were in the last year." "Thrashers"—roaming threshing crews—came to town in August and September. The *Times* reported in 1911 that "Eddie Marsh of Maynard drove a large herd of cattle through here to fatten on his farm." Three years later hoof and mouth disease struck. Despite a quarantine, herds were driven through town along Columbia Avenue.

However traditional they seemed, local farmers were willing to learn. In 1909 the North Township Farmers' Alliance heard the new county agent and Purdue University experts speak on cabbage growers' problems. The *Times* opined that even "skeptical" Munster farmers thought the county agent might be worth his pay. In 1914 local men organized a North Township Agricultural Association. Meetings were held in Hessville and at the Munster School. Among its active members were C. P. Schoon, Charles Stallbohm, and Ernest Schreiber.

Cornelius P. Schoon, "A Man Outstanding in his Field." Onions grew well on the sandy soil of the Ridge. Schoon's crop was onion seeds, which he sold to nearby farmers. (MHS photo)

The finest old brick home on Ridge Road belonged to the Dirk and Dora Schoon family. Here Dora (center) stands with her daughters Mary (left) and Jacoba (right). (MHS photo)

Life in Munster in those years was prosaic enough. In the winter months farmers collected Chicago manure at a siding and hauled it to their fields. In 1912 a new farmers market in Hammond was less than successful: buyers offered wholesale prices for small lots. Munster asparagus, spinach, onions, rhubarb, radishes, and head lettuce were slow in 1913.

Weather was always important. Storms, hot muggy days, a heat wave, and then a drought threatened the town's crops in 1915. Rain was "disastrous and discouraging," corn was not ripening, and wheat was soggy. The Little Cal flooded, and "what crops not floating around are decaying in the ground." A rainy June was followed by a heat wave; a drought dominated July and August. A year later local farmers fretted over too much rain. A heat wave was finally broken by more rain and "farmers were thankful." By 1918 Oliver Kraay had had enough, sold his farm, moved to DeMotte, and bought a grocery store.

Everyday events also affected farmers. A tribe of "Gypsies" came to town in November 1909 prepared to pitch their tents, but were ordered to move on. In 1917 Jake Andrews discovered an escaped "lunatic" happily munching oats in his barn. The poor fellow, it turned out, liked oats, drank water from a trough, and slept on a bed of straw. Andrews gave him a kick, but the "human horse" returned one of his own. The town marshal finally returned the man to the asylum. Farmers complained of "autoists" helping themselves to fruits and vegetables, and called for arrests. In 1917 lightning struck Henry DeMik's barn, killed a horse, and burned the structure to the ground. No one ever said farming was easy.

Young Jansens and neighboring children harvesting onion sets. (MHS photo donated by Marion Postma)

Many Munster residents worked at Meeter's Onion Warehouse on Wentworth Avenue in Lansing. (Bud Meeter photo)

Onion sorters pose by a conveyor belt at Meeter's Onion Warehouse. (Herman Paepke photo)

School Days

In 1908 Munster assumed responsibility for public education within its boundaries, not particularly to improve the schools, but rather because it would be cheaper. Hugo Kaske, Peter Tanis Jr., and Gerbrand Kooy were named to the School Board by acclamation, at a salary of $40 per annum.

Miss Etta Henderson, late of Beloit, Wisconsin, was the first principal of the Munster Town School. Miss D. Frers of Whiting taught combined classes in Room 2, and Miss Ruby Wilson of Crown Point, in Room 1. Only Miss Henderson returned to teach a year later. Teachers' salaries, ranging from a miserly $57.50 per school year to $85, guaranteed a constant turnover.

Childhood diseases were everyday matters. The schools were closed by the Board of Health for two weeks in November 1910, because of a "prevailing epidemic of measles." A chicken pox outbreak was ignored for a time, and schools remained open, but poor Peter Kooy was quarantined. An epidemic of whooping cough afflicted Munster youth in the summer of 1916, and typhoid and scarlet fever followed in 1917.

Smallpox appeared in 1913; Dingeman Jabaay and Mrs. Peter Tanis Jr. survived that deadly disease. Vaccinations were offered to all schoolchildren, but many parents, fearing "sore arms" or worse, refused to allow them. Another smallpox scare in 1914 led to another vaccination drive, but a year later, little Helen Vierk contracted the disease, and school was again closed for a time.

The disease was "on the increase" even in the 1920s. When infected people casually walked about town, the town fathers mused that "possibly a stricter quarantine is needed." Communicable disease outbreaks caused school closures into the middle years of the last century. The annual epidemics that usually arrived with the new school year ended only after "shots" were mandated.

The influenza pandemic of 1918–19 afflicted everyone. In the fall of 1918 Lake County Health Commissioner Raleigh P. Hale ordered monthlong closures of schools, churches, theatres, and even imposed a ban on public gatherings. Yet the Spanish flu raged on, in Munster and around the world. In December, after many families and ninety pupils were down with the flu, the Dutch school closed for a respite.

Munster opened a "night commercial school" for adults in 1917, and awarded certificates to its first graduating class of ten a year later. But the night school, a good idea in itself, was considered a wartime measure, and was soon discontinued. Few Munster folk had educational aspirations beyond the eighth grade. The Kooy brothers, Albert and Cornelius, completed a six-month course at Chicago Business College. Only three Munster students, Alice Kortenhoven, Ray Kaske, and Samuel Kooy, attended Hammond High School in 1907. In 1916 four Munster pupils attended classes in Hammond, and only three a year later.

Enrollment in the Munster Public School was small in the early years of the last century. Fifteen students sat in Miss Etta B. Henderson's Room No. 3 in 1908. In 1910 Miss Mary Herlitz taught grades six, seven, and eight and served as principal. Miss Louise Carter of Hammond taught grades four and five, and Miss Clara Matthies, also from Hammond, taught the lower grades. A total of 180 students attended classes in 1912, just over two hundred in 1913, 188 in 1919, and 177 in 1920. Miss Hopp came from Crown Point to teach music, a weekly event Munster farm boys later remembered as a "Day of Infamy."

In 1916 the school divided the various grades between two teachers. In 1915 two students graduated from the Munster Public School, and in 1916, Louise Kaske, Kate DeMik, and William Flynn passed the eighth grade exam, and would graduate in May. Numbers rose sharply in 1919, when nine earned diplomas.

Extracurricular activities were modest. In 1910 the children organized a school box lunch social. A reading contest brought participants to Crown Point in 1916. A dozen more students "rooted and shouted for fellow school mates." Helen Kaske won top honors in "Class A—5th and 6th Grades," and repeated her performance a year later, with a score of over 97 percent.

Afterwards the students visited the public library, the county jail, and the children's asylum. Lunch was served at the home of Mrs. Frank Hammond, a former Munster teacher. In that same year seventh and eighth grade girls canned peaches and sewed curtains as part of their domestic science class.

Economy was the paramount principle in the public schools. With the Dutch parochial school carrying a part of the town load, enrollment remained small. As late as 1919 Munster employed only two teachers. The most visible change in the Munster "system" in these early years of the twentieth century was a new school building.

In January 1914, the Town Board decided to build a new school, at a cost of $25,000. The money came from cash on hand and bonds. The architect was Mac Turner, John McClay the builder. Both were Hammond men. The building was constructed on the south side of Ridge Road between Columbia and Calumet Avenues, on a site now occupied by the Center for the Visual and Performing Arts. The bricks were made in Maynard and delivered to Ridge Road by the Monon Railway.

A two-story brick structure on ten acres, the school was designed "along modern lines with metropolitan interior arrangements." There were classrooms, offices, a library, and "additional space" in the basement. Dedication Day, March 13, 1915, featured speeches and a pantomime by pupils, "Columbia the Gem of the Ocean." Louise Crawford of Crown Point sang; Lucille Velmer and Dineen Whiting performed piano solos.

The new Munster Public School was built in 1914 high on the Ridge. (MHS photo)

Cornerstone of the Munster Public School on Ridge Road. (MHS photo)

The Munster School was renamed in 1950 for James Franklin Doughty Lanier, a Civil War–era financier from Madison, Indiana, and later, New York City. It was the town's only public school for thirty-four years. In 1928, the first of several expansions added a gymnasium to the rear of the building. In 1942, with enrollment at 233, a front wing with four classrooms and an auditorium was tacked on, at a cost of $50,000. Originally a grade school, Lanier also housed a junior high school after 1949, when a new Munster Elementary School went on stream.

In 1960, as the town's new and very flossy Wilbur Wright Junior High School entered service, the School Town considered closing Lanier, but decided to renovate the old building and restore it to elementary school status. The structure then stood three stories tall, with a dozen classrooms, administrative offices, a gym, band and music rooms, an art room, and a home economics "sewing room." A small library and a cafeteria occupied the basement.

The Class of 1927 at the Munster Public School. Seated, left to right: Annabelle Munster, Maurice Kraay, Miss Merle Stone, George McKee, and Frances Gill. Standing: Helen Jabaay, Harry Horton, Elizabeth Kirsch, John VanDerTuuk, and Susie Porte. (MHS photo conated by Maurice Kraay)

School bus of the 1920s. (MHS photo)

CHAPTER VI THE NEW TOWN • 73

But Munster was increasingly tuned in to "modern" education, and enrollment at the old school was declining. Lanier was closed in 1980 and the student body divided between Eads and Elliott Schools. A debate over future uses ended with a pricey rehab estimate, and Lanier School was demolished.

The "Dutch" School

The Christian Reformed School opened in September 1907, next to the Munster Christian Reformed Church in a "very good appearing" $1,600 two-room, block building. One year later a principal's home was built next door. A. Cleveringa was hired as the first teacher and principal, for a princely $60 per month. A second teacher, Miss Christine Knoll, was hired in 1908 for $35 per month. The little school's fifty-six pupils came from Munster, Highland, Lansing, and other Illinois towns. A horse-drawn school coach carried the children to and from the school.

By 1914 enrollment had grown to 124, and two classrooms were added to the little building. Instruction in the earliest years was in a "fractured" Dutch-English. Eight students were awarded eighth grade diplomas in 1917. Tuition was set in 1921 at $1.90 per child for the first two children and half price for the third. Enrollment continued to grow, and in 1924 a one-room building was moved to the property, and another in 1930.

Munster Christian School, established the same year as the town of Munster, 1907. It stood beside the Christian Reformed Church until 1942. (Munster Christian Reformed Church photo)

Christian School classroom in 1915. The teacher was John Tuls. (MHS photo donated by Martin Jabaay)

74 • MUNSTER, INDIANA: A CENTENNIAL HISTORY

As in the public schools, teachers came and went frequently. Mr. Cleveringa left after three years. Miss Tilma taught from 1910 to 1912, Miss Smith came the next year, and Mr. John Tuls served from 1913 to 1917. Four teachers were employed at the growing school in 1919 when Clara Dyskstra, William Lautmy, George DeJong, Cornelius Kikkert, William Zigteman, Benjamin Ooms, and Andrew Porte graduated. Nicholas Yff was the principal in 1939, and five teachers, the Misses Kats, Bouwkamp, Jabaay, Hoekema, and Van Til, taught grades one through seven to a hundred pupils. Twenty-two graduated in 1939. Commencement ceremonies were held in the church. The 1941 ceremony featured a student pageant, "Scenes in American History."

The school was moved to Lansing in 1942. The old schoolhouse was demolished two years later, and the site became part of the church parking lot. But it had been busy until the end. The wartime theme of the final commencement in May 1942, "demonstrated methods of loyalty to the U.S.A. and patriotism in class work." In a rather sad ceremony, diplomas were awarded to twenty-three youthful members of Munster and Lansing Dutch-American families. The final banquet for alumni probably wasn't a very cheerful occasion, either.

But the combined resources of two Christian Reformed Churches were behind the Lansing Christian School, which opened in 1943 in a new, two-hundred-student building at Randolph and Lange Streets. School bus service from Munster began in December. Nick Yff continued as principal, although some of the teachers resigned. In the mid-1950s fifty or more Munster children were in attendance. By 2000 over five hundred students were enrolled, including many from Munster.

Social Life in the New Century

Town picnics and box socials were always popular events. Lunches were prepared, boxed, and auctioned off to the highest bidders. Decorations on the boxes provided hints to eligible swains. The box auction of 1917 raised $40 for a new piano. Beginning in 1902, concerts by John J. Kraay's Munster Community Band enlivened festivities. An October 1913 event featured

---

Children play in the front yard of the Kaske house, which was built in 1910 after the old Brass Tavern/Stallbohm Inn was destroyed by fire. The building is now the home of the Munster History Museum. (MHS photo)

dramatic readings and songs by a male quartet. Other occasions, like the "well-attended" cantata *David the Shepherd Boy*, performed by the Munster Choral Society in May 1915, were sponsored by the "Holland" church. The Munster and Highland churches also sponsored Labor Day "feasts" to support home and foreign missionaries.

The Glorious Fourth featured parades that made Munster look "more like a city than a country town." The *Lake County Times* reported in 1914 that "autos, motors, and vehicles of all sorts by the hundred, came through a large crowd." In parade formation, the Munster Band tootled along the Ridge from Lansing to a church picnic under the trees "near the big ditch" at either Wicker's Grove or Kraay's Woods. Folks from Saxony on the Hammond side of the Little Cal and Highlanders joined with Munster folk each year for that event.

For the improvement-minded, the North Township Agriculture and Literary Society met regularly at the Munster Public School. In March 1915, County Agent S. J. Craig showed stereopticon slides of Lake County farm improvements. More politically, the Society opposed joining the Hammond sanitary district, concluding that plumbing and a municipal water supply such a system were unnecessary, and would—horrors!—raise taxes. The Society called on Munster voters to vote "NO" in an upcoming referendum.

Civic-minded fellows formed the Munster Commercial Club in 1915 and elected Henry Bolt as its first president. In February 1916, the club provided speakers and a band for a community "booster meeting." In April a voters' league was formed. In June the club sponsored a "mass meeting" to discuss the "town hall proposition." Little Munster was getting to be a busy place.

Halloween was not so innocuous in those days. The typical boys "pranks" involved "dumping outhouses" and carrying off gates. Pulling bluegills and bullheads from the murky waters of the ditch and hunting rabbits also appealed to youth. Young ladies pursued the more genteel arts of quilting and sewing. The Misses Henderson, Wilson, and Minnie Kaske gathered at Miss Eugenia Knott's home in Hammond for quilting bees and juicy gossip. In 1915 a group assembled at Mrs. F. E. Schultz's to stitch up a quilt with a blue and white star.

The Munster Sewing Club spent many pleasant evenings playing games and singing. Attending the club's May 1915 gathering were those social lionesses the Misses Grace and Bessie Kamar, Lizzie and Mary Flynn, Kate Pittlik, Henrietta Kooy, Tillie Postma, Lillian Kelly, and Louise and Helen Kaske. A group of high school girls called themselves the "Herem Club" and gathered at the Kaske home. Six guests "hiked" from Hammond for an event there one day in chilly January 1917. Those were simpler days: the *Times* reported in September 1913 that "Miss Heilitz and Beulah Brundige took a walk to Hammond Wednesday evening."

The I and I State Line Band—Munster's very own. (MHS photo)

The fellows also occasionally made the social news. In April 1908 the *Times* noticed that Munster's "leading citizens," Jacob Munster, Cornelius Schoon, Dingeman Jabaay, Charley Stallbohm, Henry Daugherty, Jacob Bakker, Fred Long, George Johnson, August Richter, and Peter Klootwyk, "visited old friends" in Hammond. In August of that same year, Joe Munster married Miss Delia Kikkert in her family parlor, and left for Iowa the next day.

Business

Making a living was serious business. While most men farmed, a few found other work. In 1907 C. P. Schoon—he of many posts—became a census taker for the *Lake County Directory,* while Miss Winnie Schoon worked in Hammond for the OK Champion Potato Digger Company. Ernest Stallbohm was a Hammond fireman in 1911. In 1913 Jake Kooy built houses along Columbia Avenue for Peter Tanis. Egbert Aring ran the Munster Blacksmith Shop in 1915, and hoped to find a partner. The *Times* noticed that he was "making good," and that his charges were reasonable.

Local farmers made good winter wages hauling river and pond ice from Hammond to the Maynard Depot for the Chicago stockyards. John Branch, who sold Rawleigh products door-to-door, was described as one of the town's two "medicine men." Ray Kaske, on the other hand, moved to Indianapolis for a job installing stoves. In 1911 Cornelius Kikkert worked in Hammond, then moved to New York.

In 1914 letter carrier Joseph J. Munster delivered the mail to Munster and Hessville for a comfortable $1,200 per annum. Operating out of the Hammond Post Office, Munster covered some forty miles a day in his carriage behind a "handsome bay horse." When Joe was ill, Harry Jabaay, the "rural delivery man," carried his mail. In 1916 Joe Munster bought a Ford, and in December, added a sidecar to his motorcycle.

The Brick Plant

Industry arrived a year before the town was chartered. The National Brick Company (NBC) found a twenty-two-foot-wide layer of "blue-rubber" clay at Maynard. It was relatively free of impurities, and, mixed with sand, was perfect for making Chicago common bricks. NBC bought 160 acres in Maynard in 1906.

The National Brick Company employed many local farmers seeking extra cash and young people saving money for their own farms. (MHS photo)

NBC's first local employee, electrician Martin Bultje, joined the company in 1905. Forty years later Bultje was the plant superintendent. In 1906 he and dozens of newly hired workmen built a plant and several huge, wood and coal-fired kilns on site. Draglines and steam shovels removed topsoil, dug clay pits, and loaded an electric train for the run to a conveyer, which delivered it to a huge grinder. The clay was then sent to "the brick machine" for molding, and, finally, to the kilns. In the early years a railroad siding beside the plant made shipping the finished product easy and efficient; trucks did that work later.

The company added dyes to made bricks of various hues. Mottled "clinker bricks," once discarded, became a popular choice. Much of the Windy City was built of clay from Munster and similar pits in Hobart, Chesterton, and Chicago Heights. Prominent architects like George Keck and Frank Lloyd Wright favored Chicago common.

NBC provided seasonal and sporadic employment for many years to hundreds of local men. The company opened and closed its brickyards according to the marketplace and the seasons. In mid-1907 the company reneged on a union-scale piecework agreement. A brief strike by the plant's ninety-four laborers, fifteen molders, and twenty-one "green" brick workers idled the plant for a few days. When orders fell later in the year, NBC closed the plant for the season. Everyone was laid off "for an indefinite time" in September 1908.

In November 1909, NBC shipped eight hundred carloads of topsoil to sandy Gary, but snow and cold weather forced the plant to close in December. The plant was again idled in March 1914, by a lengthy Chicago brick passers' strike. But the brickyard shut down in August, and, according to the *Lake County Times,* "a number of Munsterites are out of work."

Carl Dittrich, National Brick employee, in the always-hot brickworks. (MHS photo)

In busy 1927 fifty men worked at the Munster plant. In the 1930s, as construction ground to a halt everywhere, the company made bricks only in warm weather. Stock was made, stored in the kilns, and sold year-round. By 1939 the company could make three hundred thousand bricks a day. After the war NBC kept 115 AFL-affiliated International Brick, Tile and Terra Cotta Workers in Local 72 very busy.

The usual production rate was one eighteen-hundred-degree fire per week per kiln, including a three-day cool down. For a day and a half a thirty-foot-long, oil-fired firestorm was aimed at kilns loaded with bricks. The building boom propelled orders, but then a regional shortage of bricklayers led to a slowdown at NBC. In the 1950s the Maynard operation could make five million bricks a month, sufficient for a thousand homes.

After 1930 the clay holes were used as municipal dumps and landfill. Early in 1941 the town was notified by the "Illinois Brick Company" that the brickyard had been sold, and that after July 1941, it would be closed to further dumping. That proposition was voided, but the issue resurfaced in 1949, when National Brick Company, apparently still the actual owner of the plant, notified the town that it had leased the clay pit to both Hammond and the City of Chicago (for up to thirty carloads a day) as a dumpsite.

The town, in some shock, withheld permits from the company, on the thin grounds that the Munster master plan had reserved the area for future residential use. A packed antidump meeting supported the Town Board, and many complained about the company's secret negotiations with Hammond, and cited a Rockford, Illinois, polio epidemic that was attributed to an "untreated garbage dump." The town settled that feud with a "two-fisted determination to adhere to its master plan."

The more recent history of the plant is unclear. Its owners simultaneously mined clay, made bricks, and operated a garbage dump. Bernard F. Weber was the president of NBC in 1952 and Clarence Weber was the vice president. In 1966 the brickyard was sold to Alfred Gawthrop, who renamed it the American Brick Company (ABC), and then sold it again, five years later, to Robert Carey. Marty Benes, a former trucker who delivered brick for the company, remembered that a large number of Mexicans were employed at the plant in those years, and were paid by piecework.

The inherently smoky plant, now encroached by suburban homes, faced a difficult future. It had arrived first, had a long history, and paid taxes on its $6-million-a-year business. But its smoke and ashes were unacceptable to new homeowners who had moved to Munster to escape air pollution. Encouraged by the town, the EPA and the state closed in on ABC, waving a bundle of pollution ordinances.

Carey spent a million dollars converting his kilns to natural gas and experimenting with various filters and scrubbers, but found that firing bricks inevitably caused air pollution. The company stayed in business until 1987. The site was purchased by the Community Foundation of Northwest Indiana, which, two years later, deeded it to the Munster Parks and Recreation Department.

30TH PL
RIDGE RD
RIDGEWAY AV
FULLERTON AV
SEBERGER DR
FAIRWAY AV
SOUTH ST
TERRACE DR
MONROE AV
GREENWOOD AV
BEECH AV
WALNUT DR
WHITE OAK AV
MORAINE DR
HOHMAN AV
SUNSET LN
BRIAR LN
LAWNDALE DR
PARK DR
OAK PARK DR
SYCAMORE
MAPLE LN
EVERGREEN
MEADOW LN
TIMRICK DR
45TH ST
MARGO LN
SUPERIOR AV
BROOKSIDE DR
BANBURY PL
GLASTONBURY ST
MILFORD HAVEN WAY
LEICESTER RD
SALISBURY DR
WHITEHALL GARDEN
INDIANA PKWY
PROGRESS AV
VALPARAISO DR
CALUMET AV
THICKET LN
REDBUD RD
CRIMSON TREE LN
CEDAR CREST DR
IVY LN
TAMARACK DR
FITZGERALD DR
TWIN CREEK BLVD
BOWEN DR
NORWICH CT
SINGLETON DR
POPLAR LN
CORNWALLIS CIR

CHAPTER VII

From War to War
1917–1941

A WAR WAS UNDERWAY IN EUROPE IN 1914, BUT the United States remained clear of that slaughterhouse for almost three years. But signs of war were plentiful. In August 1915, a troop of United States Cavalry passed through town. Some, in that less sophisticated time, believed they were German soldiers. In July 1916, a recruiting officer visited town. After the American entrance into the war, a convoy of Army trucks passed through on Calumet Avenue.

Munster fellows were ready to serve their country. Peter Schoon, a son of the redoubtable C. P., was first to enlist, in April 1917. Young Schoon received his basic training in Fort Wayne and was assigned to service in the Coast Artillery. Ray Kaske was promoted to the rank of sergeant and went to Europe with the Twenty-sixth Infantry Division. Conscription began soon after America's entrance into the war, and quickly scooped up a dozen men, among them Joe Munster, Willliam Klooster, Peter Bult, Oliver Kraay, Andrew Krooswyk, Albert Kooy, and Ernest Stallbohm. Many more followed before the war ended in November 1918. Fortunately, no one from Munster died in that struggle.

The C. P. and Susan Schoon family farmed on land south of the Ridge and west of Calumet Avenue. Seated: Rose (Kingma), Susan, Kathryn (Zybell), C. P., and Hilda (Jabaay). Standing: Winnie, Peter in his World War I uniform, and Mary (Tanis). (MHS photo)

The home front was highly involved. A Munster Red Cross Branch was organized in November 1917, and remained active until just after the war. Members rolled bandages, collected money, knitted gloves and sweaters for the soldiers, sold war bonds, and supported morale. The United War Work campaign for "benevolent purposes" set Munster and Highland's quota at $1,500 in October 1918. Young people pasted War Savings Stamps in little booklets. A Community Sing and Thrift Stamp Social at the public school, probably for the children, raised $14.50. The Reformed Church played an important part in the community war effort. Funds were collected for war bonds and for religious education in the trenches, and in November 1918, most of the community assembled there to give thanks for victory and the return of peace.

Joint Munster-Highland Liberty, and then Victory Bond drives absorbed every spare dime and dollar in town. In mid-1918 the third Liberty Loan Bond drive collected $6,600—almost three times the town's assigned quota—from 115 subscribers. A fourth campaign, in the fall of 1918, again went over the top, raising several thousand dollars over the Munster-Highland quota of $15,500. Postwar Victory Loan drives also exceeded quotas.

Munster entered the 1920s still a small farm town. Only thirty-five homes had been built there since the Civil War. But dozens of new homes were built along Hohman, Calumet, and Columbia Avenues after 1920. Between 1925 and 1929, over a hundred new homes were added to the town inventory. The 1920 census counted just over 600 Munster residents, but growth was rapid after then. Nearly 200 people moved to town in 1927 and 1928 alone. The population was almost 1,000 in 1930, an increase of almost two-thirds, and 1,751 in 1940, a startling 80 percent growth for a still tiny town over ten years. Most of the new residents were businessmen, executives, salesmen, and professionals, not farmers. By 1928 some thought the farmers' town, a "lovely district as yet unsullied by factory smoke and industrial grime," was "taking on an urban appearance."

An improved bridge over the Little Cal at Hohman Avenue opened the west end of town to developers. Broadmoor, an eighty-home "restricted" community in the northwest corner of town, was touted in 1925 as "the first step toward a comprehensive city beautiful plan." A. A. Lewis and Company of Chicago introduced Hollywood Manor on ten acres between Hohman and the Monon Railway tracks in 1928; their first customer was Hammond banker and contractor R. L. Hutchinson.

Hammond realtors Gostlin, Meyn, and Weis developed the Hollywood addition near Hohman Avenue and the river in 1928. Lots along Forest Avenue attracted more upscale homebuyers. Wicker Park Realty Company, which proposed to sell lots to builders of more expensive homes in the northeast corner of town, was founded in 1927 by Hammond banker Creighton Belman, with backing from A. Murray Turner, W. C. Belman, and others. A plat map posted in Town Hall in 1928 showed sixty-five new property deeds. By 1929, when the Depression put a sudden halt to construction, relatively few new homes had been built in Munster, but the suburban seed had been planted.

Under constant pressures from residential expansion and increasing numbers of automobiles and trucks, new streets and roads were laid after 1920, and old ones were

William Klooster, who served in World War I, was elected town clerk in 1920 and held that office until 1931. (Courtesy of Fred Klooster)

extended, rebuilt, improved, and widened. Developers often laid out dirt or gravel lanes. Better roads were completed from the Hohman Avenue Bridge to the Ridge, and from the Ridge to Maynard and on toward Dyer on Calumet. Calumet Avenue had long been described as the "worst piece of pavement in the county." The Highway Commission designated Calumet Avenue a state route, and later numbered it Route 141. The road became "modern" only in 1935 when the state paved it with concrete and widened it from twenty feet to forty feet from the river to Ridge Road.

In 1922, anticipating a day when Calumet would finally reach the Lincoln Highway (later, Route 30), civic-minded fellows endorsed construction of an overpass or a "subway" at Maynard to carry it over or under the tracks of the Panhandle Railroad. Of course the railroad objected. Railroad viaducts or overpasses on Calumet were again promoted in 1936 and 1937, but that project was still pending eighty-five years later.

Widening and paving were priorities. In 1924 Ridge Road lost its "country road status" and became State Route 6. A year later, now a "heavily burdened" artery, it was widened to eighty feet from Calumet Avenue to the state line, and became part of the "Yellowstone Trail," an unofficial, booster-supported, cross-country route that passed between Valparaiso and Chicago. In 1926 it was again rebuilt, from the state line to Highland.

Henry Harder, E. M. Fuller, and H. S. Daugherty joined the North Township Good Roads Committee to work for road building programs and pressure government officials to impose taxes to pay for them and get to work. That was a rare moment in American history: private citizens demanding higher taxes!

Wicker Park

Wicker Park is not part of Munster, but as a North Township entity, it had a major impact on the town. Munster folk had been picnicking in John J. Kraay's woods by the ditch for many years. In 1923, Kraay offered his land to Hammond and Munster as a park, but neither seemed interested. Two years later, in a last-minute operation—developers were already dickering with property owners—a group of sixteen civic leaders, coordinated by Hammond banker and chairman of the Hammond Park Board A. Murray Turner, organized themselves as the Patrons of Wicker Park.

They donated "time and their discriminating judgement." Turner and his friends loaned their own money to buy Kraay's 65 acres of "virgin hardwoods," Mary Wicker's 153 acres, which included prairie, farmland, and "Camp Wicker," which the local Boy Scouts had used since 1920, and Herman Meeter's 75 acres, for $200,000.

The Wicker Park project was a model of private drive, efficiency, and volunteerism. It was also a polite indictment of passive local governments.

Bystanders tip their hats in greeting President Calvin Coolidge in 1927. (Photo found and donated by Martha Wilke)

Turner lobbied the General Assembly for an enabling law to allow North Township to operate a park and for authorization of a bond issue to pay for the project. Meanwhile, his busy crews built a clubhouse, a roadway through the 226-acre park, baseball fields, tennis courts, and, inevitably, a golf course. Eighty local men took a train to Washington, and invited President Coolidge to speak at the dedication of Wicker Park, which was deeded to North Township in May 1927.

On June 14, 1927, President Calvin Coolidge came to town. Well-guarded by a detachment of soldiers, 750 police officers, and Munster Boy Scout Troop 33, the president praised the people of the Calumet for their efforts, and dedicated Wicker Park to the heroes of World War I. He was cheered by a pleased crowd of one hundred thousand. Afterward he boarded Colonel Walter Reilly's huge Rolls-Royce and was driven along Ridge Road and back to his waiting train in East Chicago. For Munster and the entire Calumet, Flag Day 1927 was a grand, never-to-be-forgotten occasion. Five months later, F. H. Warman of Hammond made the park's first hole-in-one, on the 182-yard ninth hole.

Advancing Suburbanization

In 1935 a WPA survey of Munster found a stable community: a third of all homeowners had lived in one place for ten years or more, half for over five years. The WPA tallied 306 residences, of which 285 were single-family units and seven were duplexes. The pollsters found the fewest apartment houses and businesses of any town in the area. Most homes were of wooden construction, but one in four was brick. One surprising statistic that offered an insight into extended family life on Indiana farms: more Munster homes had eleven or more persons in residence than any other Calumet Region community. The survey also found one church, one cemetery, and one sanitarium in town.

President Calvin Coolidge dedicated Wicker Memorial Park in 1927. Maurice Kraay and two other Munster Scouts from Troop 33 can be seen at the bottom right of the photo. (MHS photo)

Home valuations centered around $7,000; just over half were mortgaged. A hundred renters paid between $15 and $20 per month. Indoor plumbing had largely replaced the washtub and the outhouse. But many of those living on farms made do with iceboxes, rather than refrigerators, in their kitchens, though electricity was available. During the spring and summer of 1927 gas pipelines were extended to Munster, and the power company sold kitchen stoves, on "easy payments," to all comers.

Few homes were built in the early years of the Depression, but after 1937 the transformation of Munster from farm town to suburb accelerated. By 1935 the Federal Housing Administration (FHA) was active in the Region; six Munster mortgages were insured by the FHA in only two weeks in late 1939. Confidence was rising, and banks were again open-handed. Town Clerk-Treasurer Peter Tanis issued 180 building permits between 1937 and 1939. Munster had become the premier residential area in the Region, based on 1937 property evaluations.

Munster was described as the "fastest growing" town in the Region and seventh in the entire Chicago area. Home construction values doubled after 1939 and passed a million dollars in 1941. Restored to life, Wicker Park Estates sold lots to builders of rather pricey $7,500 to $16,000 homes. In 1935 and 1936, City and Suburban Land Company's Hollywood Subdivision installed utilities, built streets, and put over seven hundred lots up for sale. Builder Fred J. Walsh started there with ten model homes. Sunnyside was again a "restricted Subdivision for Particular People." Ellyson Realty sold home lots in Broadmoor Subdivision for $650. Kraay's Ridgeway Addition on twenty acres was sold out by 1943.

As World War II approached, Munster was a busy place. Streets were being widened, paved, and rebuilt all around the town. Streets were carved out for new subdivisions. Eighty-five new homes were built or underway in 1939. As the year ended, twenty permits were issued for new homes in November alone. In 1940 a new Walnut Drive pointed southward. Building permits were issued in July 1940, at six times the rate for the same month in 1929. In September, a tenth of all homes being built in the Calumet Region were in Munster. But in October 1940, as war became likely, the boom began to bust. Only eighteen new homes were built in town that month.

Independence Park

Independence Park was the largest and most remarkable development in Munster, and a major departure from the past. It was planned as a major subdivision to the east of White Oak Avenue on part of the former John J. Lawlor Estate. Originally planned to offer four thousand ultra-low-cost

Wicker Park Estates home built in the 1920s. (Photo in 1982 by Lance Trusty)

Lambert and Ada Jansen Schoon both grew up in rural Munster, married, and the later helped change the town to a residential community by subdividing farmland and selling lots. (Photo donated by Pearl Schoon)

homes to working people, Independence Park was to have hundreds of wooden "Cape Cods" on winding streets. Leo Lippman, a lumberyard operator, and Chicago realtor L. B. Harris presented the plan to the Town Board in February 1939. Harris was president and probably the owner of the Indiana Housing Association, a name uncomfortably similar to that of an existing state agency.

Board President Henry Harder, members Henry Konefsky, D. A. Jabaay, Nick Kirsch, and C. H. Strockman, and most of the townspeople were horrified. Harris soon bowed out of the project, tired of fending off complaints and investigations by the local bar association, realtors, the Indiana secretary of state, and the federal government. Lippman scaled the plan down (though he occasionally made noises about erecting ten or twelve thousand homes). Revolutionary-era themed courts, circles, and drives were scraped out, covered with steel mill slag, and rolled flat. In mid-1939 Lippman built a model home on White Oak and invited *Times* readers to "Drive Out Today." A thousand eager buyers tramped through the model each week.

Lippman put a crew of 350 carpenters, roofers, electricians, and plumbers to work on Independence Park. *Life* magazine noticed all that busyness, and called Independence Park the "most talked-about" project in the nation. Lippman built plain, clapboard, one-and-a-half-story homes with unfinished attics, two to three bedrooms, and oil heat. The houses were unfinished, semi-finished, or finished, depending on buyers' purses and carpentry skills. Construction quality was marginal, but Lippman's salesmen "turned over" homes as fast as they built them, for between $2,950 and $3,800. Over a hundred were occupied by June 1940, and two hundred when the project ended a few years later. Why not buy one? One could move in with only $75 to $100 down. With an FHA-guaranteed 4.5 percent loan, monthly payments were around $25, including taxes and insurance.

Lippman had anticipated postwar mass-produced communities like Levittown. In mid-1940 Town Clerk Tanis was still signing up to five applications for building permits a day. Even after the United States went to war in 1941, construction continued at Independence Park. Lippman had wangled federal "defense plant worker" priorities. In the end, two hundred families of former renters now lived in their own homes, and, if the place seemed rough and ready, over the years hard-surfaced streets and modifications and upgrades would transform it into a pleasant, tree-shaded hometown. But in 1943 Leo Lippman's company went bankrupt.

Independence Park residents William Cashman and his son Robert stand in front of their home on North Delaware Parkway. (MHS Photo donated by Robert Cashman)

Independence Park home. (Photo in 1982 by Lance Trusty)

White Oak Association building, located naturally on White Oak Avenue. (Photo in 2006 by K. J. Schoon)

In 1940 residents formed the nonprofit Independence Park Community Club, in 1966 renamed the White Oak Association. Realtor Clarence Armstrong was its first president and spark plug. It cost a family one dollar to join and fifty cents a month dues. Almost every Independence Park family joined. Lippman gave the group a small, partially finished building on the site of his original, but burned-out salesroom. Forty families pitched in and finished the job.

The club's most immediate concern was obtaining better town services. There were serious drainage and sewer problems, the streets were badly rutted, there were no streetlights and no bus service. They also wanted the town to pave White Oak Avenue.

The new Association also supported clubs, a scout troop, holiday parties, church meetings and a Sunday school, a playground and a baseball diamond, and, over the years, enriched the lives of its members. Clarence Armstrong ran the 16mm projector at Friday night kiddie movies. Potluck suppers were popular events. The Munster town marshal sponsored monthly "Teen-Age-Middle-Age Dances" in 1943. Mrs. Hazel Armitage became the club's first woman president in 1946. The wooden clubhouse burned in February 1961, but, with a loan from a member, was replaced by a block building in thirty days. The White Oak Association finally closed in 2006, and the clubhouse was given to a nearby church.

Flaming Arrow Patrol of Boy Scout Troop 33 enlisted Independence Park youth. A dozen or more members shoehorned into Troop Master Bill Shire's car for rides to meetings at Town Hall. Munster's first three Eagle Scouts were members of Flaming Arrow Patrol. Ronald Johnson was the first to fulfill the requirements; he, Dale Erickson (later a medical missionary), and Kinney Coil were all inducted on the same evening as Eagle Scouts.

Independence Park bothered Munster residents who envisioned their town as a solidly middle-class community, but it was a breakthrough for working-class folks. Americans were then slowly recovering from the Great Depression and the Soviet Union was promising a glorious *future* for working people. Meanwhile, that militant capitalist Leo Lippman was actually moving delighted working-class families into homes. And with a down payment equal to a few week's wages! Certainly Lippman cut every possible corner, but a lot of good, plain working folk now owned their own homes. Ten years of peaceful agitation would finally convince the town fathers to fix the streets and sewers. Independence Park was a triumph of democracy.

Farm Life

Farm life continued to evolve, as the first generation and their children passed on or moved away. Competition from more efficient and larger truck farms elsewhere hurt the small-scale truck farmers along the Ridge. Southern Munster farmers did well with field crops, although the market for oats and hay fell rapidly after 1920 with the passing of the horse culture. That also crimped Munster's abundant and cheap supply of fertilizer, which had come by the train carload for many years from the streets and stables of Chicago.

Truck farming moved southward in 1930 when 406 acres along the state line passed to Harold Weinacker, a Chicago realtor (for $100,000). His well-drained, rich black loam became "one of the leading truck farms in the district." Onions, grown in "vast fields" that, one observer noted, "stretched away as far as the eye can see," sold well. Cabbage and tomatoes remained good market crops. Libby, McNeill and Libby's plant in Highland gobbled up sixty to a hundred tons of cabbage daily in season. A few truck farmers remained active in south Munster until late in the twentieth century. Some brought their veggies, fruits, corn, and even horses to a monthly farmer's market on Columbia Avenue in Hammond.

Local sales were still important. Farm stands were busy all along the Ridge. Buster Mills' stand near Calumet Avenue offered vegetables and fruit from Munster and Michigan farms. Other farmer-marketers included Ben Munster, who operated several stands, Martin Boender, Walter Mills, Clarence Kooy, and Peter Kikkert. John Hamacher and H. W. Lentz were also notable Ridge Road farm stand operators.

Many had described Munster as a garden spot over the years, but not everyone agreed. In 1923, despite the town's zoning ordinance, to some Ridge Road looked a bit raffish. "The acreage tracts are so small," wrote one Hammond realtor, a tad sourly, "that most of them are not restricted, with the result that there are no established building lines, [and] no restrictions against business." The same fellow described Munster's veggie and flower stands as "cracker jack . . . thrust out like sore thumbs." In 1921 a "sand pit" on Ridge Road beside the Monon Railway tracks became a neighborhood garbage dump, which added nothing to the town's image.

Munster hosted the 1940 Lake County Truck Farmers School. County Agent M. A. Caldwell lectured on truck farming and a Purdue soil chemist told the farmers what they pretty well already knew about their land. But Munster had its own expert. Bart Huizinga entered a potato judging contest, in of all places, the Hotel Sherman in Chicago, held forth on potato grades, plant diseases, and crop bugs, and won first place.

Mechanized equipment replaced horses on the Schoon family farm. (MHS photo)

Munster's Mart on Ridge Road east of Calumet Avenue—selling farm produce as fresh as produce can be. The sign on the right reads, "We grow the vegetables we sell." (MHS photo)

88 • MUNSTER, INDIANA: A CENTENNIAL HISTORY

A Business Boomlet

The town still had few retail businesses in 1920, but that changed some over the next ten years. Former blacksmith Dick Muzzal opened the town's first garage on Ridge Road in 1921. An "oil station" opened at Ridge and Calumet in 1924. Late in the 1920s a Griffith concern bought the sandpit on Ridge Road, cleaned it up, and built a lumberyard there. Two years later it was sold to Fred Papke of Gary, who named it the Munster Lumber Company. Tom Petso bought the concern in 1954, and operated it, in later years, as a Handy Andy hardware franchise.

Angelo Trakis sold his ice cream stand at Ridge and Calumet to Peter Klootwyk in 1927. Martin Jabaay opened his barbershop in 1927. It was the oldest business site in town in 2006. As the decade closed, Davis Cleaners opened at the corner of Ridge and Forest. Prang's Delicatessen opened in 1928 on the Ridge between Hohman and Forest. Henry Rademaker sold his grocery to Mrs. Corinne DeMik in 1929.

Mr. and Mrs. John Hesterman operated and enlarged one of the growing town's most popular entities, the Ridge Road Roller Rink, just west of Calumet, which was demolished in 1937. Roller-skating was a national fad in 1928. Daughter Florence Hesterman stayed on her feet for thirty-three hours at the Chicago Coliseum to become the world's champion marathon dance-skater.

In 1936, Munster had two grocery stores, Klootwyk's, a general store that sold hardware and other stock, and Phil Schuringa's Grocery. Martin Jabaay cut hair as usual. In the summer of 1940 Arthur Rehburg opened a grocery on White Oak next to Independence Park; another grocer did business in a building at Ridge and Oakwood. And early in 1941 George H. Smith opened a $17,000 cold storage locker plant on Calumet Avenue.

Service stations were operated in 1939 by Burt McKee, Paul Littman, John H. Ooms, Walter Mills, I. Wieringa, Clarence Kooy, and Martin Boender. Helen Hopp's beauty shop was on the Ridge at State Line. A modest tourist bureau opened in Town Hall in 1934 to direct visitors to local rooms, cabins, and campsites.

Several restaurants prospered. Maurice "Mace" Allen's durable and popular Mace's Bar-B-Q opened in 1925 on the southeast corner of Ridge and Calumet. At Mace's one could enjoy a drink, admire Mace's collection of stuffed animal heads, *and* quietly bet on the horses. Burned in 1945, it reopened as The Corner, and was torn down in 1980. Miss Ida Becker ran a dinette. Mrs. Milo Rockovich's Ultra Moderne Tea Room at 1723 Ridge Road catered to "fashionable parties and luncheons" and served tasty Sunday dinners. The *Times* claimed that Mrs. Rockovich enjoyed a "splendid reputation and nationwide recognition."

The Ridge Road Roller Rink, in the 1920s, was located in the Hesterman's barn up on the Ridge. (MHS photo)

JABAAY'S BARBERSHOP

Martin Jabaay opened his barbershop on Ridge Road in late 1927 on a corner of land shaved from his father's truck farm, which extended over to Hohman Avenue and down to the Little Calumet.

Marty, a popular fellow, cut hair in his store for forty years. He also led the town band. Jabaay died in the 1990s. Tom Smith, his employee and then partner for ten years, took over the shop when Jabaay retired.

The shop is still in operation as Al's Barber Shop, and is the oldest business in town.

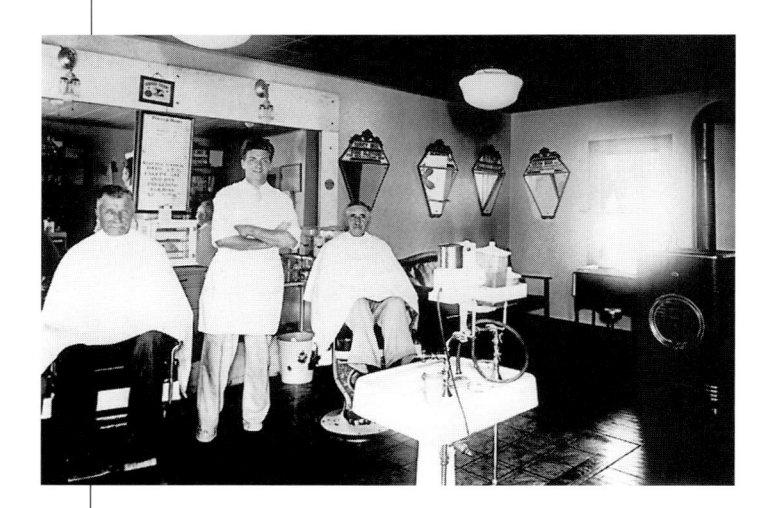

Martin Jabaay in front of his barbershop on Ridge Road, 1928. (MHS photo donated by Martin Jabaay)

A view from the north showing Jabaay's shop on a corner of his parents' farm. (MHS photo donated by Martin Jabaay)

Inside Martin Jabaay's Barbershop, 1933. Seated are Albert Flym, left, and Martin's father, Dingeman A. Jabaay, right. Jabaay earned a dollar a month for hanging advertising mirrors in the corner of his shop. One of them advertises Bock Hardware in Lansing. (MHS photo donated by Martin Jabaay)

The first three owners of the shop: Martin Jabaay (seated), Tom Smith (left), Carl Miller (right), with longtime barber, Peter Dykstra. (Photo donated by former owner Al Rossi)

Sinclair Station on Calumet Avenue just north of Ridge Road during the 1950s. (MHS photo)

Mrs. Baker's Adventures in Good Eating at Calumet and Ridge. (MHS photo)

Indiana Cafe at the northwest corner of Ridge and Calumet. The Shell Station is south of Ridge. (MHS photo)

Mace's Bar-B-Q sat in a diagonal position on the southeast corner of Calumet and Ridge. (MHS photo)

In 1937 Carl Spitler, owner of a Ridge Road campground and trailer park, challenged the town's new "trailer camp" ordinance, and won a temporary injunction. The central question for the town, and the real cause of the ordinance, was Spitler's plan to rent trailer spaces to long-term residents. The town won its point after a second challenge from Spitler.

One entity in town was never too popular. In 1927 the Sisters of Mercy purchased Ben Strong's five-acre farm. The sisters moved the house and made it an "old peoples' home," and built Mount Mercy Sanitarium on the site. A thirty-two-bed, two-story brick hospital, it specialized in "nervous cases." In 1940 the order requested a permit for a major expansion. A public hearing revealed deep unhappiness with both the asylum and the expansion plan. Two years later the good sisters gathered up their habits and moved to Dyer. Mount Mercy Sanitarium became Our Lady of Mercy Hospital in 1951, and merged with Hammond's St. Margaret Hospital in 1992.

Government and Politics

Town government changed little between the wars. Business was conducted by the Town Board, sitting, under various hats, as committees for this, that, and the other, and by cadres of volunteers. Clearly more police were needed, but little was done, and a movement to establish a town magistrate's court failed. New plumbing, structural, and electrical inspectors kept up with construction after 1936. Elections were held on schedule, and slates of candidates were fielded, as allowed in Indiana, by local parties.

Most voters were cut from the same conservative Republican cloth; even in the FDR landslide of 1936, Alf Landon carried Munster by almost two to one. The only local political change of note mirrored the national pattern: in the 1931 campaign, which centered on antiannexation and the sorry economy, the "Old Guard" candidates on the Citizens ticket were turned out of office by the Peoples Party fellows. The new crowd won election after election in the 1930s.

In fact, the differences among the candidates in Munster were more personal than political. Town officials were motivated by civic duty and public service and never, never thought of giving up their day jobs. There were no "politicians" involved in town government.

Hamacher's Nursery was located north of Ridge Road where Citizens Financial Bank is today. (MHS photo)

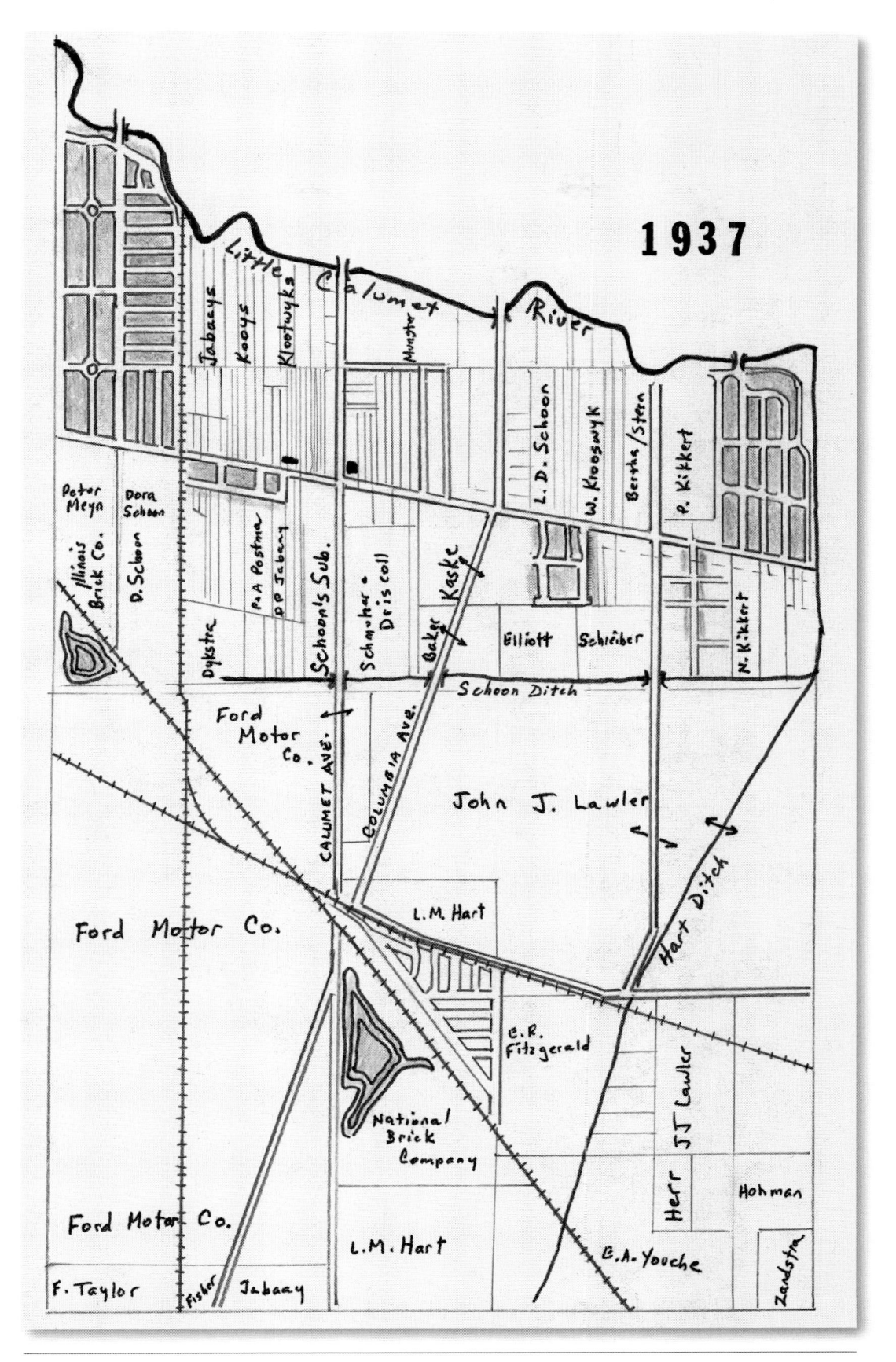

Land ownership map from 1937—one hundred years after David Gibson's log Stagecoach Inn was built on the Sand Ridge. (K. J. Schoon, 1982)

CHAPTER VII FROM WAR TO WAR 1917–1941 • 93

To cite a typical example, in 1939 the town government consisted of Board President Henry Harder, a pressman at W. B. Conkey in Hammond and a noted horticulturist and florist; Dingeman A. Jabaay, a retired farmer, who served on the Board for over a quarter century; Nick Kirsch, a truck farmer and seasonal loader at the brickyard; Clair Strockman, a foreman at Grasselli in Hammond, and Peter C. Tanis, who in 1939 had been clerk-treasurer and the town's day-to-day manager for sixteen years.

True to their principles, the town fathers were agreed on economy. Projects were often put aside because of cost. Board members heeded townspeople, individually, in referenda, and in public meetings. Tax levies in the 1920s, always low by later standards, rose and fell with the economy. Issuing bonds for sewer systems or water towers were painful events, and costs were usually passed on to or shared with direct beneficiaries. Tax bills for water, road and street lighting, and bond service increased steadily before the economy soured in 1929. The General Fund rate expanded in the good years between 1922 and 1927, from .09 to .46, and the town's assessed tax base expanded from $1.1 million to $2.9 million.

Crime became more of a problem after 1920. Much of it was the old-fashioned kind. In 1923 a local farmer spent ten days in jail for beating his wife. Robbery, both individual and group-style, was a more serious problem. In 1930 seven armed bandits charged through the door of Mace's Bar-B-Q, cut the phone line, emptied owner Maurice Allen's cash register and the pockets of patrons and employees alike, then robbed the service station next door, and escaped in two stolen automobiles with five hundred dollars. A year later John Lorscheider's filling station at Ridge and Hohman was robbed. This time the "perp" was nabbed, and sent away for ten years.

In 1934 a garage fire tipped the marshal of a moonshine operation on Crestwood Avenue. The "monster still," which used an illegal gas tap, was shut down, and the lady proprietor was taken to jail. A year later a torso was found in a swamp near Sheffield. A week after that teenagers Victor and John Kirsch of Munster and Fred Kunz of Hammond found a trunk containing a pair of legs near the brickyard. The victim was Earvin J. Lang; his killers were found. Such foul play certainly upset, and perhaps excited quiet little Munster.

Annexation Games

There were two major "outside" concerns. One was annexation, the other, for a while, was Ford Field. From the 1920s on various big city "amalgamation" plans called for various combinations of Whiting, East Chicago, Hammond, and Gary. Fortunately for Munster, no two cities were ever on the same page, which is the only reason why small potatoes like Munster and Highland survived.

Peter C. Tanis was Munster treasurer from 1920 to 1921 and from 1926 to 1935, and clerk-treasurer from 1936 to 1951. (MHS photo)

From 1920 to the 1950s, popular wisdom held that Highland and Munster would become part of Hammond. Munster was seen as the "logical location" for upscale homes. Hammond had already taken North Township lands to the north, and, after a long court fight, Hessville in 1923. Gary would presumably one day devour Griffith. Big city men argued, correctly, that annexation would bring the towns a variety of benefits and modern municipal services. Townspeople countered that higher taxes—the great bugaboo of the era—would more than offset any advantages gained, that home rule was important, and besides, they really didn't *need* better drinking water, sewers, and schools, or more police or a bigger fire department.

The first confrontation began in January 1923, as Munster residents signed a "first-strike" petition objecting to annexation by Hammond. Hammond officials, ready to pounce, harped on Munster's dependence on bad-tasting well water, and offered Lake Michigan water as bait. Rumors, based on fact, were spreading that Gary was about to devour Griffith, Highland, and perhaps Munster (though one Gary councilman thought Munster was in Illinois!). Hammond struck first on November 5, 1925. The mayor dispatched city police to round up councilmen for an emergency session. An annexation ordinance was rushed though the legalities, and Munster was bagged at 7:30 p.m., Highland, five minutes later.

Outraged, the two Ridge towns went to court, and blocked action until the Depression took the steam out of annexation. A few in Munster wavered, arguing that regular bus service and the city's downtown shopping district were worthwhile, and that perhaps even more benefits might come from a union with Hammond. Modernizers complained of Munster "backwardness" that retarded growth and discouraged Chicago investors. By the mid-1930s the question was mooted.

In 1945 Hammond Mayor Vernon Anderson went "on the prowl," arguing that annexation was the "only logical means for the postwar development of Hammond." A Munster town referendum opposed his plan. Home rule, low taxes, and cheap public services swayed the voters. In 1953 former Congressman William Schulte called for a grand union of all of North Township into the second largest city in Indiana. A sound idea, but Hammond was again asleep at the switch, while townspeople complained often and loudly. Despite many reasonable calls for municipal mergers over the years, the question, for Munster, had finally been resolved.

Ford Field

In the 1920s a popular pollster reported that Henry Ford was considered the third greatest man in history, after Jesus and Napoleon. His Model T set the world standard for popular transportation, his factories were busy, and he owned an airline. His less-than-ideal Trimotor passenger planes served Detroit and Chicago. In 1924 Ford opened a still-active assembly plant in Hegewisch, which employed some 150 Hammond men. Two years later, with pockets full of cash and grand plans, Ford bought a thousand acres in Munster from the estate of Lucius Fisher for $800,000, and some four hundred more acres across the state line in Lansing.

At the center of Ford's new "Aeroplane City of the World" would be a landing field. Along its perimeter would be a major parts center, a freight forwarding complex, and an airplane manufacturing plant where ten thousand workers would build dozens of "Flying Flivvers" every day. Ford's designers and builders were already hard at work on that tiny, dangerous, eighty-five-mile-an-hour toy. Adjacent highways and a railroad spur line would deliver raw materials and carry finished goods away.

For a while Munster folk talked like Oklahoma Boomers. Local editors, boosters, and realtors were transfixed: once Ford's plan was underway, industrial employment would double or triple the populations of Hammond and Munster overnight, and Ford was the very man to make it happen. And a few things did happen in 1927.

Ford leased much of his airport land to local farmers for sod-building crops while construction crews went to work. A new roadway and a spur line connected the airfield with highways and the Grand Trunk Railway. A steel-framed hangar, designed by architect Albert Kahn, still in use in 2006 and a designated historic site, and several smaller structures were built. Floodlights were installed for night operations and the Henry and Edsel Ford Greater Chicago Flying Terminal opened in June 1926.

All the ballyhoo of the age was uncorked. Newspapers gleefully reported the landings and departures of Hollywood stars like Wallace Beery and America's sweetheart, Mary Pickford, and gushed that Munster would be as well-known in Australia as New York City. Local manufacturer Frank Betz flew sightseers around in his fleet of seven-passenger "all-metal monoplanes."

But it was not to be. The Depression halted the project, Ford's attention wandered off to other things, and Ford Field remained a grass strip for many years. After the property somehow survived the postwar building boom, in 1948 Thomas Seay renamed it the Chicago-Hammond Airport. In 1976 it became Lansing Municipal Airport, and eventually, and more grandly, Lansing, Chicago Airport. Ford's Munster property became, variously, a Cold War missile site, an industrial park, and lastly, subdivisions.

Hard Times

The Depression years were hard on the people and the town government alike. Assessments were steadily reduced even as the number of homes in town increased. Delinquent

---

The Ford Hangar at what is now Lansing, Chicago Airport. (MHS photo)

Edsel Ford and E. N. Bennett at the Ford Field. (Photo found and donated by Martha Wilke)

taxes increased by a factor of ten between 1930 and 1933. Town income and the civil budget shrank together, although the school levy was modestly increased. Most of the town's funds were impounded after the failure of the Highland Farmers and Merchants Savings Bank, while contractors still expected payment when work was done. The Chamber of Commerce helped with poor relief in 1932, and a Munster Welfare Relief Committee was formed in late 1933.

But Munster was in far better shape than Gary and Hammond, where mass unemployment lasted until the later 1930s. Most of the town's suburbanites kept their jobs. Munster farmers were hurt when agricultural prices collapsed, but managed to keep their properties by cutting spending to the bone. They lived on whatever foodstuffs they could raise and bartered for the rest. Some farmers found jobs with New Deal agencies after 1933. Scanty records indicate that most suffered long and quietly before going, in desperation, to the North Township trustee's office for a few sacks of coal, medical care, and perhaps vouchers for some groceries.

The chief burden of relief was carried by the North Township trustee, the official "steward of the poor." But that official was bankrupt even before 1932. Traditional private charities helped, chief among them the Lake County Relief Commission and various Chambers of Commerce. Hundreds tilled "Depression gardens," the predecessor of Victory gardens, on land borrowed from the township, businesses, and private owners. Many Munster people cultivated plots in the North Township gardens on Indianapolis Boulevard in Highland.

Churches did what they could, despite sagging contributions, although the members of the Munster Reformed Church actually increased their donations. In 1938 a Munster grocer donated a thousand bushels of onions to the Salvation Army in Hammond; all were given away in a single day. In 1939 the marshal's office sponsored a Valentine Dance and Carnival, and used the proceeds to help "distressed" people coming to Town Hall for aid.

On a bitterly cold day in February 1936, a car carrying four Munster WPA workers to Town Hall to collect their pay for a street work project was struck by a train at Maynard. The cause of the accident was frost-covered windows in subzero temperatures; they apparently never saw the passenger train bearing down on them. Peter Meeter, Cornelius Ver Beek, Garret Vanderhook, and John Kruit left four widows, sixteen children, and precious few assets behind them. The Munster Chamber of Commerce made arrangements for their burial and immediately organized a relief campaign.

One positive event: in 1938 the Town Board, with Henry Harder serving as president, asked consultant Lawrence Sheridan to draw up a master plan. Sheridan studied everything, interviewed many, and prepared a comprehensive report. The plan envisioned the

Boender Open Air Market was north of Ridge Road and east of Hohman Avenue. (MHS photo)

future of a suburb, not a farm town. The Town Board studied the proposition for three years. Adopted in 1941, the Master Plan gave the Board authority to regulate zoning, home building, apartment construction, businesses, heavy and light industry, public safety, schools, the police and fire departments, and future parks and recreational facilities. Modified by need and common sense on several occasions, most notably in 1950, it served Munster very well.

Growth made the water supply a major problem. In 1923 Munster held public meetings to discuss construction of a modern municipal water works, which meant joining the Hammond Sanitary District. Instead, the town drilled a well and built a water tower behind Town Hall, and as Munster grew, drilled more wells. The first stage of a municipal water system was installed in 1924 by the Munster Water Works, with $17,000 in funds from a bond issue. Munster thereafter required developers to underwrite the installation of local water lines. A second well was drilled in 1928 in the Elliott Subdivision. A third successful well was drilled in 1932.

By 1938, after drilling a series of dry wells, and with new homes rising everywhere, Munster realized that wells, however deep and however many, weren't up to the job. And the water tasted awful. A year later, with a $20,700 grant from the Public Works Administration (PWA) and local funds, Munster finally built a connector line over the river to Hammond to bring Lake Michigan water to town. A new pumping station on Calumet helped, and Munster finally had enough water for its suburban homes and lawns. The town built a second water tower for storage and pressure, and, as required by Hammond, installed meters in every home. Over the next year the ever-resourceful Jake DeMik installed 375 of the newfangled gadgets, even as the last of Munster's crank telephones were being retired. The town on the Ridge was becoming very modern.

Education in the 1930s

Changes were few in the town's two schools between the World Wars. Student enrollments in the public school dropped from 335 in 1930 to only 247 in 1933, and hovered around 300 until late in the decade. The entire 1933 school town budget was under $30,000, including $1,775 for teachers' salaries and an annual tuition payment to Hammond of $7,200 for educating Munster's high school youth. By 1939, 70 Munster youth attended Hammond High School. The five teachers typically met combined classes. When new Principal Ernest Elliott replaced E. Perry Flick in 1940, the school building was found to be in "A-1" condition. Around a hundred attended the "Dutch" School in the 1930s.

A few improvements were made. *Girls* were issued armbands and allowed to serve on the Safety Patrol after 1933. Night classes in citizenship were offered in 1935. The Home Bureau launched a kindergarten campaign in 1935 with a

Munster Public School with the 1928 addition at the rear. (MHS photo)

weekly story hour and a demonstration kindergarten, taught by Miss Kline. In the fall, a town-wide bazaar raised funds for equipment, and a kindergarten was opened for children ages four to six. Fees for the children's physical exams were underwritten by the new PTA. In 1936 Munster used a generous WPA grant to landscape school grounds and repair facilities.

Providing noon meals for the children was a challenge. In 1936 the students were fed donated canned fruits and vegetables. In 1939 the PTA organized a kitchen in the school, collected canned goods, jellies, jams, and vegetables, and opened a hot lunch program. The cost per student was seven cents.

Clubs and Organizations

Indiana was a land of joiners, and Munster was no exception. For years its citizens had been active in a variety of nationally affiliated groups in Hammond and elsewhere. Local organizations began to appear after 1920. The Munster Chamber of Commerce emerged in 1925 at open meetings, under the guidance of William Terpstra and H. S. Daugherty. The chamber, an open civic group, invited all, including women, to attend meetings and join the fight for better roads, "instruct" town officials, and encourage business. The Junior Chamber of Commerce was organized in 1927. The Town Band was (re)formed in 1928.

In 1934 and 1935, in addition to the usual business-centered activities, the Chamber sponsored community dinners. The first event was a rabbit feast for 750 hungry Munster folk in December 1934. A year later the Chamber sent three mighty hunters northward to bag deer, "and maybe a bear" for the event. They bagged enough venison, a bear, and other critters to serve a thousand guests. Annual Fourth of July picnics in Wicker Park attracted as many as six thousand people "of Holland descent" for many years.

By 1940 the Chamber of Commerce had fought annexation by Hammond, provided much-needed relief during the Depression years, helped develop the zoning plan, and

Kindergarten class and Miss Kline, 1938. (MHS photo)

had even established a crop inspection station. In 1940 the Chamber plumped for a Northcote Avenue bridge over the Little Cal. Civic volunteerism, in and out of government, was a powerful force in those years.

Even so, by 1941 the Chamber of Commerce was moribund. After a hiatus, a Munster Businessmen's Association was formed in 1949, and reformed again in 1955 as the Chamber of Commerce. The Chamber's headquarters were located at the corner of Ridge and Hohman until 1989, when it moved to the Center for Visual and Performing Arts. The chamber continues to encourage business, works with Town Hall on various projects, and serves as the "front door" of the community.

The Munster Home Bureau was organized in April 1933, at the home of Mrs. Otto Rabe. Later renamed the Home Economics Association, the Home Demonstration Association, and, in 1936, the Munster Extension Homemakers, the group helped new residents meet "older settlers," sponsored talks on home improvements and potluck luncheons, raised funds for Goodwill Industries, helped open the first Munster kindergarten in 1939, and served hot lunches at the school "soup kitchen."

The later 1930s saw many new groups emerge. Eight outdoorsmen, led by Bernard L. Berg, organized the Munster Fish and Game Protective Association in 1940. The Association built a log cabin exhibit for a sports show, sponsored birdhouse building contests for young people, and helped wardens hatch quail eggs. The Community Players, under the direction of Homer Hitt, Herbert Montgomery, and E. Lacy Gibson, first trod the boards in 1940 with *The Valiant, Where But In America?* (with author Oscar M. Wolff in the audience), and *Courage*, presented as a benefit for the PTA Youth groups also prospered. Among them were the Young Peoples Club, which sponsored barn dances at Town Hall in the 1930s, and a busy 4-H Club. The Girl Scouts were active after 1936.

Girl Scouts in Munster were organized in 1935. This photo was taken in celebration of the troop's being the first fully uniformed troop in the Hammond area. Troop members were Betty Norris, Betty Strockman, Yvonne Baker, Marilyn Johnson, Mrs. Fergusen, Jean Bacon, Jane Banta, Mrs. Grace Anderson, Edna Frank, Ruth Schmueser, Betty McCue, Lois Kraay, Ida Schoon, Carole Carter, Elaine Rud, Virginia Elman, Nancy Miller, Jacqueline Smith, Jean Orr, Patricia Lancaster, Marcella Lancaster, and Betty Rockovich. (MHS photo)

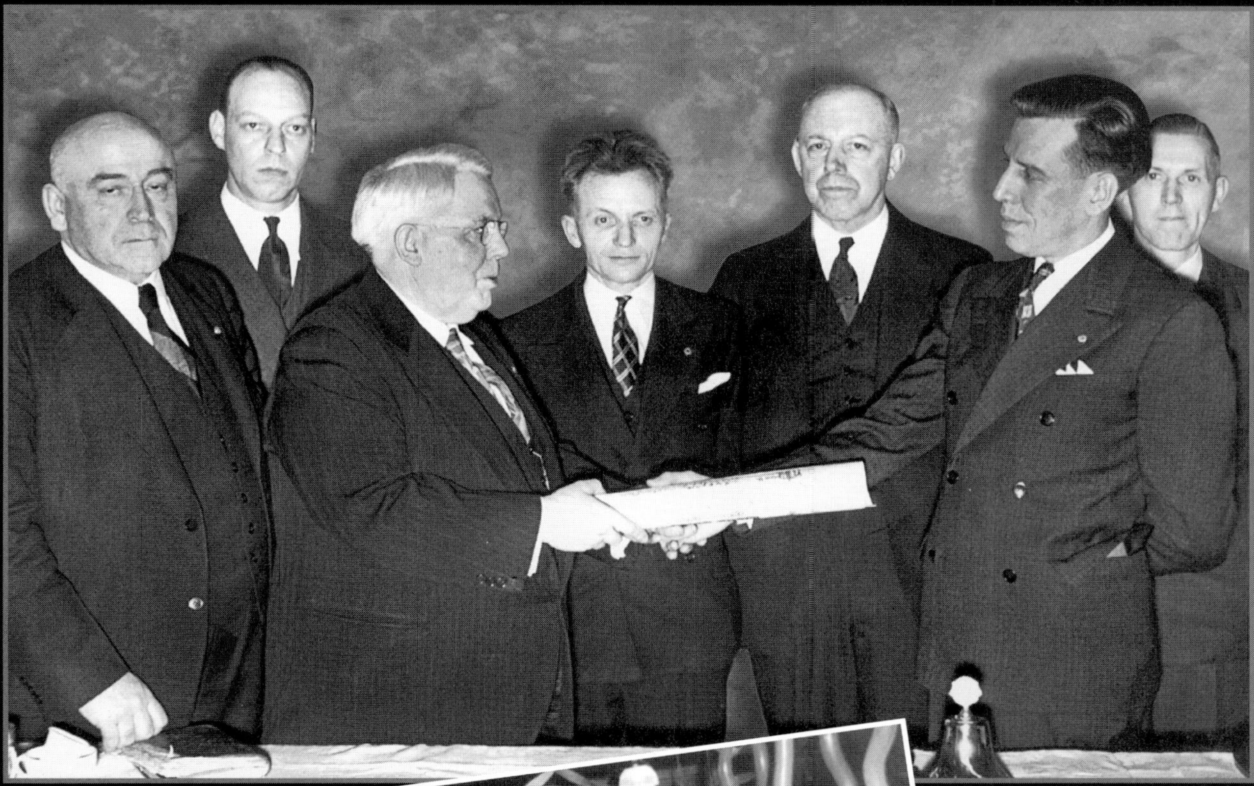

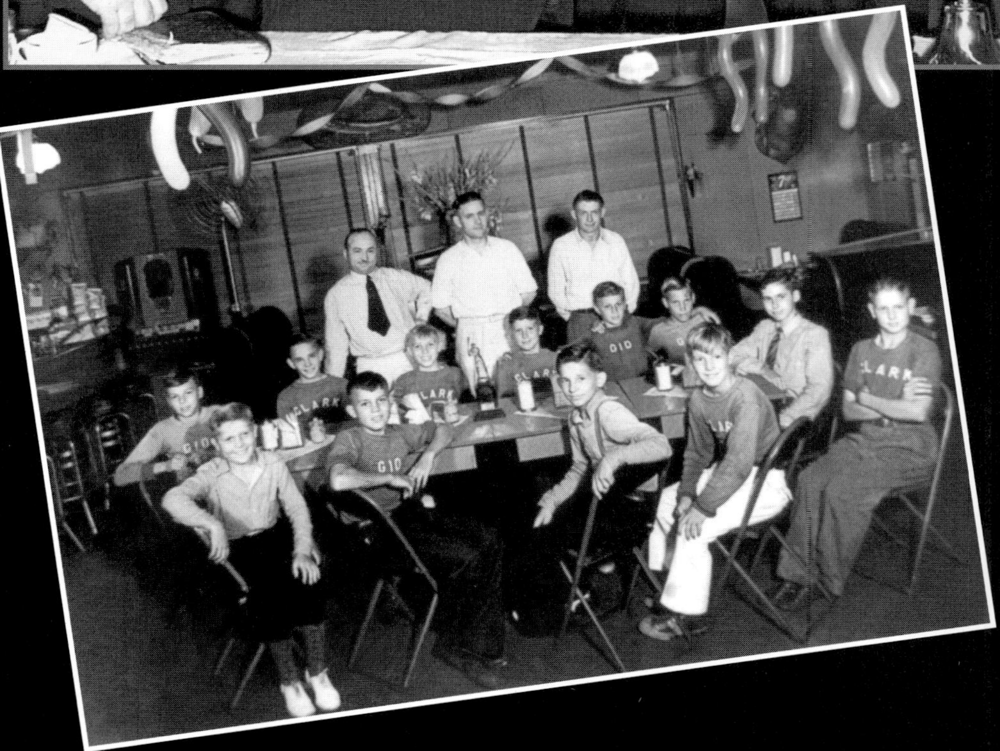
CLARK
GIO

30TH PL
HARRISON AV
MONROE AV
MADISON
FULLERTON AV
HOWARD
RIDGEWAY AV
FAIRWAY AV
RIDGE RD
SEBERGER DR
SOUTH ST
TERRACE DR
RIDGE RD
SOUTH ST
GREENWOOD AV
BEECH AV
WALNUT DR
WHITE OAK AV
CASTLE DR
MORAINE DR
HOHMAN AV
SUNSET LN
BRIAR LN
BRIAR LN
LAWNDALE DR
SYCAMORE LN
MAPLE LN
PARK DR
RIDGE RD
TIMRICK DR
MEADOW LN
45TH ST
MARGO LN
SUPERIOR AV
45TH ST
BROOKSIDE DR
GLASTONBURY ST
BANBURY PL
MILFORD HAVEN WAY
LEICESTER RD
SALISBURY DR
WHITEHALL GARDEN
INDIANA PKWY
PROGRESS AV
VALPARAISO DR
CALUMET AV
THICKET LN
REDBUD RD
CRIMSON TREE LN
IVY LN
TAMARACK DR
FITZGERALD DR
TWIN CREEK BLVD
WHITE OAK AV
BOWEN DR
NORWICH CT
IVY LN
SINGLETON DR

CHAPTER VIII

War and Peace
1941-1950

IN THE SUMMER OF 1939 EUROPE AGAIN WENT to war. The United States remained a highly interested "observer" until late 1941. Everyone felt, deep down, that America would be drawn into that "foreign war." Meanwhile, British money paid for almost anything American factories could make, and the Calumet Region hummed with industrial activity. Jobs were plentiful, and attracted thousands to the Region. Housing was scarce, builders, workers, and farmers flourished, and everyone in town had their choice of jobs.

On the surface, life seemed normal. In October 1941, Town Board President Henry Harder flattened his national competitors in a flower-judging contest at Garfield Park Conservatory in Chicago. Harder's gladiolias—including some new strains he had developed—won five first places. A horticulturist since 1925, Harder was still working as a pressman in Hammond. He cultivated 260 varieties on his Munster farm. In October, the Home Bureau managed the Munster Community Chest Drive, which raised funds for a variety of community purposes.

Munster Christian Reformed Church servicemen in World War II. (Courtesy of Fred Klooster)

Similar events and activities continued even after the attack on Pearl Harbor and were expanded by new ones, often with wartime themes. In 1942 the Girl Scouts held a fundraiser in the school gym. In January the entire town was invited to attend a Presidents' Birthday Party and an "old-fashioned shoe box social" in the gym, on behalf of the Infantile Paralysis Fund. Town Marshal Ed Bennett managed the affair, which raised $137.63 for the fight against polio. Admission was ten cents. Each "girl and lady" was invited to bring a decorated box lunch "with her name on the inside," to be auctioned to the highest bidder.

In February the Town Board banned overnight street parking during the winter months because of a rash of tire thefts, already a scarce item. Students in the upper grades at Munster School presented an operetta. Complaints about roaming dogs and stray chickens eating early-flowering bulbs suggest another ragged edge between suburbanites and farmers. In June the town voted to spend $1,003 on street and alley repairs. Hunting was finally banned within town limits in December.

In March the *Times* reported the passing of the oldest man in town, John Broertjes, eighty-eight. Broertjes was born in Rotterdam, immigrated to the United States in 1866, settled in Roseland, and moved to Munster in 1877. Emil Schreiber, also eighty-eight and the town's next oldest man, died in December. Schreiber was a native of Saxony, in Hammond, and had attended school in a log cabin with Indian children. All in all, Munster offered a fairly typical image of small-town life in America.

As the world went to war, Munster continued in its commonsensical ways. Elections were held on schedule; the Progressive Party ran its slates against the Peoples Party candidates. Munster remained faithfully Republican; in 1944, despite presidential advice about changing horses in midstream, the town voted two to one for Thomas E. Dewey over three-term incumbent FDR.

Unlike most small towns in America (and Munster, Germany, for example, where major demolition was underway), construction boomed in Munster, Indiana, during the war. Builders needed government "priorities" after 1942; the rule was, no priority, no brick, no nails. But Munster was close to defense plants that were hiring more workers every day, and those workers desperately needed a place to live.

Nearly all homes were then north of the Ridge; central and south Munster were still farmland. The only significant exception was Independence Park, with 168 houses and more rising every week. Only three homes stood in the southeast corner of town. In the twelve months after June 1941, Munster added 170 homes to its stock. In October 1942, 30 new homes were completed, including duplexes and apartments. Except for Independence Park, construction was focused in the northwest corner of town.

One of many two-story brick duplexes built in the early 1940s. (Photo by Lance Trusty in 1982).

In mid-1942 contractors built dozens of "low cost" duplex homes in Hollywood Manor Subdivision. Angered homeowners hired an attorney to stop them, and complained that the new units were "cheap," would be rented, not sold, and would hurt property values. A hundred Hollywood Manor residents filled a Zoning Board hearing, and asked that future houses be upgraded from Class C to Class B construction. The Federal Defense Housing Project Administration (FDHPA) and the Office of Price Administration (OPA) argued that the construction was for an emergency "defense housing project," and that "war production workers" needed immediate housing.

Local builder Ray Seberger had already finished several duplexes. City and Suburban Developments, Inc., which had already built others, had a contract in hand for forty more, and wanted builders for a hundred more. The Town Board was forced to acquiesce, but did insist that they must cost at least $9,500 and have brick exteriors.

In March 1943, with FHA backing and more duplexes under construction, Colonial Homes offered a row of new duplexes on Belmont for either direct sale or rent-to-buy to "persons vital to the smooth-running of the important home front." In mid-1943, permits were issued for more duplexes and the occasional apartment house. The only "traditional" new structure in town was Gerritt Van Drunen's chicken coop on Ridge Road. Things did slow down a bit after 1943, in a mere pause before an amazing postwar boom.

The Munster "tourist camp" was still at odds with the Town Board in August 1942. In 1937 the town had mandated a one-month trailer parking limit and a thirty-day maximum residency for occupants of the trailer park's cottages and apartments. But Carl Spitler, now profitably renting rooms to war workers, also wanted to rent mobile homes. Despite the urging of Governor Henry Schricker, the determined Town Board ordered the occupants to move on. The Board, which had already won a fight with Washington on construction rules for "war worker" housing, wasn't about to bend for a mere governor. Or a world war.

Munster Folk at War

The draft began with a mass registration in October 1940. Every Munster male between twenty-one and thirty-five, later forty-five, then sixty-four, had to register at Town Hall. Herman Ringgenburg chaired the Draft Board, assisted by the

Munster Christian Reformed Church servicemen in World War II: (back row) Don Klooster, John Harkema Jr., John Dekker, Herb Van Wieren, Joe Norman, Clarence Verbeek, Melvin Jongsma, unidentified, Rich Hoekstra, Bob Ooms, Jim Smit, and unidentified; (second row) Harold Scholten, Chester Boender, Peter J. Dykstra, Abel Doornbos, Douglas Boender, Gil Fennema, Peter M. Dykstra, Jake Meeter, Andrew Jabaay, and Harry Rodenburg; (third row) Harold Bultema, John Vroom, John Vander Noord, Cornelius Boender, John Dykstra, Jacob Doornbos, Tony Hoekstra, and Bud Meeter; (front row) Melvin Kamstra, Gerald Klooster, Case Dykstra, Ed Huizenga, Chaplain C. Van Schouwen, Reverend Joseph Monsma, John Doornbos, Fred Klooster, Charles Zandstra, and Arnold Dekker. (Courtesy of Fred Klooster)

Reverend J. H. Monsma. The actual draft began in December 1940, and by June 1941 some seven thousand men from the Calumet Region had been inducted into the service.

The numbers climbed after the American entrance into the war, to 67 from Munster in September 1942, to 110 by mid-1943. Seven men from Independence Park were in uniform by July 1942. When Town Attorney M. E. Belshaw was inducted in September 1942, the Town Board voted to retain his firm's services "for the duration."

The *Times* faithfully reported news of local servicemen. John Hoekema was the first to leave from Munster. Corporal Hoekema survived the war. Coast Guard Petty Officer Roy Shropshire won national wrestling honors, and posed for the press with boxer Jack Dempsey in 1943. Gerald Huizenga was promoted from the driver's seat of a Pleasant View Dairy milk truck to the Army in 1943. Private Bob Hitt returned from training at the University of Alabama for a short furlough in January 1944. Private Steve Markovich was in San Diego with the Marines in 1944. And there were many more stories.

Army Air Force fighter pilot Lieutenant Eugene C. DeBoer flew eighty missions, dueled with Japanese Zeroes in New Guinea, and won the Air medal, the Silver Star, and the Distinguished Flying Cross. In late 1943, DeBoer was honored at a grand party at the school attended by the entire town. Lieutenant Raymond H. Kahl, another winner of the Air Medal, was also honored. The school band played "Coming in on a Wing and a Prayer" and "Over There."

Private Joseph Hoekema, a paratrooper, won several citations and battle stars in North Africa and Italy, and a Purple Heart in the Netherlands. Private Vernon Moore won a Purple Heart on D-Day and a Bronze Star for valor in Belgium. Roger Boonstra of the Fifteenth Air Force was promoted to the rank of lieutenant in 1944 and awarded the Air Medal with two Oak Leaf Clusters. A Purple Heart was pinned on Sergeant Clarence J. Porte in 1943 for wounds received in the North African campaign.

Some were taken prisoner. Wounded and captured during the Battle of the Bulge, and originally reported missing in action, Sergeant Norman Schoon spent the last months of the European war in German hands. Technical Sergeant James L. Klootwyk was also reported missing in action after his Flying Fortress, the *Coral Princess*, was shot down over Germany. But, like Schoon, the radio operator/aerial gunner also surfaced in a prisoner of war camp. B-17 pilot Lieutenant Robert G. Foster, winner of the Air Medal with two Oak Leaf Clusters, ended the war in a prison camp, at Moosberg, Germany.

Armored Division Private Maurice L. Hopkins was captured in Germany and reported missing in action. But Hopkins later reported that he and three friends from Whiting were alive and well in a prison camp. The resourceful fellow managed to send his picture home from the camp, and in August 1943 actually made a shortwave radio broadcast to his parents on Kraay Avenue.

A few would never return. Air Cadet Howard H. Miller died in Tennessee on his first solo flight in 1942. Private John A. Wall was killed in action in March 1945. Some casualties were confirmed long after the war. In January of 1946, First Lieutenant Robert Bensemmer was confirmed as having been killed in action. Sergeant Robert E. Trueblood's parents hoped that he might have parachuted to safety after his airplane exploded over Germany in April 1945, but after examining possibilities for a year, the War Department confirmed his passing. Three other young men from Munster gave their lives in World War II: Gordon Cowell, Walter Karlen, and Francis Timm.

Women also served in uniform. Connie McGavin was active in the Women's Auxiliary Training Corps (WATC) at Indiana University. Margene Moore served in the Women Appointed for Voluntary Emergency Service (WAVES). Platoon Sergeant Elaine Ramage (Olson), later a leading light in the Munster Historical Society, went on active service from the Marine Corps Reserve. Her engagement was announced in the *Times* later in the war; her mother served as a Red Cross ambulance driver. In 1944 former practical nurse, steel mill employee, and SPAR ("Semper Paratus, Always Ready") reservist Violet E. Caviness went on active duty as a parachute rigger for the Coast Guard at Norfolk.

The Home Front

Rationing and shortages were everyday matters. Ration cards and books were issued by teachers and volunteers at the Munster School under the supervision of Principal Ernest Elliott. According to issued ration books, the population of Munster in 1943 was 3,584. Sugar was closely controlled. Coffee was often not available, unless one "knew someone."

In the winter of 1943 it was reported that chicken and green vegetables were plentiful, turkey scarce, and canned goods "tight," more because of the steel in the cans than the contents. Gasoline was tightly rationed, and speed limits were strictly observed, mostly because of the rubber shortage. New tires were as rare as hen's teeth, and pleasure driving was considered unpatriotic.

Victory gardens, like the Depression gardens of the 1930s, were widely planted. "Food is ammunition—it will help win the war. So march to victory in your victory garden," urged the *Times* in February 1943, as part of a nationwide campaign. March, or dig and weed, they did. Victory gardening became a wartime virtue. The Lions Club sponsored gardening classes and, under the direction of A. H. Bacon, provided town-wide plowing. Bacon, Peter Tanis, and Ed Bennett coordinated gardening activities. After a rousing speech by County Agent Lloyd Cutler, the Independence Park Club asked for spring plowing of seventeen acres, and Clarence Armstrong led hundreds of new gardeners into the fields.

Munster farmers faced several problems after 1941. While many farms in town were on the small side, and could continue with family help, enlistments and the draft gradually cut the labor supply. Farmworkers found far better wages in local war plants. Moreover, seeds, insecticides, and fertilizers were tight. Taxes rose, even as markets absorbed everything farmers could grow at higher prices.

In January 1942, Munster farmers joined with others in nearby towns in the Vegetables for Victory and Vitamins (VVV) Committee. Members vowed to raise their crops as usual, despite seed shortages and labor problems, and agreed to employ anyone willing to work, without discrimination. VVV members were described, in the heated and patriotic argot of the day, as "Dutch-American farmers of the 'green belt,' men as intrepid as the Dutch in the Netherlands East Indies, who are poking stiff left jabs at the bared teeth of the Japs."

In fact, food was plentiful, and full employment meant that everyone could afford it. The various shortages—no meat some days, sugar always scarce, out of this or that—were essentially irritants, rather than serious problems. There was plenty of unrationed stuff to eat. And, even if those in the big cities played the black markets, Munster folk generally remained dutiful and patriotic.

Sergeant Elaine Ramage Olson, USMC, and her mother Gladys Ramage, a Red Cross ambulance driver. (MHS photo donated by Elaine Olson)

Defending the town against whatever the enemy had to offer was an early concern. Homeowners were told "it can happen here," but don't panic, just prepare. Townspeople contributed generously to the Civil Defense program. The Munster Civil Defense Council was organized in January 1942 under Lake County Office of Civil Defense (OCD) Director Walter R. Mybeck. Town Board President Henry Harder served as local chairman, assisted by Dingeman Jabaay. Board members included Clair Strockman, Nick Kirsch, Peter Tanis, and Henry Konefsky.

Marshal Ed Bennett attended an FBI school in Civilian Defense. Fire Chief William Schmueser coordinated disaster responses. C. S. "Doc" Howat was the community training officer. Emergency Medical Officer Dr. E. C. Hulett trained fifty first-aid workers. Chief Air Raid Warden E. Lacy Gibson and several assistant chief wardens coordinated the activities of ninety-five block wardens.

Wardens were fingerprinted, issued white helmets and flashlights, and sent to first-aid classes. William Kaye, a Standard Oil–Whiting chemist, lectured them on "Gas Defense" in May 1942. Boy Scouts served as messengers, and loved every minute of it. Townspeople assembled in the school gym on a Friday evening in May 1942, for the first public Civil Defense meeting. A film, *The Bombing of London*, was shown twice to overflow crowds, and calls for donations and volunteers went out.

In August 1942, the Army ordered a twelve-minute, test blackout for the entire Calumet Region. At 10:00 p.m. on the twelfth, all lights were to be out or covered, smoking was prohibited, automobiles halted, telephones not to be used, and all citizens were to be indoors until the all-clear was sounded. Munster officials reported "100%" cooperation, with no accidents. Other blackouts and drills followed in 1943, with declining seriousness, as the tide of war turned. Even so, OCD rallies filled the school and raised morale. Town officials reminded people that "it could *still* happen here," and combat veterans spoke to rallies about the war and "doing your part."

Women managed the home front. In January 1942, Mrs. Nick Fagen, the Women's OCD chairman and an accomplished speaker, exhorted Munster ladies to stop waste and recycle everything possible, including rubber overshoes; train for emergencies; give blood; plant Victory gardens; buy bonds; can food early; and "prepare for sacrifice without excitement and without complaining."

The Women's Division of the OCD recruited sector captains and block matrons. Committees coordinated with community organizations to encourage morale, good nutrition, healthy recreation, and collection of "salvage for victory." The Fire Department Ladies Auxiliary provided air-raid instructions, worked closely with the Red Cross, and organized rummage sales to benefit bond drives. In 1942 Mrs. Homer Hitt chaired a fundraising campaign for the Hammond United Service Organizations (USO) and raised over $1,000.

The Home Bureau sponsored classes on restyling clothing; the "Dutch cap" was newly fashionable in 1943. Courses in first aid and home nursing care were given at the Christian Reformed Church; graduations featured a patriotically decorated table "with a first aid room in miniature" on top. The Panhellenic Club sponsored "projects," including bridge games, to benefit the Red Cross, the needy, the USO, and scholarships.

The Red Cross was the busiest organization in town. The Munster chapter was organized in June 1941, and went right to work making clothing for European refugees. Rows of sewing machines in Town Hall stitched day and night until the project was moved to the school auditorium in 1942, and later in the war, to the basement of the Christian Reformed Church and to homes. Red Cross ladies made flannel and muslin bed gowns, skirts, first aid bags, sweaters, dresses, even beanies, but surgical dressings were the major focus. In just half of 1941–42, after the ladies rolled 10,549 dressings, their quota was raised by a factor of ten. Small wonder they occasionally ran out of materials.

Production Chairman Mrs. Stanley Stone kept careful records: from May 1942 to May 1943, forty-eight workers spent 6,829 hours making almost two thousand sewed and knitted articles of clothing. In that same period two hundred volunteer "surgical dressing workers" spent 3,482 hours making almost fifteen thousand dressings. The Red Cross also collected magazines for servicemen, raised money in annual Christmas Drives, and welcomed blood donors. In 1943 there were 250 women active in the Munster chapter.

Young people did their part. War stamps were sold in every classroom. A March 1943 drive collected over $500 from 388 pupils and staff. Mrs. Nock's class led the parade with $93.85 collected in two weeks; Mrs. Sohl's students brought up the rear with $7.30. A boys club sponsored by the Lions built model airplanes for the government. Senior Girl Scouts sewed kit bags for servicemen.

In September 1943, the children joined a parade with the CD Wardens, Boy Scouts, and school bands from nearby towns to rally the town to buy more bonds. In February 1944, Munster School hosted a Victory Dance; admission was three ten-cent war stamps or a bond purchased at the school office. And in October, the Lake County Truck Farmers Association awarded a Victory Farm Volunteer Corps insignia to 130 school children for their successful victory gardens.

The recycling drive for the war effort was an excellent model for later environmentalists. A nationwide search for aluminum was under way even before America joined the war. Coordinated by a number of local clubs, seven hundred kids participated in a "pan swim" at

War bond parade proceeded down Ridge Road, led by Munster Girl Scouts and the Munster School Band. (MHS photo)

A horse troop begins another war bond parade at the corner of Forest Avenue and Ridge Road. (MHS photo donated by Fred Klooster)

Fred Klooster participated in a bond parade in 1942 then the next year shipped off to Fort Benjamin Harrison and the European theater. (MHS photo donated by Fred Klooster)

CHAPTER VIII WAR AND PEACE 1941–1950 • 109

Wicker Park Pool on July 29, 1941. Admission was an aluminum pot or pan, to become fighter planes. In October, the Munster Panhellenic Society collected old leather goods to be made into jackets for British pilots.

By spring 1942, anything salvageable was collected and recycled. Rubber, rags, metal, and paper were the most important materials, and were soon joined by fats. "Now is the time to clean out attics, basements and garages," announced the OCD, "to be ready when the collection is made."

In April 1942, Munster Boy Scout Troop 33 collected newspapers, magazines, and cardboard for the war effort. Julius "Jake" DeMik, the town trash collector and truck driver, delivered everything to a freight car on a siding. The last drive of the year netted over seven tons of goodies. Mrs. A. J. Schuler directed scrap metal collection. Calling a single can in the garbage "un-American," Pearl Schuler, Assistant Scoutmaster Bill Hitt, and every Boy Scout in town went on the warpath for metals.

Because of the shortage of galvanized steel, in September Pearl Schuler asked people to return their old mailboxes to the hardware store for repainting and resale. Citizens were asked to bring their flattened cans to collection centers on "tin can day," the first Saturday of each month. By October the Scouts had collected over a hundred tons of various metals. In March 1943, they rounded up 1,150 pounds of tin cans, and exceeded that a year later. Recycling continued until the end of the war.

The Girl Scouts and the Brownies led the fat recycling drive, for soap and ammunition, they were told. The campaign began in October 1942, and immediately collected 183 pounds of fat. Under the direction of Mrs. Walter Kussmaul, rendered and strained fats in tin cans were collected and delivered to a dealer. Butchers also accepted fat donations. Cooperation was splendid, and "shows a fine spirit and will be continued as long as the government needs the fat." Rubber was equally valuable; one could donate old tires to benefit the local defense fund, or sell them to gas stations for a penny a pound.

War or Defense Bonds were sold everywhere. Rallies, drives, and "Victory" parades were regular events coordinated by the OCD. The nationwide Third War Bond Drive in October 1942 prompted a rally, a parade from Forest Avenue to the school, and a flag ceremony. Booths were manned by servicemen. Bonds were also sold at Town Hall. The event raised over $25,000, despite a delay in the parade caused by the sudden departure of the town fire truck, in full bunting, to extinguish a pair of burning haystacks in Schreiber's Woods.

Bond sales passed $80,000 in 1943, and the *Times* congratulated Munster, "a strictly residential town of 3,000 and less than a dozen small businesses" for "a fine achievement, averaging more than $25 for each man, woman and child in the community."

In early 1944, Munster Town Clerk and bond chairman Peter Tanis reported sales for the Fourth War Bond Drive of over $90,000, nine times the town's assigned quota. A Victory Concert—admission was three ten-cent war stamps or one twenty-five-cent stamp—by the forty-four-member school band under the baton of Mrs. M. Schrader, and the Girls Glee Club packed 'em in. It was, the reviewer said, "a stirring performance of patriotic and classical numbers, especially "little Meta Freeman, third grader, who sang a song." The Sixth War Bond Drive in late 1944 raised $44,000 through a great deal of "personal contact," according to Peter Tanis.

Annual Honor Roll Ceremony at Independence Park. (MHS photo)

The Schools in Wartime

The central problem facing the little school system was finding room for the children of families who had moved to town during the building boom. Enrollment doubled between 1938 and 1941; eighty new pupils arrived in 1941 alone. In 1941 the school partitioned the auditorium and the music room into classrooms and held classes in the gym, until an addition was completed. Two new teachers were hired in mid-term.

In 1942, with six new classrooms in service and a staff of thirteen teachers, the Munster School squeezed in almost two hundred children. Ernest S. Elliott was now the full-time principal with no teaching duties. Forty-two children attended kindergarten in 1942. The PTA supported and managed the "hot lunch" kitchen. Twenty-three students graduated from eighth grade in 1942, thirty-nine in 1944, forty in 1945.

Life in the old building seemed normal. In 1942 Mrs. Max Schrader directed *Polished Pebbles*, an operetta, and was given a bouquet and a gift for her efforts. Twenty-eight Munster young people attended various colleges in September 1942. Twenty-one Munster kids graduated from Hammond High School in June 1942. In December 1943, "Munster Mothers," led by Mrs. Theo Schwenke, raised funds for instruments and equipment for the Munster School Band. A Pearl Harbor Day concert was presented to the school children and the public. As the concert was announced, John J. Kraay, who had founded the town band many years earlier, passed on to his Maker.

In the ten years after 1940 seven hundred new homes were built in town, making Munster one of the fastest-growing communities in Northwest Indiana. The population increased two and a half times, reaching 4,753 in 1950. Moreover, growth was steady, fueled during the war by home construction for defense plant workers, and, after the war, despite all the warnings of an inevitable postwar depression, by universal confidence. The housing market was driven by money from war bonds, returning servicemen with pockets full of mustering out pay, years of steady employment and rising wages, and busy mills and refineries. Munster, perched on the southern border of the gritty industrial Calumet, was in exactly the right place at the right time.

Munster Public School with the three-story addition put on the front of the building. The building was later renamed Lanier Elementary School. (MHS photo)

Munster Public School Band proudly poses in the school gymnasium. (MHS photo)

CHAPTER VIII WAR AND PEACE 1941–1950 • 111

The town was still no business center. It had fairly standard rows of service stations and garages along Ridge Road and Calumet Avenue. Automobiles were increasingly favored for shopping; the "walk-in" days were ending. In 1948 Peter Schoon moved his car agency from Hammond to Calumet just north of the Ridge. Sutter's, a smallish grocery on Ridge Road just east of Calumet, moved across the road in 1947, and became the town's first "supermarket."

In 1946 Phillip Schuringa added a tiny post office to his grocery at 817 Ridge Road. The "P.O." was nestled behind a window in the rear corner of the store. Bunnell's Grocery was at the corner of Ridge Road and Oakwood in a building that would later house a barbershop and a dry cleaner. And the Munster Freezer Locker stood ready to freeze whatever one could catch, shoot, and cut up. South of the Ridge on the east side of White Oak, Al Skwirtz's Royal Blue Grocery, which had opened in 1940, catered to Independence Park customers. Nearby, the Dutch Bowl, a classic walk-in diner-restaurant, provided the three essential food groups: sodas, hamburgers, and French fries.

Munster farmers prospered with crops of onions, beets, rhubarb, cabbage, and asparagus. In 1946 they were pressured to form a cooperative to trade with the lucrative Chicago market. Schoon Ditch, originally dug as a drainage route in 1906, had become a sewer. Clogged by 1946, it was scoured at a cost of $3,000. Some three thousand cubic yards of debris, including trees, was hauled away. The "decades old problem of open-air markets that line Ridge Road" continued to irritate realtors and suburbanites, who considered them "messy." The state highway department called them traffic hazards. Town Marshal Adam Funk politely disagreed, but asked the farmers to "clean up" and least try to keep the sidewalks clear. The little farm town was fading away, into neatness.

Postwar Home Building

Home construction rates in the postwar years were uneven, but averaged fifty homes per year between 1945 and 1950. The immediate postwar years were slow, but builders were busy in 1948 and 1949. Munster led the area in value per unit, although Hammond led even Chicago in building rates. By 1948, with 1,224 "units" occupied, Munster had become quite the suburban town. Wicker Park Estates steadily sold lots for upscale brick or stone homes. After a squabble with existing landowners over his smallish lots, Henry Downey's City and Suburban Land Company moved ahead with the sale of lots in Hollywood Manor Subdivision to builders of $13,000 to $19,000 homes.

In the spring of 1946 a proposal for an apartment house on Hohman Avenue met determined opposition from hundreds of homeowners. They sent an angry petition to the Town Board, grousing that "we moved out here from Chicago to get way from crowded apartment houses . . . if they're going to put up more apartments here we might as well throw

The Swan family lived west of the Monon tracks on Belmont Place. Here three-year-old Tim Swan waves at a passing Monon train in August 1944. (Photograph by his mother.)

These brick apartments on Hohman Avenue are still handsome after sixty years.

everything to the winds and get out." The builder's few friends in town offered the defense that he was providing "more homes for returning vets." And build he did.

Road Work

Access to the north changed steadily after the war. In 1946 the county built a new bridge over the Little Calumet at Northcote. The wood-and-concrete structure replaced an earlier bridge that had collapsed four years earlier. Overpasses carried Hohman, Calumet, and Columbia Avenues over the new multinamed Tri-State, Kingery Highway, or Interstate 80-94, which crawled by in 1949, on its leisurely way to the toll Road.

In 1947, over homeowners' opposition, several streets were widened to allow fire engine access to the new school. Someone finally realized that hundreds of children had to cross the busy Monon Railway tracks twice a day coming to and from Eads School. The PTA collected six hundred signatures, mostly from parents of children living west of the tracks, on a petition asking for construction of a pedestrian underpass. Belden Place residents objected, citing cost, noise, traffic, safety, and potential flooding problems. In 1950 the obviously necessary little passageway was built under the track, at Manor and Belden, and was still in daily service in 2006.

Getting a traffic light installed at the intersection of Hohman and Ridge required approval from the State Highway Commission, and that was no easy task. The state deemed it unnecessary, but Marshal William Retzloff, who spent many of his weekends there sorting out traffic jams, disagreed. A year of applications from town officials, town surveys of the site, support from the Lions Club, the Independence Park Club, and citizens-at-large finally converted the commission. The light was installed in November 1948, and, lo, the traffic problem was solved.

Educational Advances

At war's end, the Munster School, a farm town structure built for a few hundred elementary school students, was packed with almost 600. The student population grew from 610 in 1947, to 685 in 1949, and reached 729 in 1950. Every square foot of space, including the gymnasium and the auditorium, had become classrooms.

The school employed nineteen teachers in 1947. Most joined a new, but short-lived AFL-AFT teachers' union early that year. Salaries were about the same as were then paid in Brown County. They ranged from $1,800 with two years of college, to $2,400 with a degree and four years experience, and to a maximum of $3,600.

A hundred Munster youth still attended out-of-town high schools in Hammond and elsewhere in 1947, and 130, three years later. "Commuter" students rode South Shore Line buses. Two school buses carried students between their homes and Munster schools in the later 1940s. Ron Johnson recalled a long and sometimes cold walk from Independence Park to the school bus stop at the foot of Oakwood. At first the students' route veered over the "Big Ditch" through Highland, but then Independence Park residents built a narrow footbridge over the "Little Ditch" (the kids called Schoon Ditch the "Little Ditch," and Mr. Hart's namesake, the "Big Ditch").

In August 1946 the school band was disbanded, for lack of a practice room. Mothers complained that Munster had reverted to a "typical rural school, not the type of school a

---

The pedestrian tunnel under the Monon Railway tracks at Belden Avenue, as it was in 2006.

growing town like Munster needs." They suggested that the band be allowed to practice upstairs in Town Hall. "No way," replied "white haired" Town Clerk Peter Tanis. "Let him take his nap some other time," said the irate mothers. Things were getting serious.

But, naps aside, the town was responding. In 1949 the School Board, perhaps in response to the new Munster Teachers Association, decided to end its "rural" pay system, and place Munster's twenty teachers on an "urban" salary schedule. Salaries were bumped up 15 percent. Generously supported by a community already complaining about taxes, Munster drew up a five-year expansion plan to compete in the race with homebuilders.

Munster's second public school was built on Harrison Avenue, a location that reflected Munster's recent population growth. The project began with the purchase of land from Dr. William Weis and Jacob Blink. But farmers Dingeman Jabaay and Arthur Harkema refused to sell. Jabaay didn't want more money, didn't want his farm cut in two, and did want to keep his asparagus field. Both men lost in court, after delaying groundbreaking for three months. The meeting of old and new was not always so peaceful in Munster.

The $200,000 Munster Elementary School, designed by Bachman and Bertram of Hammond, opened for classes in 1948. Students came from homes west of Calumet Avenue. Two years later it became the James B. Eads Elementary School, as part of a program to name Munster schools in honor of "Indiana Industrialists." Munster now had a school "system." The first stage of the building contained nine classrooms on eight acres and was designed for 350 students.

In 1957 six more classrooms, a kindergarten, and a cafeteria were added, and six more classrooms and other spaces in 1964. In 1969, with over five hundred students and a staff of sixteen teachers, Eads added a six-thousand-volume library/audio-visual materials center. Eads was a "K–6" school until the new middle school opened, at which time it became a K–5 school.

St. Thomas More Parish School opened in 1949 on Calumet Avenue next to a new church. Grades 1–6 classrooms, with ninety-two children in attendance, were staffed by Benedictine Sisters

---

Eads Elementary School, then on Harrison Avenue. Note the vacant land around the school. (MHS photo)

St. Thomas More School on Calumet Avenue. (STM photo)

114 • MUNSTER, INDIANA: A CENTENNIAL HISTORY

from Nauvoo, Illinois. Sister Mary Jean Feeney was the first principal. A year later, as parish membership passed three hundred and student attendance reached 135, a seventh grade was added. St. Tom hired its first lay teacher in 1953.

Expansion was steady; by the mid-1950s attendance had reached four hundred in Grades 1–8. Many St. Tom's graduates continued their education at Bishop Noll Institute in Hammond—fifty-plus in 1956. In 1955 a gym activity center, band room, and other facilities were added. Enrollment passed five hundred in 1959, and four more classrooms were added a year later.

In 1970 a new church was completed, and the former church building became part of the school. Two kindergarten rooms were added in 1986, and a preschool opened ten years later. In 2002 a nearby former Baptist Church became the Cornerstone Center, which housed a preschool and a kindergarten center. By 2006 enrollment had expanded to over six hundred students. Thirty teachers conducted three classes in each grade, and a principal and two assistant principals managed the busy institution. By 1999, when the school celebrated its fiftieth anniversary, thirty-two hundred students had graduated.

The base of the Munster educational system was occupied after 1946 by Mrs. John (Thelma) Harder's Happy Hour Kindergarten, probably the first private kindergarten in Indiana. Mrs. Harder was a former Munster schoolteacher. The little school was expanded over the years to include a nursery school, and, in 1977, Barbara Dixon added a day-care program.

Governing a Suburb

In 1945 Munster began a lengthy "suburban crisis" identical to many towns across America. Growth, steady work, optimism, and prosperity were just fine, but caused no end of problems for small governments. Opportunity and challenge had arrived on the same bus.

The builders of Independence Park had put people in homes, but had given little thought to streets and sanitation. The dirt-and-slag streets of the subdivision were a rutted mess, and drainage and sewage disposal was somewhere between poor and nonexistent. Every heavy rain caused more damage. In 1941 the White Oak Community Association asked the town to make repairs and improvements. But the Town Board had its hands full with problems of population growth and keeping the home front alive and well in World War II, and nothing was done.

In 1946 a special meeting between a "large group" of residents and the Town Board melted some ice, and the town decided to make street repairs. But the Board failed to even get one bid from a contractor. The residents were offered use of the town truck to fill in the ruts. Actual street paving began in 1947. Barrett Bonds were issued for sewer and drainage systems, and Independence Park began to be a good place to live.

The Munster Master Plan was little changed until late in 1949, when the town fathers decided to expand the business zone in the Calumet Avenue–Ridge Road area. The Zoning Board asked the Town Board to define another business zone from the river to Fisher Avenue on Calumet, and from Tapper to the state line along Ridge Road. Businesses were required to provide off-street parking on "dust-proof" lots, meaning asphalt or concrete, and signage was closely regulated.

In the later 1940s Munster wrestled with a common suburban problem: finding enough tax money to run things. The Board was inundated with requests from the "new people," who wanted more schools, better streets, more police, an upgraded fire department, low taxes, and *right now!* Increasingly outnumbered older settlers opposed most of these ideas, because they were expensive and of little benefit to farmers. Even the construction of a road near the Monon Railway tracks in 1949 caused farmer-suburbanite friction, because it would pass through a working field. To be sure, that "community of fine homes" was in better fiscal shape than most of the others in the area. "Growing pains" might be the best description of the situation.

The new school and construction of the pedestrian underpass pushed the town's borrowing power to the state-mandated limit by 1950. Taxes for streets and schools almost doubled between 1945 and 1949. Property values, the town's overall assessment, and tax rates all ascended in parallel with inflation and the booming postwar economy. New homes generated taxes, but also large numbers of school-age children. Property valuations rose from $4.4 million in 1945 to $6.4 million in 1951, and tax rates climbed in those years from sixty-three cents per hundred to ninety-three cents.

Held down by a "log cabin tax system," the town was officially seen as "near bankrupt" in August 1948. Munster was in bondage to bonds, and held to a dated tax formula by state and county mandates. Meanwhile, people needed water and sewer connections immediately, and there was no escaping the fact that Hammond, the only available provider, wanted more than just pipe connections.

A 1945 editorial in the *Times* made it plain: Hammond was "as necessary to Munster as a mother cat is to a nursing kitten." Hammond was being asked to build water and sewer facilities "to accommodate another community" to which it "has lost many of its leaders in business, the professions and in labor." Annexation, concluded the clearly jealous editor, was the only solution.

Munster strongly felt otherwise, valued its home rule, but needed services that only Hammond could provide, especially modern sewage disposal, at presumably fair rates. Times were changing: communities could no longer dump raw sewage into local streams. The town was ordered (not seriously, as it turned out) by the Indiana Stream Pollution Board to stop polluting the Little Calumet after July 1, 1945. And, while the town was already getting Lake Michigan water from Hammond, pressure was often low, especially in summer.

The town needed to build storage tanks, extend water mains, and treat its wastes, and *now*. In the summer of 1949, as second-floor plumbing in homes often had no water pressure at all, Town Board President A. J. Schuler declared a state of emergency. Merger with the Hammond Sanitary District was unavoidable, even though that seemed the first step toward annexation. Most were resigned to the necessity, and the cost, but James A. Mooney, who farmed almost a thousand acres in the southwest corner of town, claimed that costs would rise excessively, without giving any benefits to Munster farmers. In 1948 the Board voted to join the Sanitary District, and prepared to build water towers and mains. Taxes did indeed rise, but far less than if the town had addressed its water and sewage problems on its own.

New streets and roads, increasing traffic, and safety concerns were also pricey issues. In 1945 James Hart led a committee of the Munster and Highland Lions Clubs in a study of road safety, traffic, parking, and railroad crossings. Ridge Road, for years a part of State Route 6 (and would remain so until 1976), was the scene of numerous accidents. Small wonder: for years the speed limit on that largely residential passage was fifty miles an hour. A barrage of pleas and complaints from town officials convinced state highway officials to lower the limit to forty in 1949.

Organizations and Daily Life

Family, work, home, and church were at the center of daily life after the war. Little League games and the Sunday drive were pleasant events. Rising expectations finally made life worthwhile, after a long depression and an ugly war.

Few clubs and organized social groups were active in town before World War II. Perhaps the Hoosier inclination to join, maybe all the Home Front cooperation, or possibly suburbanization explains it, but more than two dozen social and civic groups were active by 1950. Some were older, like the American Legion and Panhellenic, but many were new. The very active Lions Club, which sponsored the Community Park Association, and the Munster Businessmen's Association, which became the Chamber of Commerce in 1955, were major forces for community improvement.

The Munster Women's Club was founded in 1951, and started the town's Cold War Civil Defense program, raised funds for the library, supported the Girl Scouts, and originated the Munster Pool project. Among other active groups were the Junior Women's Club, which was established in 1949, the Home Economics Club, and the Independence Park Community Association. Little League, Pony League, and Youth Leagues were organized in 1950, and played on two diamonds in Community Park on Calumet Avenue. Eleven troops of Girl scouts were active in 1946, with more coming.

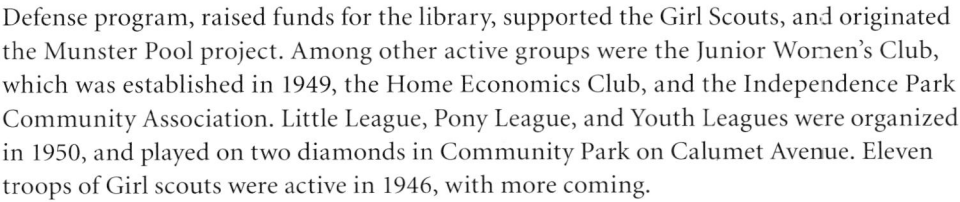

The Conservation Club sponsored turkey shoots, deer hunts, picnics, and stag parties. In 1946 the club organized a foxhunt in south Munster. Nothing too fashionable there: the critters were dining on farmers' chickens. Participants met on Saturday mornings at Myron Smith's garage on Calumet. Bounties fattened the club's treasury.

The Community Chest had originated in World War II bond drives, and afterwards remained focused on Munster. In June 1945 it became a permanent organization; Cyril A. Smith was its first president. Fundraising events were held in the fall, with an annual goal of over three thousand dollars in the forties. Money was distributed to the scouts, veterans, home emergency relief, the cancer society, and other deserving groups. The Munster Community Chest joined the Lake County organization in 1968, and eventually became part of the Lake Area United Way.

The *Times* reported on life as usual in the later 1940s. In July 1945, J. P. App opened the town's first "modern" drugstore at the corner of Ridge and Hohman. Two weeks later, Mace's Barbeque burned. Poor Mace Roberts lost all his hunting trophies in that fire. Some excitement: in late 1948, Oscar Keith, a Munster brickyard laborer, won $30,000 on a popular radio quiz show, *Truth or Consequences*.

In 1949 the "white horse mystery" confounded Independence Park. For several days a riderless steed galloped up and down the subdivision's streets. Town Marshal Adam Funk and Night Marshal Harold Pritchard had no luck in corralling the elusive horse, much to the glee of local reporters, who thought it might be the Lone Ranger's mighty horse "Silver." Eventually man triumphed over beast, and it was caught and returned to Cecil Hamacher.

Monon Centennial train passed through Munster in July 1947. (Tim Swan photograph)

App's Drug Store, later Munster Pharmacy, at the corner of Hohman Avenue and Ridge Road, circa 1950. (MHS photo)

MUNSTER MEAT MARKET
MUNSTER MEAT MARKET
QUALITY MEATS
PARKING IN REAR
PARKING IN REAR
MUNSTER MEAT MARKET
QUALITY MEATS

CHAPTER IX

The Busy 1950s

AS ROWS OF CORN STEADILY BECAME ROWS OF new homes in the 1950s, the changes in Munster closely reflected a national pattern. By 1950, the town's population had swollen to 4,750, a 171 percent increase in ten years. According to a special census, the number reached 6,548 in 1955. It was around 8,000 in 1957, and the 1960 census counted 10,313.

Average income was at the top of the Indiana list. The population was homogeneous; the nation's once-fragmented and contentious Euro-ethnics had become "white." Families enjoyed abundant leisure time—fewer wives worked then—and civic volunteerism was an everyday matter, from the Town Board to the Fire Department and the town's many organizations. Those who served on Munster's municipal boards and committees were of the highest caliber; few places in the Calumet Region were so well and honestly governed. Small town democracy worked well in Munster.

In 1957, according to a study conducted by Professor Clarence Pound of Purdue University for the Munster School Town, two-thirds of the town's 2,243 families had come from "elsewhere" in Indiana—most often from the Lakefront cities. Well over half of the residents had lived there fewer than five years. One family in five had come from Illinois. Only eighty-eight families were "natives" of Munster. The old settlers had become a small minority in a prosperous sea of suburbanites.

Munster Meat Market, beginning in 1952 operated in the same building as Klootwyk's General Store had been in much earlier years. (MHS photo)

The Purdue professor found a middle-class society in Munster, relatively well educated, racially homogeneous, but ethnically and religiously heterogeneous. It was young: four in ten were under the age of twenty-one. Four in ten were businessmen, professionals, or managers, the highest percentage in Indiana. Nine of ten owned their own homes, also the highest percentage in the Region. Only 246 families lived in duplexes, and a few more, in apartments.

Munster was economically integrated with the industrial Calumet. The Purdue study reported that one in three worked in Hammond. One in five worked in the East Chicago steel mills, a low number for the Calumet, one in ten at the Standard Oil Refinery in Whiting. There were few connections with Gary, fewer with Chicago. Less than 1 percent (twenty men and one woman) worked in "agriculture."

Life was almost entirely upbeat in the postwar years. The 1951 Community Chest Drive raised $4,400 for the Scouts, the Heart Fund, and the Cancer Fund. The Girl Scouts attracted nine of ten girls of enlistment age to one busy troop or another. Troops were sponsored by the PTA, Pan-Hellenic, St. Thomas More Church, and others. Traffic was a growing problem in a town of people who would rather drive than walk. Law enforcement officials spent their days dealing with too many cars going too many places too fast.

Life grew "modern." Dial telephones—finally—were installed in the homes of all 1,850 subscribers in 1954 and 1955. TEmple 6 and TEmple 8 were assigned to Munster, which later became the familiar 836 and 838 exchanges. Beginning in 1954, the Munster Garden and Home Club offered flower arrangement lessons and sponsored garden shows. In 1957, rather than confiscate young fellows' BB guns, Police Chief William

---

Boy Scout Troop 33, renamed later Troop 533, the oldest troop in Munster, now meets at Elliott Elementary School. (Calumet Regional Archives Photo, donated by the Munster Lions Club)

Explorer Scouts in Post 33 participate at the 1960 Klondike Derby, which tested Scouts' skills in winter. (Calumet Regional Archives Photo, donated by the Munster Lions Club)

Retzloff organized a Junior Rifle Association, and invited boys and girls alike in either the Scouts or the Junior Police Association to complete a gun safety course, and then blast away, with supervision, on the new police shooting range near the brickyard. The site was donated to the town by B. F. Weber Jr., president of the National Brick Company, and included ranges for rifles and pistols.

If big-time crime was no problem, the occasional juicy murder interested many. In the spring of 1950 George and Josephine Pappas were found dead in their home on Forest Avenue. The case made headlines ("Crazed Veteran Runs Amok") for several years. "Strange Aura Surrounds Death Home," chirped the *Times*. At first it was deemed a murder-suicide, but a brother-in-law, Victor Smelko, soon confessed to the murders, but offered no motive. On trial in Hammond, Smelko repudiated his confession. His attorney portrayed him as a war-disabled, "psycho-neurotic" veteran who should be committed for treatment. Three trials over two years each resulted in hung juries, and Victor Smelko went free in 1952.

Less villainous was the discovery in 1959 of some old bones in a load of sand taken from an excavation for Joseph Burger's Ridge Road grocery store. After analysis, a doctor described them "recent," and not those of an Indian. Then Della and Myrtle Munster and Mrs. Nick Kirsch, "whose family had lived in Munster for over 100 years," recalled that the area had once been a potter's field. With that the twittering died down. Aw shucks, no ancient Indian burying ground!

Small businesses flourished. A 1950 *Hammond Times* survey found forty active members of the Munster Businessmen's Association. Eight offered food service, from grocery stores to a frozen food locker. The Munster Meat Market opened for business in 1952 in the former Klootwyck's Store.

Cub Scout Pack 33, the first pack in Munster, met at the Town Hall in 1955. (Calumet Regional Archives Photo donated by the Munster Lions Club)

Also active: three restaurants or ice cream stores; three plumbers; three realtors; one drugstore; one barber, the perennial haircutter Martin Jabaay; and three automobile-related businesses. Karlen's Cottage Cheese was made in a garage on Crestwood Avenue; it would evolve into Sealtest Cottage Cheese. Munster also had a hardware store, Else Perdicaris' Munster Conservatory of Music, O'Donnell's Music Store, and a thrift shop. The Munster Lumber Company was a five-man operation in 1954, and would grow to fifteen times that size by 1972, perhaps a good indicator of the town's growth.

In 1957, according to a Town Directory published by the Junior Women's Club, Munster's business roster included six grocers, among them two national chain stores, Food Fair and Kroger's, and the Munster Meat Market. Six contractors, six homebuilders, five plumbers, Munster Hardware on Calumet, and seven realtors were active. A Calumet National Bank branch was in operation. Two used-car dealers, DeYoung's and Jabaay's Motors, competed for customers. Barber John DeMaar now competed with Martin Jabaay. Also new on the list: two dentists, two beauty shops, one bakery, three motels, and five service stations. And one physician was listed in the telephone book.

The industrial base was occupied by the aging brick factory and Munster Steel Company, which opened for business in 1958 on a site purchased from the brick company. O. C. Robbins' little plant welded and bolted-up steel structures for schools, bridges, and highways. Business was good, and by 1974 Robbins employed a hundred men. Ronald Robbins, the son of the founder, and his family owned and operated the plant, with sixty employees, in 2006.

Munster and the Cold War

The Cold War came to Munster in 1956 with a $1.2 million Nike surface-to-air (SAM) missile site, one of six, and, eventually, twenty-two in the lower Lake Michigan area. Located in southwest Munster farmland, Battery No. 46 was America's "last line of defense" for the Region's industries against attacks by manned aircraft. The "Nike Site," as it was always known locally, was built in two units. The north site, south of Forty-fifth Street and west of Columbia, housed the command center, computers, radar units, barracks, and service facilities. The south base, on Columbia Avenue just north of Main Street, contained three missile silos and a storage facility.

Munster Conservatory of Music on Calumet Avenue. (Calumet Regional Archives photo)

Munster Lumber on Ridge Road next to the Monon Railroad. (MHS photo)

122 • MUNSTER, INDIANA: A CENTENNIAL HISTORY

GRAND OPENING

THURSDAY AND FRIDAY, AUG. 29th and 30th 1957

DUFFY'S DARI-CASTLE

942 RIDGE RD.   MUNSTER

(2 Blocks East of Calumet)

— FREE —
SOFT SERV ICE CREAM
FOR CHILDREN UNDER 12
THURS., AUG. 29th
3 P.M. to 5 P.M.

— EAT AT OUR SNACK BAR —

Milk Shakes   Malted Milks
Hamburgers   Steaks
Shrimp   Sandwiches
Fish   French Fries
Red Hots   Chicken-In-Basket
         Sundaes

CARRY-OUT-ORDERS

FREE SOUVENIRS FOR EVERYONE

Ruby Duffala cooks up some food for hungry customers. (Duffala photo)

Duffy's Dari-Castle opened in 1957 in a new building on the front lawn of Emil and Ruby Duffala's Ridge Road House. (Duffala photo)

Calumet National Bank branch office at the corner of Calumet Avenue and Ridge Road. (MHS photo)

CHAPTER IX THE BUSY 1950s • 123

Munster Steel Company south of the Pennsylvania Railroad on Calumet Avenue. (MHS photo)

Munster Christian Reformed Church burned on the cold morning of Thursday, January 3, 1952. Fire departments from Lansing, Highland, and Griffith assisted the Munster department, but were unable to save the old wooden structure, which burned to the ground in less than one hour. Henry Boender, a photographer whose studio was across the street from the church, captured the scene in this photograph. (MHS photo)

The flood of October 1954 turned Wicker Park Estates into the Venice of Northwest Indiana. (MHS photo)

The base also included a hobby shop, a barbershop, and a Post Exchange. A hundred officers and men lived there and shared a mess hall. The Nike base and Community Park were dedicated on the same day in 1957 by Governor Earl Handley.

Munster's missiles never went to war. A microwave relay tower was constructed on the base in 1965, and linked missile sites between Gary and Milwaukee. The Nikes were replaced by a second-generation Nike-Ajax missile, and, in 1960, by long-range, nuclear-tipped Hercules SAMs. Despite the presence of those doom machines, in that same year the base commander held an open house for the community, showed movies of missiles in action, and gave a demonstration of the radar system. Local kids were occasionally invited "over the fence" for site tours.

In August 1968 the Pentagon deactivated the entire system. The missiles were removed and the soldiers were transferred. For some years the base served as the headquarters and missile-coordinating center for the Sixtieth Artillery Brigade, but in 1973 that group also moved away.

The base was declared surplus and sold "as is." By 1972 it was the property of the town, the school city, and the Lake Area Retarded Children Association (who later sold the silo site to Salyer Plumbing). The Munster school band proposed to salvage and sell whatever hardware remained on site as a fundraiser, but that sensible proposition drowned in legal snarls over safety and liability.

For years the town and the School Board dithered, unsure, partly because of dismal environmental study reports, of what to do with the place. The north site eventually became the site of Hartsfield Village and Hospice's William J. Riley Residential Care Facility. Salyer Plumbing continues to use the other base for supply and equipment storage.

Growth and Development

By 1950 Munster was a builders' and home buyer's paradise. As the price of farmland soared, a decade of nonstop expansion followed; 1,528 new homes—an average of 150 per year—were built both north and south of the Ridge over the next ten years, twice the rate of the 1940s. Most of the construction occurred after 1955.

The nasty but distant war in Korea, the draft, and a stream of war-related casualties were background noise to the busy, middle-class suburb between the Little Calumet and still-sleepy Dyer. The war brought prosperity; the steel mills were flat-out busy, jobs were plentiful, and pay envelopes were fat across the Calumet. With few farms remaining, the era of "buy a piece of land from a farmer, and build a house" ended. The era of the larger-scale developer and contractor had arrived. Local Dutch-Americans crabbed about all the changes, then joined established firms in the expansion business. Realtors dubbed their prairie-like sites Hill and Vale Estates, Knickerbocker Manor (with six additions), and a variety of other toney-sounding monikers.

In 1951 C. D. and Lambert Schoon launched Schoon's South View Subdivision, a twenty-five-acre project for seventy-five homes on Monaldi land south of Ridge and west of the Monon Railway tracks. Two hundred mostly frame and shingle homes valued at over three million dollars in six subdivisions were built in 1953. In 1955, as a dozen or more building permits were issued monthly, White Oak Manor began on sixty-four lots near Greenwood. Walnut Hills built

Bud and Martha Meeter's house at 8209 Forest Avenue was the first house on the block in 1952. (Meeter photo)

thirty new homes just over the Ridge. Monaldi's First Subdivision near Ridge Road had thirty-seven homesites. Monaldi's Second Subdivision was next to Jacob Kooy's land. A Monaldi-Kooy project built seventy-five brick and stone homes on twenty-five acres north of the Ridge, connected by Kooy Drive.

Seven development proposals came before the town in 1956, including Chase Manor, Castle Estates (Thirty-third Street to the Little Cal, east of White Oak), Kraft Addition (Walnut Drive to White Oak, facing Thirty-fifth Street next to Elliott School), Ridgeland Park, and two additions to Baldwin Builder's White Oak Manor, a multi-million-dollar project. Ridgeland Park occupied the land from the Little Calumet to Broadmoor between Jackson and Calumet.

In 1957, 2,243 families lived in town (but only 250 in duplexes, and 100 in apartments). Between 1950 and 1957, the town's real estate assessment rose from $5.8 million to $9.9 million. In 1958, despite a serious recession, the town issued over three hundred building permits, with a $2 million increase in value over the preceding year. Another Lambert Schoon Subdivision was located on Ridge Road on the east side of town. The home building continued unabated into the next decade: two dozen new homes were started just in April 1959.

In 1951 and 1952, in an event that might have determined the future of the town, the Purdue Research Foundation (PRF) purchased the 715-acre John J. Lawler Estate (once Hart land, then a Fisher property) and some 73 adjoining acres. At the time, the university trustees viewed the site as either a future regional campus or a long-term anti-inflation

---

New Houses on Kooy Drive, north of Ridge Road. (MHS photo)

River Drive and Hawthorne, Crestwood, and Parkview Avenues in the far northeast corner of the town. (MHS photo)

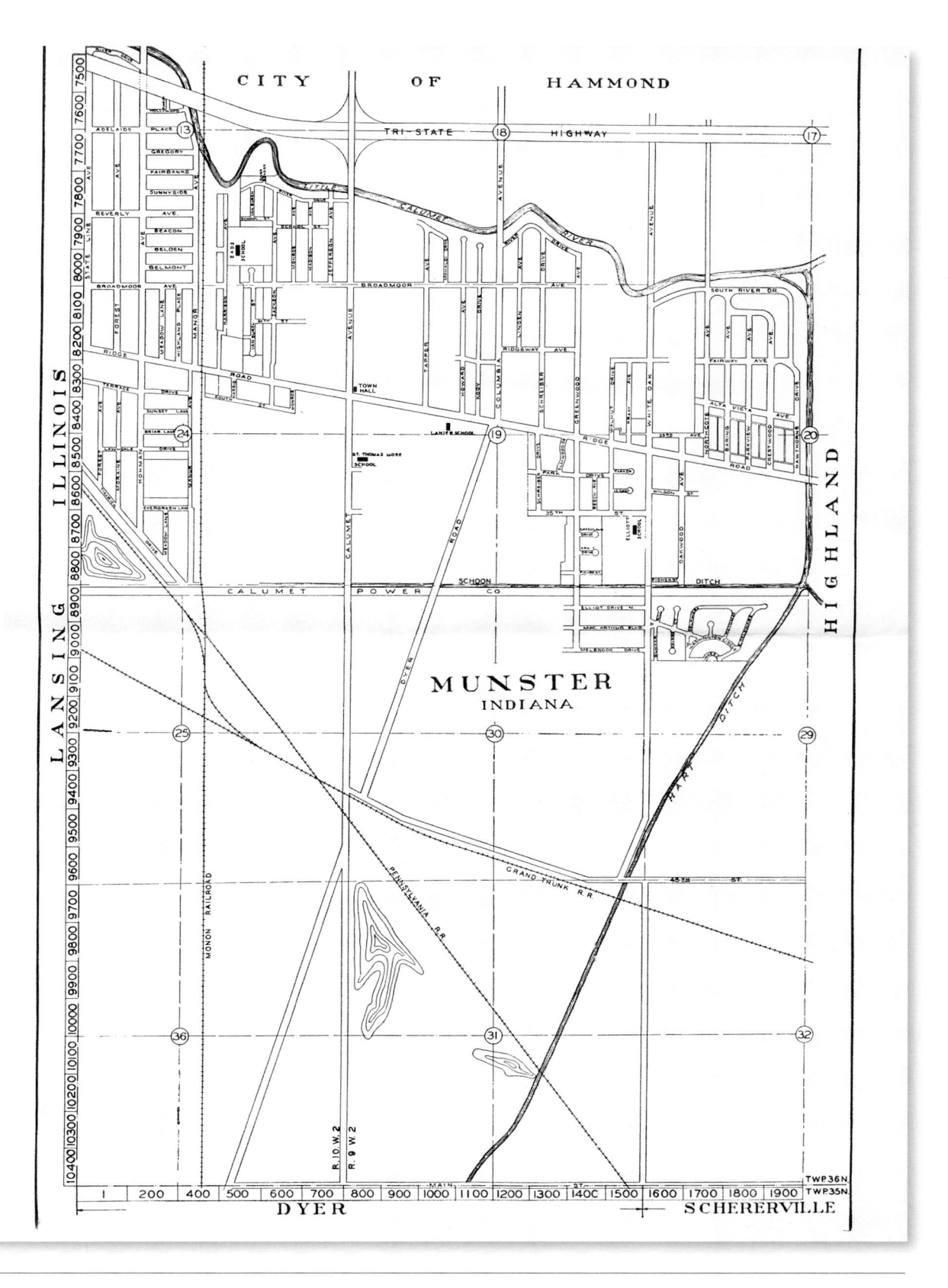

Street map of Munster, 1957. (Published by the Munster Junior Women's Club and donated by Sue Hendrickson)

CHAPTER IX THE BUSY 1950s • 127

investment. With lots in the area already selling at a thousand dollars and up, PRF, hoping to underwrite its property taxes, leased most of its Munster land to local farmers, and awaited events.

But the university built its regional campus in Hammond, and planner Lawrence V. Sheridan was asked to cobble up a model plan for the PRF site. Sheridan prepared a glossy report and handsome drawings showing "Munster Plains," a land of substantial homes on large lots with broad, curving streets, neighborhood parks, churches, shopping centers, and green belts. Finally, Purdue decided it was interested in education, not real estate, and profitably transferred the site to the Munster Development Trust, an entity controlled by developer and later Purdue University Trustee Donald Powers, Harold Rueth, and William J. Brant. They gradually executed much of what Sheridan had proposed. By 1982 eighteen hundred homes had been built on the Trust's lands, at an average rate of seventy-five a year.

Town Governance, 1950–1960

Munster had long divided its votes between the strictly local Independent, Citizens, and Better Government Parties. The Peoples Party had long been Dutch and farmer dominated, and in power. Newer folk revived the Citizens Party name, and charged the older group with being "unresponsive." The real issue was the soaring cost of providing public services to a fast-growing community. The Citizens Party slate won the 1951 election, four good men replaced four good men on the Town Board, and winner Hazel Randolph ended Clerk-Treasurer Peter Tanis' quarter century of service in Town Hall. A Better Government Party was organized in 1955 by former Peoples Party members and "new" people. Town government continued in its familiar paths.

In 1957 the state replaced the local party caucus with major party primaries. That decision was not popular in Munster, a town the *Times* casually described as a conservative Republican oasis "in the middle of a Democratic desert." But Democratic and Republican precinct organizations were duly formed, candidates were found, and in 1959 Munster held its first town primary.

The Meeter family—Sylvester (Bud) and Martha Meeter and their four children, Edna (tallest), Lester, Nancy, and Elaine—helped celebrate Munster's fiftieth anniversary by reminding folks of the town's Dutch heritage. (Meeter photo)

The Meeter family in the Fourth of July parade, 1957. (Meeter photo)

128 • MUNSTER, INDIANA: A CENTENNIAL HISTORY

The local party system had one solid virtue: Munster political affairs were conducted independently of Lake County's remarkable political system. Voters shared a bipartisan desire for clean government. Munster Democrats in particular now had to walk a narrow path between attending to town matters and the long arm of the Lake County Democratic machine. Munster Republicans had no difficulty in nominating and electing their slates, without serious outside interference, year after year. They continued to do so fifty years later, without remorse.

Budget-wrangling, rather than partisanship, was the order of the day. It was generally agreed that street lighting, mosquito control (DDT was then popular and effective), a new water main along Calumet Avenue, and electrical and plumbing codes hardly warranted national partisanship. What mattered was a wrecked budget caused by a tenfold increase in dump fees, or the price of water mains to a new subdivision.

Burgers Little League Team played at the new Community Park in 1955. Back row, left to right: W. Bailey, J. Clabby, and M. Cummings. Second row: T. Rossin, M. Blake, D. Brogan, J. Clabby Jr., R. Slathar, D. Rossin, and R. Adley. Front row: R. Dawson, R. Keilman, T. Dawson, R. Jevyak, J. Mitchell, W. Bailey Jr., and B. Slathar. (Calumet Regional Archives photo donated by the Munster Lions Club)

The second annual Lions Club Pancake Breakfast was held in 1957. Seated are Jack LaForce, James Clabby, and Adam Kirschner. Standing are Lee Hendrickson, Randy Bellows, Joe Burger, and Pat Berghian. The Pancake Breakfast is today Munster's longest-running fundraiser. The fiftieth annual breakfast was held in 2006. (Calumet Regional Archives photo donated by the Munster Lions Club)

Everyone preferred citizen volunteers on the various town boards and in the Fire Department. "Salaries" were still essentially honoraria. The town was governed by public-spirited professionals, worthy volunteers to a man; not one could be described as a "politician." The 1956 Plan Commission was a model: its four members were Douglas Boender, a sales engineer; Leo J. Burke, an Indiana Harbor Belt Line railroad man; Harry R. McDonald, a supervisor at Lever brothers in North Hammond; and John E. Stephens, the assistant to the president at Edward Valve in Hammond.

The 1938 Master Plan, while uniformly admired, was modified as necessary. Board members argued about tax rates, agreed to hire more police officers and buy more patrol cars, and moaned whenever Hammond called for another increase in water rates. In 1956 everyone agreed on the wisdom of a "summit meeting" of every town board, commission, and official to hammer out the town's future in a time of almost runaway home building. Citizen-officials were learning the ropes for the high-quality-high-service governing philosophy of American suburbia. They also learned to listen politely to choruses of angry citizens demanding lower taxes and higher services. The outlines of modern Munster were in sight.

School Problems

Enrollment grew relentlessly in the fifties, from just over 700 students in 1950, to 1,096 in 1955, and over 2,000 in 1960. Growth was concentrated in the lower grades, which almost tripled, and at the high school level, which rose in ten years from 130 to 550. Upper-grade students still attended Hammond High, Bishop Noll Institute, or "Hammond Tech." Some attended Griffith or Illiana Christian High Schools. For this service, in 1957 the Munster school system paid an average of almost $500 per student.

The 1957 Purdue study noted that Munster, had "one of the most rapidly developing school corporations in the state," would need fifty-seven more classrooms in the near future, and even more "when the housing developments south of Ridge Road come about." The professors observed that Lanier School was "inadequate," and that it should be replaced. The schools also should increase their emphasis on science, mathematics, and "gifted" students. A gusher of post-Sputnik science-education money flowed from Washington after 1957, which helped, but education was becoming very expensive in a community that now emphasized "college prep" courses.

In the 1950s a new educational mentality replaced embedded "village" conservatism. Most parents now wanted the "best," meaning college-prep education, for their children, and were willing—with complaints—to pay for it. The School Board, the administrators of the schools, and the teachers agreed, and responded with new courses, enrichment programs, and a variety of other improvements.

Leon Hendrickson was named "Father of the Year" in 1958 by the Hammond Downtown Council. Leon is seen here with his family at 245 Sunnyside Avenue. He was an officer in the Munster Lions Club and president of the sixteen-team Munster Little League. With him are Karen, seven; his wife, Mary; John, eleven; and seated, Susan, eight. Leon and Mary were also instrumental in starting the Munster Pool. Susan brought more fame to the family in 1990 with the discovery of the largest, best preserved, and most complete Tyrannosaurus Rex skeleton ever discovered.

At a more modest, but practical level, Marshal Funk hired part-time crossing guards, erected school zone signs, and painted crosswalks at intersections. Funk also cracked down on motorists who ignored patrol boys and—finally—lowered the speed limit on Ridge Road to thirty miles per hour. These were good beginnings.

In 1951 Principal Ernest R. Elliott became Munster's first superintendent of schools, but had to resign because of ill health a year later, and died in Florida in 1977. Elliott was replaced by Frank Hammond, who served until 1971. In 1958 Donald H. Peckenpaugh was hired as a combination attendance officer and school psychologist. In 1959 eighty gifted elementary school pupils were placed in a German language course taught by Heidi Kopper (later known as "Frau Meyer"). Grants helped underwrite improved science education.

A two-track, "college–general ed" system was in place by 1960. Superintendent Hammond noted that half of his students had an intelligence level in the "highest" quadrant. A University of Illinois-designed "Accelerated Math" program for the college-bound was added to the curriculum for Grades 3–9 in 1960. Elitism was now a "good thing."

Munster desperately needed a third school. The first stage of the Ernest R. Elliott School, on White Oak Avenue near Independence Park, was completed in 1953. Elliott opened with eight classrooms for 300 students, a kindergarten, offices, and a clinic. Built on an eight-acre campus next to a working farm, in the early years teams of horses crossed the school playground on their way to work in the morning, and returned for their oats at night. Four years later six more classrooms, a library, and other facilities were added at a cost of $140,000. Elliott School was still unfinished: an L-shaped wing, containing seven more classrooms and other facilities, was added in late 1965, and raised the school's capacity to 750 students.

As a busy and growing decade ended, Wilbur Wright Junior High School was completed in 1960 for grades 7–10, and Lanier reverted to its elementary school status. Eighth grade student Julane Kraay wrote the winning essay in a contest to name the school. When Wilbur Wright opened, it was a T-shaped building with fourteen classrooms, a shop, a science laboratory, and a cafeteria, surrounded by a cornfield. Team teaching began in 1962. A year later, two 160-seat lecture halls, seminar rooms, and a resource center (=a library) were added at a cost of $400,000. Later it was absorbed into Munster High School. Homeroom was abolished in 1964— was nothing sacred?

Ernest R. Elliott was named principal of Munster Elementary School in 1940. In 1951 he became Munster's first superintendent of schools. Elliott Elementary School bears his name. (MHS photo donated by the School Town of Munster)

Elliott Elementary School, opened in 1952 next to open farmland, was named for Munster's first superintendent.

CHAPTER IX THE BUSY 1950s • 131

132 • MUNSTER, INDIANA: A CENTENNIAL HISTORY

Aerial view from over forty-fifth Street near Calumet showing the Simmons Plant at the left and the T-shaped Wilbur Wright Junior High School at the top. (MHS photo donated by the School Town of Munster)

Munster Bowling Alley on Calumet Avenue, 1955. (Calumet Regional Archives photo donated by the Munster Lions Club)

Sock Hop was the first function of the new "Senior (high school) Canteen Group" organized by the Munster Lions Club and held at the Lanier gymnasium. Pat DeMure and his orchestra provided the music. The *Times* reported that about 250 teenagers attended. (Calumet Regional Archives photo donated by the Munster Lions Club)

30TH PL
HARRISON AV
MONROE AV
MADISON
CALUMET
WOOD
FULLERTON AV
HOWARD
KOOY
COLUM
LINDEN
SCHREI
GRAY DR
RIDGEWAY AV
FAIRWAY AV
RIDGE RD
SEBERGER DR
SOUTH ST
TERRACE DR
SOUTH ST
RIDGE RD
GREENWOOD AV
BEECH AV
WALNUT DR
WHITE OAK AV
CASTLE DR
SUNSET LN
MORAINE DR
HOHMAN AV
BRIAR LN
BRIAR LN
LAWNDALE DR
RIDGE RD
PARK DR
SYCAMOR
MAPLE LN
EVERGREE
MEADOW LN
TIMRICK DR
45TH ST
MARGO LN
SUPERIOR AV
GLASTONBURY ST
BANBURY PL
MILFORD HAVEN WAY
LEICESTER RD
SALISBURY DR
WHITEHALL GARDEN
INDIANA PKWY
PROGRESS AV
VALPARAISO DR
CALUMET AV
NORWICH CT
BOWEN DR
SINGLETON DR
THICKET LN
REDBUD RD
CRIMSON TREE LN
CEDAR CREST DR
IVY LN
TAMARACK DR
FITZGERALD DR
TWIN CREEK BLVD
REDBUD RD
IVY LN
WHITE OAK AV
POPLAR LN
Burgers
T BONE STEAK 2o9LB
ENTER ONLY

CHAPTER X

The Fast-Growing 1960s

EXPANSION AGAIN REMAINED THE CENTRAL challenge for Munster town officials. The population increased from around 10,000 in 1960 to 16,514 ten years later. A "white flight" sent thousands southward from East Chicago and Gary, and suburban developers and builders profitably welcomed the newcomers. Munster offered a sleek "executive suburb" image, with clean government, high educational levels, and excellent schools. And the town was also the emerging medical center of the Calumet Region. But where would the town find the money to meet the challenge? In addition, Munster still had no high school, and, despite the completion of new buildings, the school system remained undersized and still operated in a partially dated physical plant.

The town faced a moving target as new split-levels and ranches spread southward. Other demands for public funds and services came from medical facilities, streets, and, less visibly, water and sanitary services. Town and school officials wrestled with highly restrictive, state-mandated tax caps. One structural reform of note; the Town Board bundled years of ordinances into a new municipal code that governed construction, electricity, water, restaurants, and the like.

Burgers, at its new location on Ridge Road.

The town's senior government officials remained, with one exception, part-time and volunteer. Elective offices and nearly all appointed offices were still held by civic-minded professionals and businessmen. Salaries remained almost token. One town executive, John Bunnell, kept daily working hours. In 1960 Bunnell, a Munster resident since 1940 and a former Town Board member, was director of public works, sanitation superintendent, water and street commissioner, building inspector, mosquito control officer, Zoning Appeals Board and Town Plan Commission member, and a day-to-day buffer between townspeople and town officials. Thirteen municipal employees reported directly to him. All that for an annual salary of $8,500! Yet Bunnell was the father of much of the town planning and development of that time.

As residential construction continued, building and maintaining streets and sewers and water pipes became a challenge. Street dedications were almost everyday events as the builders of one subdivision after another laid pipe, rolled asphalt, and poured concrete. Residents demanded modern services, but griped about the cost of curbs and sidewalks, however much they added to the value of their property.

The vastly uninteresting subject of sewers caused considerable excitement. Munster was now part of the Hammond Sanitary District, which was modernizing under orders from the state. Munster still pumped raw waste into Schoon Ditch and the Little Calumet. Home septic systems percolated sewage into Hart Ditch. In 1961, under pressure from the Sanitary District, which was responding to the Indiana Stream Pollution Board, Munster authorized a million-dollar bond issue for a connection to the Hammond Waste Treatment Plant. At the same time the town was extending more water and sewer lines to more new subdivisions.

Easy on the Mustard cast members Jerry Buehler, Bob Hulett, Jim Cieplucha, Julian McConnell, Dick Lanman, and Dick Rudzinski perform at Eads Elementary School, March 24, 1962. The play, written by Lee Allen, raised money to purchase and install drain tiles at Community Park. (Photo donated by Gloria Rudzinski)

Huge concrete interceptors and oversized pipelines were buried along Columbia Avenue from the Ridge to the Little Cal, along the river, between Independence Park and Schoon Ditch, between Broadmoor and the river, along Greenwood, and elsewhere. Developers installed sewer lines in their new subdivisions, and builders assessed homeowners for local connections. Although Barrett Bonds eased the pain somewhat, few wanted to pay for these "invisible" benefits.

In 1965 the state moved Route 6 to the Interstate, and "abandoned" Ridge Road, where traffic had increased by 40 percent in three years. The town was now responsible for policing and maintenance on its main street. Three years later the state abandoned State Route 141, which transferred responsibility for Calumet Avenue to the town. In 1976 the town paid an unanticipated $2.1 million to resurface Ridge Road. Meanwhile, Columbia Avenue, still a narrow byway, was one of three busy connector roads passing over the Interstate between Munster and Hammond. Widening and resurfacing that road was just one more headache for a cash-starved Town Board.

Garbage disposal costs suddenly moved into the twentieth century. For years the town had a cheap arrangement with the National Brick Company to dump and burn in the clay pit. In 1958, the property was sold to the DeVries brothers. Progressive dump managers, the DeVries adopted the more modern and far more expensive practice of bulldozing, packing, and covering refuse, and, as businessmen, also accepted trash from Dyer and Lansing. In 1960, after constant complaints about noisy garbage trucks, the Town Board forbade out-of-town dumping. The town also notified the DeVries that they were not running a proper landfill. The DeVries retorted that they had a business to run, had several customers to satisfy, and simply continued to accept garbage from all three towns. Modernization had its costs.

Water problems roiled public life for several years. Low pressure brought seasonal bans on outdoor water use. Lawns turned brown, cars became dirty. This was not the suburbia of dreams! Despite steady increases in capacity in the 1950s, by 1960 the town's water storage system was seriously inadequate; the town's three tanks provided a maximum of 1.5 million gallons per day, well below fire underwriters' requirements. In hot weather water consumption was about equal to storage capacity.

In 1964 the Town Board proposed to raise a huge, elevated tank in a park-like setting at Fisher and White Oak. Rated at a million gallons, it would be the fourth-largest spheroid

Munster Junior Women's Club's tour of Inland Steel's newest blast furnace, October 30, 1962. (Donated by Gloria Rudzinski)

Director of Public Works John Bunnell. (MHS photo)

tank in the country. That highly visible structure and two new ground-level tanks would raise town water reserves to a comfortable 4.5 million gallons per day, and provide a sound, long term water supply.

It also raised hackles. The cost seemed astounding, and loud, long, and widespread opposition followed the announcement. Residents complained to the Board and then to the Indiana Public Service Commission (PSC) about the Board's "secrecy" and "high-handedness," muttered about "dictatorship," and questioned both the necessity and the cost. Residents on Fisher and White Oak were understandably angry about the idea of a big ugly water tank looming over their homes. They argued that the tank ought to be built further south (the NIMBY principal at work) in one of the town's newer developments.

Rarely had the Town Board faced such concentrated public ire. Hearings were acrimonious and long. Residents threatened to sue the town. Meanwhile, more dry summers and low water pressure made lawn watering and car washing capital offences. Supported by the PSC and the Zoning Board, the Town Board voted to go ahead. Construction began in February 1966 and was completed by September. At the end of an unusually dry summer, the tanks were tapped and filled. Water shortages ended, the upstairs shower worked again, lawns were greener, cars were cleaner, and water bills were higher.

Small Business, Some Industry

Munster had always shopped at "Mom-and-Pop" grocery stores, but the modern supermarket arrived in the sixties. Kroger made its first, and unsuccessful, try in a building on Hohman near Ridge, now the home of American Savings, FSB. An A&P opened in Market Square and some years later departed in the general wreckage of the national company. The A&P building later became the home of Tilles Interiors. A much-modified building on the northwest corner of Ridge and Hohman was first occupied by a Ben Franklin "five-and-dime," then a bakery, next, a men's clothing store, and, in 2006, the Dawson Eye Clinic.

The Jewel Company, anticipating Wal-Mart or Meijer, sought permission to build a huge Jewel-Osco Drug-Turnstyle store in a very big box building at Calumet and Ridge. The town fathers vetoed part of that proposal on "excess traffic" grounds. In fact, many citizens did not want a discount house in town. But they did consent to a joint Jewel-Osco Pharmacy store (which was half a discount store in itself). The store(s) opened in 1970, and was quite successful.

Joseph Burger, a native of Nashville, Indiana, began his grocery business in Glen Park in 1944. Two years later he moved his IGA to a smallish building on Hohman near Ridge Road. Business flourished, and in 1959 Burger built a supermarket on Ridge Road at the state line. For a short time in 1960 the old Burger site housed Burke's Furniture Store, then, for many years, a surgical supply company. Burger's food quality, selection, and service were exceptional, and customers from two states filled his store. Four expansions of that building brought it to almost sixty thousand square feet of floor space. In the 1970s the Burger family operated four stores (two in Munster, one in Hammond, and one in Dyer) and employed over five hundred local people in Munster's leading nonindustrial business.

This A&P Food Store is now Tilles Interiors. (MHS photo)

Burger's IGA was on Hohman Avenue, just north of Ridge Road in 1945. (MHS photo)

Mrs. Burger, head cashier, knew most customers by name. (MHS photo)

Joseph Burger was Munster's master grocer. (MHS photo)

In 1970, as the center of population shifted southward, Burger opened a second store on Forty-fifth Street; it would later become Banner Foods, then Sterk's. Joe Burger died suddenly in 1975, aged sixty-nine. The Ridge Road store was eventually purchased by the owners of the Key Market chain, which was sold in turn to Strack and Van Til. Strack passed it on to Central Grocers Co-Op in 1997. Munster's good experiences with locally owned grocery stores certainly defied the established wisdom about competing with proverbially efficient chain stores.

Smaller businesses and restaurants prospered, at least for a while, then departed. Carpetland opened a Munster store on Calumet in 1960, and by 1966, then with sixty employees, had expanded three times. The store eventually closed, and the building was demolished in 2006. Wendy's kept its grill hot for a few years after 1966 on Ridge Road near Calumet; the building was subsequently occupied by a variety of seafood and Mexican restaurants.

A more durable place to eat: in 1966 "Pro" and Nancy LoDuca bought Giovanni's Restaurant, and made it one of the town's most successful dining rooms. Pro passed on in 1994, but Nancy and her daughter-in-law, Mary Leary, continued to manage it. Much expanded and remodeled by 2006, Giovanni's, still serving "classic Italian pastas," remained a busy place.

SCHOOP'S RESTAURANT

Schoop's is a Munster tradition. More of a fifties diner than a fast-food place, it offers a variety of burgers and diner-style meals at booths, tables, and a lunch counter. One favorite is the Mickey, a single burger with two cheeses, named in honor of Jake DeMik, once the town garbage collector.

In 1948 Alan Schoop and Art Fogarty bought Miner-Dunn's Hammond restaurant, and opened a second store in Munster in 1959. Fogarty sold his interest to Alan Schoop in 1964. Schoop operated both until he died in 1973.

Under son Mark's management, the Munster Schoop's has expanded twice, once in 1969, and again in 1998, into the former Baskin-Robbins store.

Today the Schoop's banner flies over twenty-three stores in four states. And the makin's are good: Schoop also owns Howard and Sons Meat Market.

To order like a pro at Schoop's, ask for "two and one with the old everything, and a Green River."

Fogarty and Schoop Hamburgers was the forerunner of Schoops Hamburgers, now known throughout the Calumet Area. (MHS photo)

Ridge Garden Center was for years a great place to get plants for the garden, and in later years fireworks for the Fourth of July. (MHS photo)

The Corner (formerly Mace's) and Bohling Florists on Ridge Road east of Calumet Avenue. (MHS photo)

Howard's Meat Market with Howie the Cow, a Munster icon. (MHS photo)

CHAPTER X THE FAST-GROWING 1960s • 141

Calumet Shopping Center

In 1962 the Town Plan Commission faced another angry crowd in Town Hall. The members were handed a petition signed by eleven hundred residents opposing Ohio developer Edward J. DeBartolo's plan to build a modern shopping mall beside Calumet Avenue. Residents complained about the noise and traffic that would "disturb the peace and quiet of the bedroom suburb." Those who lived nearest the proposed facility were livid. But DeBartolo, who had already built seventy-six malls, already owned the land. The Munster Chamber of Commerce was pleased to endorse his "high class" mall with parking in *front* of the stores, for which he needed rezoning of a strip of residential land.

But the Plan Commission voted to proceed, and rezoned the site. Progress had its costs, and a sharply divided citizenry was one of them. Residents mounted a legal war that lasted into 1963. Town Attorney Eugene M. Feingold defended the town's right to rezone property in the interest of growth and development against three separate suits. In February the last anti–shopping center suit was dismissed by Judge Felix A. Kaul in Lake County Circuit Court, and two months later—presumably time enough for tempers to cool a bit—Public Works Director John Bunnell issued a construction permit. Vic Kirsch Construction began preparing the site in November and quickly poured foundations. Calumet Construction Company built the stores.

By late summer 1964 the Calumet Shopping Center was ready for business. The anchor store, Montgomery Ward, occupied the southern end of the nineteen-shop mall. The north end was occupied by a Kroger Grocery, which was sold to Sterk's in 1972. Later it became a dollar store. In between them were a SuperX Drug Store, a Gary National Bank branch, McCrory's Variety Store, Anton's Calumet Restaurant, Porter Cleaners, a beauty salon, and other smaller stores. "Monkey Ward" was mobbed on opening day, August 20. Clearly not everyone was opposed to big time malls.

The Simmons Plant

Munster's first large factory arrived in 1957 with a warm invitation from the Chamber of Commerce. The town fathers agreed, and thought that "mattress manufacturers will do just fine." The Simmons Company of New York, a "clean" industry, shifted its Midwestern manufacturing facilities from Kenosha to Munster. In 1958 Simmons built the 356,000-square-foot first stage of its plant on forty-five acres beside Calumet Avenue. Five hundred workers began making Beautyrest Mattresses, couch-sleepers, and institutional furniture. Within two years the site was expanded to seventy acres, and eventually the plant and Simmons' Midwestern headquarters totaled over one million square feet. Employment reached thirteen hundred in the late 1960s.

In 1978 the company halted all production in the Munster plant and dismissed its labor force, with no explanation. The company later cited "rising distribution costs" as the reason. Simmons operated a warehouse and distribution center in the building for a while, but finally moved everything to the South, a land of cheaper and more tractable nonunion labor.

Calumet Shopping Center, Munster's largest retail venture, in the 1960s.

Simmons' acquisition by a conglomerate may partially explain these events, but a long history of acrimonious labor disputes and a poisonous relationship between management and two unions seems equally likely. Upholsterers International Local 455 and Machinists Local 209 were militant, and that certainly influenced the decision.

A series of planned and wildcat strikes, occasional walkouts, firings, refusals to cross picket lines, and general ill will roiled the plant from the beginning. A 1959 strike brought firings, violence, and a platoon of state police to keep order. A 1961 wildcat strike by the upholsterers followed the "arbitrary" firing of Thelma Guntharp. Another upholsterers strike over wages in 1962 lasted for weeks with off-and-on negotiations until a federal mediator stepped in. Bomb scares in 1966 plagued managers.

A twenty-four-day upholsterers strike late in 1967 over wages and vacations took eleven hundred workers off the line and persevered through confrontations, picket line crashing, arrests, and a lot of overtime for Munster police officers. In 1968, in the second strike in five months and the fifth at Simmons, ninety machinists walked out over wages, vacations, and benefits. That event idled thirteen hundred workers.

E. J. Higgins' Pepsi-Cola General Bottlers was a fizzier and friendlier employer. East Chicago Police Chief Edgar T. Higgins founded the company in the Twin City in 1917 as the Indiana State Bottling Works. He began bottling Pepsi in the late 1920s, using paper labels on recycled beer bottles. In 1968, E. J., his son, moved operations to Calumet Avenue in Munster and a new, $3.5-million automated plant totaling 120,000 square feet.

The "Pepsi Plant" originally employed about 100 workers, but had 250 on its payroll by 1970. Higgins then produced and delivered a half dozen different canned and bottled beverages to a dozen counties in two states. In 2006, now PepsiAmericas, the company was one of the top ten bottling plants in the Pepsi world, and with planned expansion, would enter the top five. Four hundred workers brewed and distributed four hundred different products.

Simmons Mattress factory, a huge plant for a still small town.

The Pepsi-Cola bottling line on Calumet Avenue before expansion made the plant one of the largest and most efficient anywhere.

Subdivision Fever

An almost runaway building expansion in the 1960s began with apartments on Manor Drive on land formerly owned by the Munster Lumber Company. In 1962 Munster issued permits for 113 homes, five apartment buildings, and one convent. A year later the total reached 100 homes, valued at $2.6 million. The rate accelerated: in 1966, 200 new homes, three commercial buildings, and a library were added to the town's inventory. In 1967, 238 homes, two churches, and a brace of apartment houses were completed. The next year, 1968, set the record for the decade: 264 homes valued at $7 million, and four commercial buildings.

Subdivisions came in all sizes from very large to small. Each retained one name, but expanded in manageable, Zoning Board–approved, bite-sized chunks called "additions." Lawrence Monaldi's Janice Lane Subdivision was a building in 1960. Wicker Park Estates was built out by then. White Oak Manor led the southward march. The largest development by far was Donald Powers' Fairmeadows, which eventually saw eighteen hundred homes built on almost six hundred acres in southern Munster. The developers of Hill and Vale Estates, south of Ridge Road, also built steadily, in small units.

In the only slightly slower final two years of that busy decade over three hundred new homes (average value around $34,000, up from $25,000 in 1966) and ten commercial buildings were built. Among the latter were the short-lived Yankee Doodle restaurant, now the Commander, Burger's Grocery on Forty-fifth Street, Mr. Donut on Calumet, a $2.9 million extended care facility, and three apartment buildings. The total for the decade: two thousand new homes.

Apartments buildings were still not welcomed by established residents. Whenever a builder asked for a permit for apartments, homeowners mobbed Zoning Board hearings to complain about changing the character of the neighborhood and the "undesirable density of population." When Lawrence Monaldi applied for rezoning of a tract on the east side of Euclid Avenue for apartments, irked residents countered that Munster "had enough apartments," and warned that "we are going to get into trouble." A request before the Zoning Board for permission to build thirty-six apartments on MacArthur Drive and Eliott Drive "for high-class persons" brought the usual response from local homeowners. Munster residents very much preferred to live in a town of single-family homes.

Education at the Gallop

Certainly the central educational event in that remarkable decade was the construction of Munster High School. In 1952 Munster and Highland discussed the idea of a joint school district, but nothing was done. Sending Munster kids to Hammond High School, while cheap enough, had worn thin. Munster parents complained of excessive teacher turnover and discipline problems at Hammond High, and argued that their children were "not getting a sound education in basic fundamentals." Each of the five hundred Munster students at Hammond and other high schools cost the town $600 a year. Superintendent Frank Hammond realized it was time to move on.

By 1960 Hammond had space problems of its own, and hoped to see the out-of-towners gone. The Munster school system was equally crowded. It had entered the 1960s with just over 2,000 students. That number expanded relentlessly, to 2,816 in 1965, to 3,827 in 1968, and to 4,257 in 1970. Elementary school enrollment almost doubled over the decade, and high school student population climbed from 550 in 1960, neared 800 in 1965, and passed 900 in 1969–70.

Frank H. Hammond was the longest-serving superintendent of Munster schools, 1952–1971. (MHS photo donated by the School Town of Munster)

Architectural firm Bachman and Bertram of Hammond began designing the high school in 1962. Meanwhile, financing was delayed by public meetings, petitions, opposition from the State Tax Commission, and threats of suits, mostly centering on cost rather than need. The State Tax Commission approved Munster's second, and much reduced, application for approval of a holding corporation to finance the school. In mid-1964 contracts were awarded for a trimmed (much that had been eliminated had to be built later, at a higher cost), but still excellent, high school. Construction began of two, instead of three buildings in the summer of 1965.

Munster High School, with space for 1,200 students, opened just over a year later. The field house was completed in January 1967, the pool, in April. A formal dedication of the completed 293,700-square-foot facility was held in May 1967, one month after the High School received accreditation from the North Central Association Commission on Accreditation and School Improvement. In June, the 184 members of Munster High School's first graduating class gathered to receive their diplomas and hear Senator Birch Bayh deliver the commencement address. Munster finally had a complete school system, at a cost of over $4 million for the high school and shared facilities, and $1.2 million for improvements at Wilbur Wright Junior High School.

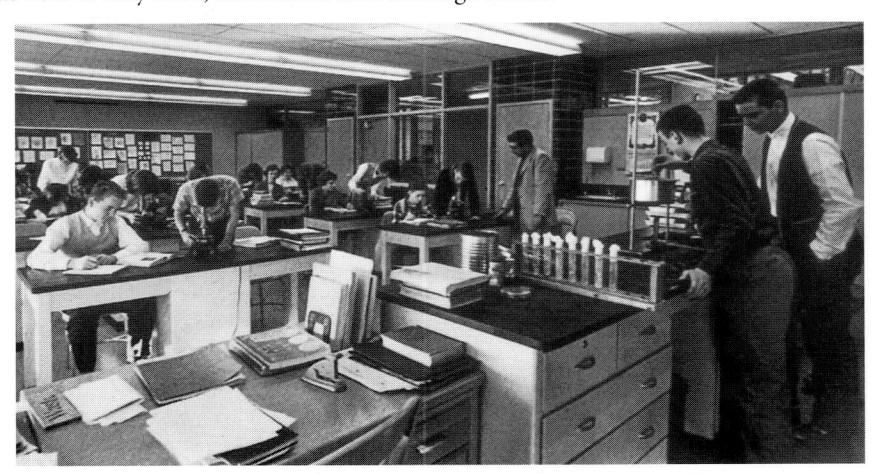

The new Munster High School from the air, 1967. (MHS photo donated by the School Town of Munster)

Science laboratory at Munster High School. (MHS photo donated by the School Town of Munster)

CHAPTER X THE FAST-GROWING 1960s • 145

Lecture room at Munster High School. (MHS photo donated by the School Town of Munster)

Language laboratory at Munster High School. (MHS photo donated by the School Town of Munster)

The first Munster High School Speech Team (*The Paragon*). (MHS photo donated by the School Town of Munster)

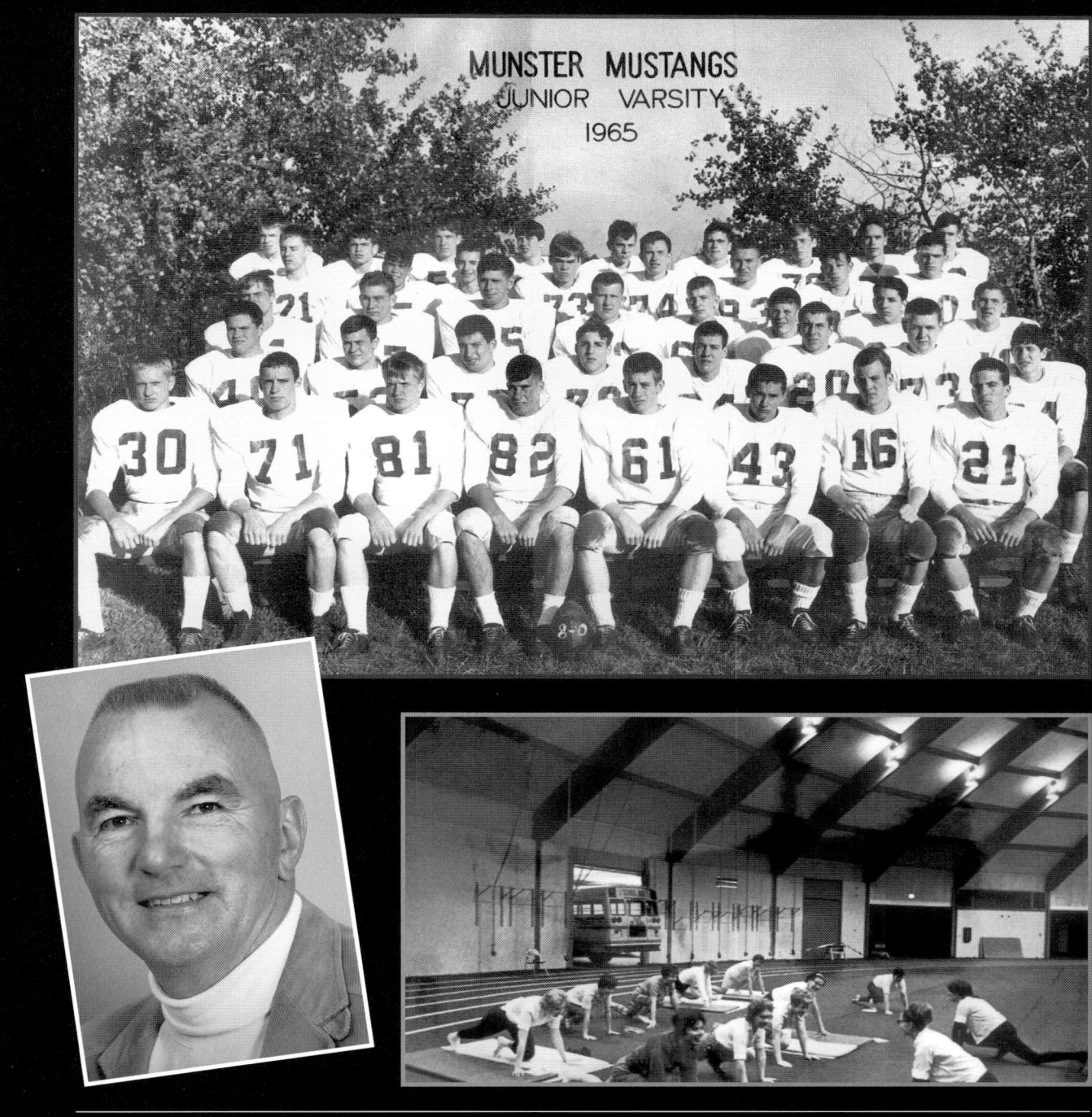

Munster Junior Varsity Football. Munster's first team had an impressive overall record of 8 wins 0 losses (7 wins were against Junior Varsity teams). Front Row: B. Butkus, G. Baker, E. Hass, S. Merten, D. Paul, L. Ulbrich, J. Horan, and J. Livingston; Row 2: D. Massa, R. Duffala, T. Dalfonso, P. Reinstein, P. Forsythe, B. Nowak, E. Cunningham, and M. Bogusz; Row 3: F. Malo, J. Pavolich, B. Walt, M. Niksic, M. Kautz, B. Garzinski, N. Rader, and W. Glaros; Row 4: S. Bolls, M. Cain, B. Boender, J. Buehler, P. Polak, M. Edwards, J. Milliken, and R. Maroe; Back Row: T. Beckman, L. Glaros, J. Nondorf, J. Bogusz, M. Adley, M. Ford, M. Sprovtsoff, R. Baudino, and L. Wayland. (Photo courtesy of John Friend)

John Friend, Munster's first football coach, basketball coach, and athletic director. In later years, Friend was a member of the Park Board, the School Board, and the Community Veterans Memorial Committee. (MHS photo donated by the School Town of Munster)

The field house, soon to host P.E. classes, exciting basketball games, and solemn graduation ceremonies. (MHS photo donated by the School Town of Munster)

CHAPTER X THE FAST-GROWING 1960s • 147

In exchange for much indebtedness, Munster now had forty new classrooms; four large group rooms; two science labs; two resource centers; two art rooms; a shop; an auditorium with a 52-foot-wide, 30-foot-deep stage and seating for 1,100; a 45-by-75-foot swimming pool with one- and three-meter diving boards, and 600 spectator seats; a 226-foot diameter, 45-foot-high field house with three hundred "pupil stations," a one-eighth-mile track at the perimeter, and 2,270 bleacher seats; a lighted football field with bleachers and a quarter-mile track; and a baseball field. John Friend, the school's athletic director since 1964, had first-rate facilities for his new Munster Mustangs.

The entire complex underwent a major remodeling in 1973 and 1974 after the junior high school was moved to a new building a short distance away and became a middle school for grades 6–8. The vacated building was incorporated into the high school. The high school was also reconfigured into college-like departments. The north building became the academic center, and the south building housed departments of math, business, art, and others. The former auditorium became a professional-grade performing arts center. In 1979 more classrooms, a science lab, and other spaces were remodeled or added, and the field house and the pool were updated. A fire in 1980 in the northern building forced still another reconstruction program.

Nor was the town through building schools. The $1.4-million Frank H. Hammond Elementary School at Fran-Lin and Elmwood Drive was dedicated in May of 1969, and named for the superintendent. The "Fran-Lin" school—so dubbed during construction—was a sixty-three-thousand-square-foot, ultramodern school on twelve acres (with twelve more on reserve) in the Fairmeadows Subdivision.

"Frank H." could accommodate almost eight hundred students in twenty-five classrooms and two kindergarten rooms. It also contained a small auditorium, a three-hundred-seat student commons–cafeteria, a student bookstore, an arena-style audio-visual center, and was air conditioned. The new K–6 school, which served students from south Munster, immediately took pressure off the overcrowded Lanier School. By 2000, it was heavily used, had limited facilities for modern electronic access, and the gym was dinky. There had been updates over the years, but Hammond School again needed reconfiguration and expansion.

The Munster school system had been dramatically transformed, and by 1970, despite massive increases in enrollment, seemed close to equilibrium. In 1968 Munster operated three elementary

SUE HENDRICKSON

The "female Indiana Jones" is a native of Munster, attended Munster schools, and was a gifted and "curious" child. Sue left Munster in 1966, and soon began a career in ocean diving and historical salvage of shipwrecks.

In 1974 Sue joined paleontologists in an expedition to the Dominican Republic, and was "hooked." Hendrickson later collected amber specimens and excavated fossil whale bones in Peru.

On August 12, 1990, while working for the Black Hills Institute in the Badlands of South Dakota, Sue discovered fossilized bones projecting out of a cliff wall. A nearly complete, 67-million-year old, thirteen-foot-tall, forty-five-foot-long, two-ton skeleton of a Tyrannosaurus rex was unearthed. It was named "Sue" in her honor.

After a long custody battle, the bony "Sue" was sold to the Field Museum in Chicago for $8.4 million. Cleaned and reassembled, the fierce-looking T-Rex was unveiled to the public in 2000, and is a highly popular display.

Sue Hendrickson later wrote an autobiography, and, in 2004, was awarded an honorary Ph.D. from the University of Illinois.

Sue is an expert on amber, ancient shipwrecks, and, of course, really big fossils. She has received many awards and honors, including a woman of the year "Glammy" from Glamour magazine in 2000. In 2006 she was a professional archaeological diver. (Photo courtesy of Sue Hendrickson)

148 • MUNSTER, INDIANA: A CENTENNIAL HISTORY

schools with a fourth under construction, and a new junior high school–senior high school complex. A study conducted in that year by Purdue University experts gushed over the Munster school system. This was a remarkable feat for a small town that had had entered the 1960s with a rather ordinary and certainly underbuilt school system, and had more than doubled in students in ten years.

By 1970 the schools had also developed a strong academic curriculum with a strong focus on languages, math, and science. Most Munster graduates continued their educations, and certainly benefited from a curriculum aimed at universities like Purdue and IU. In 1966 Frank Hammond cautiously observed that in coming years an engineering student entering Purdue might have to know how to use a computer.

The Purdue professors anticipated, perhaps too pessimistically, that the school population would increase by two hundred students each year "until all the land area of the district is saturated with residential developments." They recommended major long-range planning by the school officials. The junior high school was rated as exceptional, both academically and architecturally. Munster High School students—now settled into a brand-new state-of-the-art high school building—were "marked by exceptional academic capability." The report concluded, expensively, that Munster should replace its junior high school with a $6.2-million middle school with grades 6-7-8 instead of 5-6-7-8, and recommended that the curriculum for the less able and the non-college-bound be strengthened.

A good system attracts good teachers, and Munster was fortunate in its recruiting. It was generally recognized that teacher morale and dedication were exceptional, and that most teachers went that "extra mile" for their students. Twenty were hired in 1963, thirty-three in 1964. Starting salaries for teachers in mid-decade were $5,600 for those with a bachelor's degree and $6,100 with the master's. By 1968 the former one-room school system employed 153 teachers. A number of new administrative posts were created as well.

Munster lost as many young men in distant Vietnam as in World War II. Those from Munster who died in that nasty war: Michael Ford, Richard Ham, Robert Kikkert, George McCoy, Donald Slack, George Stivers, and Richard Schroeder. Surprisingly, that improbable conflict had little overt effect on the busy and prospering Town on the Ridge.

"Viet Nam" at the Community Veterans Memorial honors service men and women who served in the Viet Nam conflict.

30TH PL
MONROE AV
RIDGE RD
SEBERGER DR
FULLERTON AV
RIDGEWAY AV
HOWARD
RIDGEWAY AV
FAIRWAY AV
SOUTH ST
TERRACE DR
SOUTH ST
RIDGE RD
GREENWOOD AV
BEECH AV
WALNUT DR
WHITE OAK AV
MORAINE DR
HOHMAN AV
SUNSET LN
BRIAR LN
BRIAR LN
LAWNDALE DR
RIDGE RD
PARK DR
MAPLE LN
TIMRICK DR
MEADOW LN
45TH ST
MARGO LN
SUPERIOR AV
BROOKSIDE DR
GLASTONBURY ST
BANBURY PL
MILFORD HAVEN WAY
LEICESTER RD
INDIANA PKWY
PROGRESS AV
VALPARAISO DR
CALUMET AV
THICKET LN
REDBUD RD
CRIMSON TREE LN
IVY LN
CEDAR CREST DR
TAMARACK DR
FITZGERALD DR
TWIN CREEK BLVD
SALISBURY DR
WHITEHALL GARDEN
BOWEN DR
NORWICH CT
SINGLETON DR
REDBUD RD
WHITE OAK AV
POPLAR LN
MUNSTER
PARK and RECREATION
DEPARTMENT

CHAPTER XI

And Still More Expansion
1970–1980

IN THE 1970S GROWTH WAS AGAIN THE MAIN story in Munster. Now a sleek suburb, the town entered the 1970s with 16,514 in residence, a 60 percent expansion over the preceding ten years. A special census found almost 19,000 three years later, and the numbers topped out in 1980 at 20,671, a figure not far from the population reported twenty years later. Nearly all were whites, and most were prosperous. Half of all wage earners in town earned more than $25,000 per year. In 1977 the *Chicago Tribune* ranked Munster in the top quarter of all towns in the eight-county Chicago metropolitan area.

Even so, many wrestled with recession, inflation, and a new attitude about town government. People now wanted a professional administration, city-style services, and, as always, low taxes. Volunteerism was fine at the top, but municipal employees, and plenty of them, seemed better. There was something of the Tooth Fairy about those expectations, as the cost of governing skyrocketed with general inflation. Munster was a rising regional medical center, which brought both advantages and problems. The general dislike of apartments and condominiums eased.

The Town Hall and Parks Department Building on Ridge Road.

The Kaske House at Heritage Park, on the National Register of Historic Places, is now the home of the Munster History Museum operated by the Munster Historical Society.

A Girl Scout Tea at the Kaske House Museum, now Munster History Museum. (Diane Kitchell photo)

Cindy Watson tells of early Munster to students outside the Munster History Museum. (Nancy Johnson photo)

152 • MUNSTER, INDIANA: A CENTENNIAL HISTORY

In 1974 the *Times* described Munster as "one of the finest residential areas in Northwest Indiana." A Munster Chamber of Commerce survey of the town found a very high and rising percentage of professionals, executives, and educators. In 1979 IUN Professor Herman Feldman studied Munster for the Lake County Community Development Committee. Feldman reported that the town led the Calumet in community satisfaction with municipal services, including law enforcement, schools, medical and hospital care, general maintenance of public property, and even garbage collection. High recognition for Munster government!

In 1975 the town's pride in its past was advanced with the founding of the Munster Historical Society. The original Board of Directors included Norma Benoit, Robert Griffin, Evelyn Freese, Mary Martin, Dorothy Tanis, Michael Aurelius, and Jerry Gillespie. The Historical Society collected historical documents, photos, and physical evidence of town history, made it available to researchers, and eventually placed much of its collection in the Kaske House Museum. The Society lost a collection of antique tools and implements when the old Stallbohm barn burned in 2002.

The Historical Society, together with Parks and Recreation, first sponsored Olde Munster Day in 1990, an annual historical fest, and a Holiday Open House. For some years, it sponsored the Heritage Music Festival in cooperation with the Parks and Recreation Department. It also participated in the Fourth of July Parade and cooperated with various community groups in historically flavored activities. The sixty-member Society was a co-sponsor of the Munster Centennial.

Town Government

Munster town government functioned smoothly in the 1970s, while steadily growing in size and complexity. After Public Works Director John Bunnell—town manager in all but name—retired in 1978, and with a rapidly growing number of employees, the Board hired Eric Anderson as town manager. The town also created a Civil Rights Commission in 1971, an Economic Development Commission in 1974, and an Animal Control Commission in 1975.

Annual budgets continued to climb, but tax rates, while sometimes bumping the official limit, remained lower than most towns in the area, thanks to the high value of property. Assessments rose from $37.6 million in 1970 to $44.2 million in 1975, and passed $50 million as the decade ended. By 1979 the town's annual budget had reached $4.8 million.

Another change of note: an unprecedented Democratic success in a town election. In 1971 Munster Republicans coasted to victory with three-to-one margins. But, after the 1975 election, the *Munster Sun-Journal* described the town as "stunned." Democrats had scored their first-ever victory: John Mybeck had defeated Donald Webber, 3,354 to 2,987. And Democrats did well in other races, even in defeat: Democrat Richard Waxman garnered a respectable 2,879 votes to Republican Russell Snyder's 3,352. Mybeck, the first Democrat on the Munster Town Board, took his seat, and somehow the earth still spun on its axis. In reality, Mybeck was a popular fellow, and his win was more personal than partisan. Clerk-Treasurer Lois Schoon easily won a fourth term, 3,709 to 2,689, over Jean Karas.

Eric Anderson was Munster's first town manager. (MHS photo donated by Eric Anderson)

Lois A. Schoon was Munster's longest-serving clerk-treasurer. Practically a lifelong resident of Munster, Lois was appointed town clerk-treasurer on March 15, 1967, to fill an unexpired term. She was then elected to that office that fall and served nearly seventeen years before retiring. Lois helped lead the move from the old Town Hall to the new one. (Henry Boender photo donated by Lois Schoon)

John Mybeck, first Democrat elected to the Munster Town Board.

Munster's "sleeping giant," water rates, returned to life in the mid-1970s. Under an order from the Indiana Public Utilities Commission, for some years the town had distributed water below cost, but by 1978 its reserves were gone. A lengthy debate with the Hammond Sanitary District over water rates ended badly for the town. With little choice, the Town Board imposed a startling 124 percent water rate increase in September 1978, the first bump in twelve years.

Hoping to anticipate needs for the next thirty years, the Board also approved construction of a million-gallon water tower for Aetna Industrial Park, a 6.5-million-gallon ground-level storage tank, and new water mains. The Board, either a tad optimistically or simply scared, guesstimated that Munster population would reach thirty-five thousand by 1985.

Public reaction was loud and long, and political. Town Board meetings were filled with protestors. Some argued that the future ought to pay for its own water tanks. Others picked at the town's engineering study. Democrats opportunistically accused the Board of "taking the flourishing water utility and almost bankrupting it." But Town Board President Russell Snyder stood his ground. In the end, the ordinances were passed, and the town moved ahead.

Following a rate hike by the Sanitary District in 1980, the Board actually tacked on another increase. Whatever the merits of the arguments of the day, by the next century, Munster had seven water tanks in service with a combined capacity of 12 million gallons, multiple pumping stations, and enjoyed plenty of just about the best water in America.

Local and state officials gather to officially open the extension of Forty-fifth Street from Calumet Avenue to the State Line. (Trent family photograph)

Bicentennial logo embroidered by Elizabeth (Betty) Ferry. (Photo donated by Nancy Johnson)

154 • MUNSTER, INDIANA: A CENTENNIAL HISTORY

Despite their occasional crabbiness, the citizens of Munster actually liked their government pretty much the way it was. A League of Women Voters survey asked citizens if they would prefer a "city" form of government. Few said yes.

The Bicentennial of the American Revolution was widely celebrated in Munster. Bill Hensey chaired the Bicentennial Commission, and cooperated closely with the Community Park Foundation. Many events centered on Bicentennial themes. Munster architect Douglas Warner designed an obelisk and a star-shaped base for three flagpoles that were installed at the Heritage Entrance to Community Park.

The centerpieces of the celebration were a Washington's Birthday Heritage dinner-dance and an especially grand Fourth of July celebration dubbed "America: Two Hundred Years of Progress," with a concert and fireworks. Hundreds of trees were planted in Community Park, and not one but four time capsules were buried, to be opened on different dates over the next century.

School Days

Popular support of the Munster schools remained strong, though severely tested by several issues. Townspeople grumbled when asked to pay hefty taxes for new schools, or equipment, or faculty raises, but usually assented. After all, most had moved to Munster precisely because of the school

Dedication of Rotary Park. As part of the Bicentennial celebration, the Rotary Club sponsored the first public art in a town that thirty years later would be recognized for its extensive public art collection. The three figures, of an Indian, a farmer, and an ironworker, representing three stages in Munster history, were designed by Fred Holly and built by Bill Ores. Note the Bicentennial flag in the background. (MHS photo taken by Emil Duffala)

Bicentennial Obelisk erected by the Munster Bicentennial Commission in honor of the nation's two-hundredth birthday still stands at the entrance to Community Park. (Photo by Lance Trusty)

CHAPTER XI AND STILL MORE EXPANSION 1970–1980 • 155

In 1971 the public schools had room for 4,400 students, and anticipated steady growth in enrollments. Another eight hundred seats were added a year later after the new middle school opened. But to everyone's surprise, enrollments were flat from 1971 to 1975—certainly a new thing in the Munster schools—then fell steadily, from 4,542 in 1975 to 3,479 in 1980. Elementary school enrollment dropped from over 1,800 in 1972 to 1,189 in 1980. High school enrollments remained steady over the decade. Even so, there was little evidence of overbuilding in a system that had done a fine job of coping with decades of rapid growth. And Munster was hardly fully populated in 1980.

In 1970, after digesting much professional advice, the School Board decided to build a middle school on a site just north of the senior high school. The middle school idea, which offered team teaching and more individualized learning, changed the traditional division of classes among elementary, junior, and senior high schools from grades K–6, 7–9, and 10–12 to K–5, 6–8, and 9–12.

The new Wilbur Wright Middle School opened in a hurry in 1972; when classes began, Principal Raymond Rittman was still waiting for his desk. WWMS was configured with an open interior, rather than traditional classrooms, and a trendy focus on individualized instruction and team-teaching. The babble rising over the area dividers bothered students and teachers alike. Adoption of the "New Math" added to the confusion. Some quiet, and a tighter, more traditional academic *structure* soon became more important than open spaces. Interior walls and twenty more classrooms were added in 1979.

Construction slowed in the 1970s after the Middle School came on stream. A sixty-thousand-square-foot addition to the High School was authorized in 1978, which added twenty classrooms and more administrative offices, remodeled the science labs, and updated the field house. With Eads and Elliott Schools remodeled, the Board closed Lanier School. There was also some *de*struction: a major fire in October 1980, ruined the eighteen-thousand-book high school library, two lecture halls, the commons area, and a science lab. Though mostly covered by insurance, the fire caused no end of disruption. Eleven classrooms were temporarily closed for restoration.

The New Wilbur Wright Middle School. (MHS photo)

The 1973 boys swim team was the first team from Munster High School to win a state athletic championship. Pictured, left to right, in the top row: Ted Jepsen, Scott Sutter, Bill Hasse, Tom Ogren, Brent Smith, Bill Knutson, Matt Chelich, and Jeff Miller; middle row: Coach Jon Jepsen, Dirk Wonnell, Bob Mueller, Dale Sorenson, Bill Watson, Jay Stewart, Mark Wickland, and Hugh Kuhn; bottom row: Assistant Coach Jerry Croll, Mark Blocker, Ron Wennekes, Larry Micon, Jim Lee, and Tom Stine. (Munster High School Athletic Department)

The 1975 girls swim team, pictured with Principal Karl Hertz (far left), was the first girls' team from Munster High School to win a state athletic championship. Left to right in the front row: Marci Niksic, Melanie Sorenson, and Roberta Wohrle; second row: Jane Kiernan, Katy Flynn, Gayle Johnson, Betsy Less, and Karen Easter; top row: Assistant Coach Gloria Kemp, Janet Niksic, Janet Muta, Claudia Mott, Alice Easter, and Head Coach Betty Leibert. At the meet Jane Kiernan won the 50-yard freestyle event. She, Karen Easter, Gayle Johnson, and Claudia Mott set a new state record for the 200-medley relay team. (Courtesy of Betty Leibert Lukoshus.)

Munster High School Concert Choir, 1977, directed by Dick Holmberg. (Nancy Johnson photo)

Left wing Bob Trusty rushes for the ball during a Munster–Gavit soccer game in 1977. (Photo by his dad)

CHAPTER XI AND STILL MORE EXPANSION 1970–1980 • 159

Excellence extended well beyond the classroom. Munster athletes were the envy—and the despair—of Indiana. For years Munster High "fielded" an unbeatable swim team. Year after year the Munster Seahorses demolished their opponents. The team swept the state IHSAA competitions from 1973 to 1977. South Bend Riley proved too much in 1978, but Munster beat them for the state championship in 1979. In 1974 the Seahorses came in second at the Indiana Amateur Athletic Union swim meet in Indianapolis. In 1975 the girls swim team defeated the defending sectional champion, Valparaiso, and went on to claim the state title. The MHS Girls Gymnastics team, led by Donna Echterling, who took two first places, won a sectional title in 1974.

Munster chessmen Ilya Schwartzman and Stan Zygmunt set a new world record in 1980 with a 158-hour–25-minute nonstop chess match. Their marathon raised over a thousand dollars for a Chess Club trip to a national competition. Band and Orchestra members were quite successful in various competitions. The high school Distributive Education Club won a regional trophy three times in a row, and retired it in 1974. Fresh out of high school, Douglas Amber became the youngest elected delegate to the Indiana Democratic Convention in 1974. In 1974, a typical year, forty Munster students were elected to the National Honor Society.

The Speech and Debate Team was a special item in itself. Founded in 1965 by teachers Helen Engstrom (later elected to the National Speech Coaches Hall of Fame) and Al Brinson, the team won its first state championship three years later. Other closely involved coaches included Mary Yorke, Donald Fortner, James Thorp, and Eileen Thorp, all of whom are members of the Indiana Coaches Hall of Fame.

The team qualified for the national competition every year without interruption from 1968 to the present. Carol-rae Kraus won the state championship for Dramatic Interpretation in 1968. In 1970 the team won its first state championship and Jeff Gubitz placed third nationally in dramatic interpretation. The team was ranked fifth in the country in 1975, 1976, and sixth in 1979 and 1981. In 1975 the team won a first and a second in the

The 1970 Speech and Debate Team, the first team to achieve a state championship. (Donated by Helen Engstrom)

The Chicken Barbeque, has been an annual Speech and Debate Team fundraiser since the beginning. In the early years, the chicken was cooked outside the school on oversized grills. (MHS photo)

state-level debate meet in Indianapolis and a sixth in a national speech tournament sponsored by the National Forensic League. Munster was ranked fifth in the country in 1975 and 1976, sixth in 1979 and 1981, third in 1989.

In the 1980s team rankings were replaced with "Excellence Awards." Munster continued to place in the top 1 percent nationally. It received awards for excellence at the Nationals. In 1990, when Munster was ranked eighth of seven hundred schools at the National Speech Tournament, Andrea Foltz was named the national champion in poetry interpretation over fifteen hundred contestants. After 2000 the team sent between ten and fourteen students annually to the Nationals in both speech and debate. In recent years the team has been ranked in the top 1 percent nationally. Excellence indeed.

And Still More Homes

Between 1971 and 1980 just over fifteen hundred new homes with a total value of around $75 million were built in Munster. Moreover, construction was steady, year after year, averaging about 175 houses annually until 1979 and 1980, when the totals dropped to 85 and 30, respectively. In 1972 a record 273 new homes costing $9.5 million were occupied. During that busy decade the average value of a new home rose from around $34,000 to almost $100,000. Allowing for steady inflation and a deep recession, new homes were clearly getting larger and more expensive. Another notable change: in the past, whenever construction of a new multifamily structure was proposed, existing homeowners loudly objected. That attitude eased after 1970, and workers built eighty-four multifamily buildings with almost five hundred units.

Much of the new housing stock was still produced by smaller developers and builders. In 1972 approval was given to Castle Estates Third Addition for fourteen lots, Mayers' Addition for seventeen lots, Ladd Addition for twenty-three lots, and many more homes in Fairmeadows and University Estates. In 1974 the Town Board approved rezoning of part of Fairmeadows from duplexes to apartments, and that did generate some homeowners' objections, centered, as before, on "the type of people" the apartments might attract. In 1976 Donald Powers undertook Twin Creeks, a 219-lot subdivision on eighty-seven acres. Central Munster was filling up by 1980.

Andrea Foltz, in 1990 became Munster's first national speech champion in 1990. She won the poetry interpretation competition. (Munster High School photo)

Multifamily buildings on Camellia Drive are still attractive in 2006.

Twin Creek subdivision residents cross this picturesque bridge over Hart Ditch on their way home every day.

CHAPTER XI AND STILL MORE EXPANSION 1970–1980 • 161

Business and Industry

Still without a defined central downtown, small businesses expanded steadily, and some rather large ones opened after 1970. Some 283 businesses were in operation in 1975, and well over 400 in 1980, including physicians, ranging from AAA Carpet and Furniture Cleaners to Robert Zurad, CPA.

Malls multiplied. Harrison-Ridge Square opened in 1973 with seven shops and a parking lot on the north side. Developer Paul Ladd built a two-building, fourteen-store shopping center on the south side of Forty-fifth Street in 1975, between an office complex and a Citizens Federal Savings Branch that had opened in 1973. In 1974 another strip of stores east of Burger's on Forty-fifth opened with McShane's, which moved from Hammond, as the anchor store, and several smaller stores. In 1979 a small professional plaza was built immediately east of the Calumet Shopping Center.

Ridge Road changed steadily. Mercantile National Bank opened a branch in front of Market Square Shopping Center. McDonald's opened at 515 Ridge Road in 1971 with a visit from Ronald McDonald. Calumet Avenue south of Ridge Road became a favored retailing site for businesses, among them, the Olympic Raquetball Club and a Smuggler's Inn Restaurant, which opened in 1980.

Two thousand held industrial jobs in 1974. Simmons, the largest, employed 1,600; Munster Steel, 76; National Brick, 90, and Pepsi, 235. Two of the four would close over the next five years.

Ecology arrived tentatively in the 1970s. Pollution of Hart Ditch by towns in North and St. John Townships finally attracted the EPA's eye in 1979. Tests conducted at the ditch revealed dangerously high bacterial counts. Odors were noxious, especially during low water. The EPA ordered Dyer and Schererville to begin effective treatment of wastes. Calls for dredging and flushing were issued, without results. Monitoring—an economical, all-purpose solution to environmental problems—was initiated by the EPA. Finally, in 1980 the St. John Township communities did begin primary treatment of waste.

Modern times and new ideas gradually closed in on American Brick. In 1974 the brick plant was cited for air pollution by the EPA, and a year later town officials considered filing suit—not for the first time—against the smoky company. American Brick insisted that it could find no practical way to reduce emissions of "particulate matter" and sulphur dioxide. The smoke was probably more annoying than dangerous, but the new "neighbors" wanted a "clean-up" and *action*.

Fighting for his company's life, in 1976 Robert Carey met with officials of the Indiana Air Pollution Control Board and the EPA. Carey, who had already spent large sums on compliance, argued that, with available technology, bricks could not be made without emissions. The EPA countered bluntly that his company had to clean up or close. Time was running out for the oldest industry in Munster.

The Hammond Clinic and Munster Med Inn. Burger King is recognizable at the bottom of the photo. (Hammond Clinic photo)

Other environmental actions included an audit of the school system's energy usage, an ecology open house at Wilbur Wright in 1974, and the establishment of a recycling center at the former Nike Site by the Munster Recycling Committee. A year later it became the Region Recycling Committee and the operation became the Region Recycling Center. With volunteer assistance, the Recycling Center collected metals, paper, and glass. The plan was to recycle, reduce solid waste and perhaps to raise some money for community improvements. Residents brought items to the site on Saturdays. Constant vandalism kept people nervous until the site was sold to Kaiser-Aetna, and the ecology effort ended.

The League of Women Voters placed repositories around town to collect steel and aluminum cans, but excessive overhead ended their "Can-paign." And in 1976 Helen Bieker received an Environmental Quality Award from the EPA for her work with the Great Lakes Basin Task Force.

The ghost of Henry Ford visited Munster, in the form of Lansing's proposed "bi-state" Jetport. In 1976 the Town of Lansing bought the little airfield from the estate of Thomas Seay, and began to develop Lansing Municipal Airport. The town collected over thirty million Illinois and federal dollars for airport expansion from a hundred to six hundred acres and to extend the north-south runway (there was also an east-west runway) at both ends, for smaller jets. Few in Munster liked the sound of that, citing noise, the cost of moving roads and infrastructure, and its effect on growth and development.

In 1980 Lansing asked the Town Plan Commission to ban construction of tall buildings from the runway approach zone. Munster was not pleased to be asked to transform its planned industrial park into a "clear zone" for Lansing. The Town Board was handed a petition with over three thousand signatures opposing airport expansion. It discussed and debated the issue, then voted against rezoning. For its courage, the Board was given a standing ovation from a highly partisan crowd. But Washington finally ruled, and the runway was extended almost to Forty-fifth Street.

American Brick Company, before its closure. (Russell Snyder photo)

Munster's bike route was designed in the late 1970s by the Junior Women's Club working with the town government and the Police Department. Signs around town still give directions for this round-the-town route.

BRIAR LN
LAWNDALE DR
SYCAMORE LN
MAPLE LN
EVERGREEN LN
GARFIELD AV
HARRISON AV
MONROE AV
MADISON AV
JEFFERSON AV
BRIAR LN
34TH ST
RIDGE RD
PARK DR
INDIAN PATH
SCHREIBER DR
OAK PARK DR
PARK DR
TWELVE OAKS DR
TIMRICK DR
MEADOW LN
45TH ST
MARGO LN
SUPERIOR AV
GLASTONBURY ST
BANBURY PL
MILFORD HAVEN WAY
LEICESTER RD
WHITEHALL GARDEN
INDIANA PKWY
PROGRESS AV
VALPARAISO DR
CALUMET AV
Maynard Reservoir
BOWEN DR
NORWICH CT
SINGLETON DR
CAMELLIA DR
45TH ST
BROOKSIDE DR
CEDAR CREST DR
THICKET LN
REDBUD RD
CRIMSON TREE LN
IVY LN
TAMARACK DR
FITZGERALD DR
TWIN CREEK BLVD
PARKSIDE DR
IVY LN
WHITE OAK AV

CHAPTER XII

Modern Suburb
1980–2000

IN THE LAST TWO DECADES OF THE LAST century, the citizens of the Town on the Ridge enjoyed a high quality of life, excellent homes, nationally recognized schools, honest government, high-quality public services, and a "bustling" business and industrial environment. Most agreed that the key to the town's success was planning, strict zoning, strong building codes, and careful management of growth.

The dramatic population growth of the previous decades finally petered out. In 1980 the population was 20,671, after a modest ten-year increase. The 1990 census found only 19,949, a small, but surprising decline. Ten years later, as Munster was running out of buildable land, the census reported 21,511 residents (up 7.8 percent). That was among the smallest decennial changes in fifty years. In 1990 there were 7,344 housing units in town, and just over 8,000 in 2000. At point, over seven thousand families owned their own homes, while fewer than nine hundred were renters.

The New Town Hall on Tapper Avenue houses the Police and Fire Departments on the north and south ends.

Munster demographics were typical of upscale Chicago region suburbs. In 2000 nine in ten were white, almost 5 percent were of Asian origin, and one in twenty was Hispanic. One in a hundred was black. Age distribution was also typical: one in five was of school age. Four in ten families had no children living at home. Munster was a good place for single fellows: in 2000 females outnumbered males by ten to nine. Actually, few were looking; two of three residents were married. From a broader perspective, Munster enjoyed abundant religious diversity, but the population was relatively homogeneous, and lived in a rather uniform, middle-class cultural climate.

The number of college graduates grew from one in four in 1980 to one in three in 1990, and to almost 40 percent in 2000. Occupations reflected that high educational level. By 1990 four in ten were members of a profession. About as many were "service" employees, including teachers, and 14 percent were engaged in "production."

Munster was a financially comfortable town. The 1990 median household income was a lofty $48,483 and neared $70,000 in 2000. In 1990 the median price of a home in town was just under $150,000, ranking Munster first in the state in average home sale value. That figure passed $216,000 in 2000. Even so, buyers found Munster attractive, and a steady stream of Hammond city folk and Illinoisans moved to the Ridge town. Some accused Munster folk of "snobbery," but residents were pleased with their town's high standards and low taxes.

Government

Despite occasional differences over specific issues (a proposed joint fire department district with Highland rained fire and brimstone on its proponents), the people of Munster were manifestly pleased and proud of their town government. Its long-term adherence to the original 1938 Town Plan had manifestly worked, even if Fran-Lin's curves contradicted the neat grid plan. Everyone benefited from strong parental commitment to the schools and quality of education. The town's pro-business policy had built a stable "micro-economy" and a fine tax base for the community.

In 1988 Town Manager Tom DeGuilio described Munster government as "apolitical" and "progressive." By then DeGuilio, the town executive officer under the Council, was the central figure in everyday town management. DeGuilio, a native of Chicago Heights and a graduate of Illinois State University, succeeded Eric Anderson in 1984. Named Citizen of the Year in 2002, DeGuilio was an expert at staying calm, making improvements, and keeping costs low. In 2002 his office had a staff of seven, including an assistant town manager, secretaries, two computer persons, and a public information officer.

The town administration 2000–2003, Munster's only Council evenly divided with two Republicans and two Democrats. Elected officials in the back are Clerk-Treasurer David Shafer and Council Members Steve Pestikas, David Nellans, John Hluska, and Helen Brown. In front are Assistant Town Manager Matt Fritz, Town Manager Tom DeGiulio, and Town Attorney Eugene Feingold. (MHS photo)

The town operations budget doubled in the ten years after 1981 from $4.5 million to $8.6 million. The costs of water, utilities, and solid waste disposal brought the budget to around $15 million. Munster was very good at attracting federal funds. Town Board President Don Johnson observed that "Munster is always ready with a project." It wasn't very Republican, but it was darned effective. Tax rates declined as property values soared to $120 million in 1990. Landfill operations earned a nice but temporary income—$1 million in 1987—that funded other city services.

The Town Council was evenly divided between parties in 2000, and often deadlocked, according to the *Times*. Everyone denied that "politics" had any role in Council voting, but "terse exchanges" were not infrequent. Citizens seemed complacent: in the 1999 primary only one race, in the Third Ward, was contested, between two Democrats. The Town Board became the Town Council in July 1989. Helen Brown, the first woman to serve on the Council, was appointed in 1998 to complete the term of David Shafer, who had resigned to take a full-time position with the town. That revolution only took ninety-one years!

DeGuilio described the town as "landlocked," but still following the 1938 Master Plan. Munster continued to adhere to the spirit, if not the exact details of that plan, and the result was a community with clearly defined separation between residences, businesses, and light industrial sites. Now if the Town Council could move railroad tracks....

A number of other changes took place. An eight-acre site between Tapper and Ridgeway was chosen in 1977 for a new Town Government Complex. It was time: the old Town Hall needed "emergency aid." Its walls were "crumbling" from seepage and cracks

---

New Town Hall dedication, July 4, 1982.

Lousiville and Nashville train heads north in July of 1983 crossing the bridge over the Broadmoor Avenue viaduct. (Mark Stanek photo)

in the mortar. The chosen site had been subdivided in the 1920s, but had not been built on, a rare thing for the area north of the Ridge. The Town Board approved the design of a Colonial-style, thirty-eight-thousand-square foot, $5-million structure in 1979.

The new Municipal Center was dedicated on the Fourth of July 1982. The twenty-thousand-square-foot central unit housed the government, including the Town Manager's Office, Town Council and public meeting rooms, and an assortment of other town offices. The northern wing housed the Police Department in twelve thousand square feet of space. The southern end of the complex was a six-thousand-square-foot, four-bay fire station. Covered walkways connected the buildings. Years later a complete renovation and partial reconfiguration of Town Hall cost another $2.5 million.

In 2000 a noisy confrontation emerged over the proposed installation of cellular telephone antennae atop the water tower near Ridge Road. Some forty people living in the area, organized as the Munster Town Watch, vigorously opposed this profitable leasing venture. The Watch rallied with signs proclaiming "Don't Radiate Our Kids" and "Education Not Radiation," threatened to "impeach" town officials, and filed a suit against the Council. The community was perhaps more amazed than upset by all this. Bound by federal rules, the Town Council signed a contract late in 2000, and the antennae were installed. A year later the opponents withdrew their suit.

Already the winner in 1983 and 1987 of the Indiana Association of Towns Community Achievement Award, Munster went all-out for recycling in June 1990. An invasion of blue plastic bins was preceded by a blizzard of notices, talks, a public access channel video, brochures, and a not-so-subtle threat that homeowners who failed to use them would pay extra. Recycling began with curbside trash separation. The town had anticipated that half its customers would participate, but in the first week the level was nearly 100 percent.

A year later, as Munster won the Governor's Recycling Award, the town's recycling program was "comprehensive," with an ongoing 90–96 percent participation rate. Years later, after the town privatized trash collection, everything was poured into a single bin truck at the curb, and was later separated at a buy-back center.

The Munster public art program was another success story. In the mid-1990s Councilman Hugh Brauer offered a genuinely bright idea: ask businesses and industries who accept tax abatements to apply 1 percent of their expenditures for construction and equipment to public art projects. Munster, the only

---

This horse sculpture by John Kearney stands in front of Staley General Transportation on Forty-fifth Street. (MHS photo)

Sculpture by Kathleen Farrel of Joliet, Illinois, in front of Strack and Van Til's on Ridge Road.

town in Indiana to do so, created a Public Art Committee to connect the public good, artists, and funds.

By 2004 thirteen outdoor sculptures were either installed about town or planned at a cost of $640,000; two years later more were installed, and the expenditure was over $1 million. The program was copied elsewhere. In 2005, Munster's public art project won a major award from the Indiana Association of Cities and Towns, which commented, "sometimes the best programs are the simplest ones."

In 1999 a $1.2 million federal Transportation Enhancement grant and $300,000 from the Munster Civic Foundation funded a town-wide bike path. The eleven-mile-long path—with more planned—connected residential areas with parks, forest preserves, and other communities. No local tax money was involved in its creation. Plans were made for a Pennsy Greenway that would follow the route of an abandoned railroad track from Lansing to Crown Point.

Munster remained a safe place to live. The overall crime rate was low. A double homicide in a home on Thirty-third Street in 1989 was given abundant press coverage, but turned out to be the work of a rather dense contract killer hired by family members to settle a business quarrel. Two years later another double murder on Garfield was committed by a former boyfriend. The police quickly collared the "perps." Both of these lurid events were family or personal, rather than random crimes.

The senseless killing of a dry cleaner's clerk in 1993 in the Calumet Shopping Center was the town's only major unsolved violent major crime. In 2000, Munster hosted a $31 million cocaine bust; the goods were actually intended for Chicago distribution, but were stored in a garage on Manor Avenue. Bank robberies continued, perhaps inevitably, given the rising number of banks and the proximity of I-80-94.

Good management and planning had finally conquered one ancient problem. Other than grumbles about rates, few had much to say about the water supply, unless it appeared in their basement after a storm. The town was finally comfortable with seven storage tanks with a total capacity of 12 million gallons, and two pumping stations to keep them full of Lake Michigan water.

Among the civic improvements made after 1980 were a new pumping station at River Bend, more parks, and new, remodeled, or expanded schools. The widening of Calumet Avenue to Dyer offered fast travel to the new south Munster homeowners. While 45th Street was a relatively fast route to Indianapolis Boulevard, it also gave drivers plenty of time to read their mail at Calumet Avenue, a major chokepoint by 2000.

The PepsiAmericas sculpture by Mark Lundeen on Calumet Avenue creatively incorporated a can of Pepsi in the girl's hand.

The Bike Path parallel to the NIPSCO easement north of Elliott Drive.

CHAPTER XII MODERN SUBURB 1980–2000 • 169

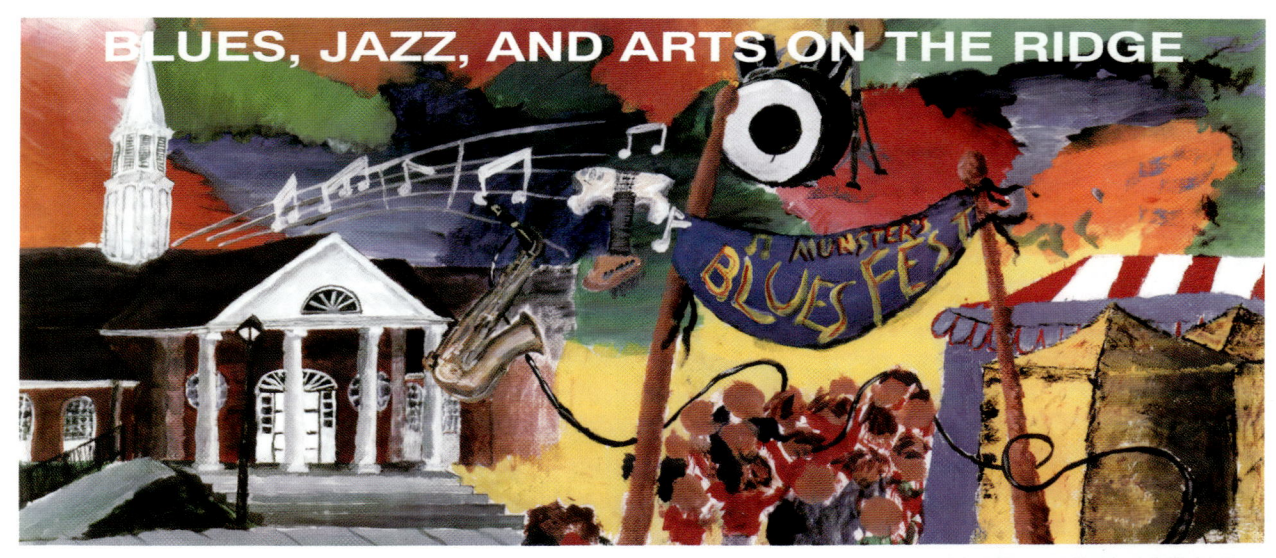

SATURDAY	JULY 13, 1996	10 am - 10 pm	MUNSTER TOWN HALL	Presented By: MUNSTER CHAMBER OF COMMERCE
SUNDAY	JULY 14, 1996	10 am - 6 pm	1005 RIDGE ROAD	MUNSTER FOUNDATION, INC.

The Munster Civic Foundation was not a government agency, but certainly a major element in community enrichment. The Foundation was created in 1991 with a $2 million grant from the Community Hospital Foundation. It sponsored Fourth of July fireworks and other activities, contributed to the bicycle path project, and for some years before the Parks Department assumed responsibility, co-sponsored the Blues, Jazz, and Arts on the Ridge Festival, which filled the Municipal Complex parking lot every July, and underwrote community plantings and the Munster Centennial celebration.

And More Home Building

After 1980 residential growth was concentrated almost entirely in the far south side of Munster. Tom DeGuilio remarked in 1988 that one "can't find a dozen buildable lots north of Forty-fifth Street." The focus of the construction was between Forty-fifth Street and Main Street, once a quiet road, now a busy route. Farmland steadily disappeared: the last twenty acres of the William C. Herr Farm, site of Munster's last large farm and true farm stand, was sold to Northwest homes in 1990.

An array of upscale subdivisions emerged. Most were complexes of single-family homes, but condominiums and townhouses were a growing part of the mix. Home construction rates were about evenly distributed over the years between 1980 and 2000. In 1950 Munster had about 1,100 housing units. Between 1950 and 1980, the total number of homes quintupled. In the 1980s 542 homes were added, and in the 1990s, 1,091.

The town's philosophy remained one of steady expansion, contained well short of a boom. Zoning laws and building codes continued to determine who did what, and where. Briar Creek, just east of Somerset, was planned by Donald Powers as a 118-unit single-family development, the first south of Forty-fifth Street since Twin Creek was launched in the 1970s. Every lot was sold in nine months, mostly to individual buyers and investors, rather than builders. Two years later half the lots had completed homes

---

The 1996 Blues, Jazz, and Arts on the Ridge Festival poster was drawn for the Munster Chamber of Commerce by Munster High School students Mike Nishimura and Ed Roy. (Complements of the Munster Chamber of Commerce)

Flag Day parades, organized by the Munster Historical Society, were held for several years in the 1980s and early 1990s. Kids and adults marched from Town Hall to Community Park for a flag raising.

Maisy the Bag Lady (a.k.a. Sylvia Columbus) entertains participants at the Flag Day Parade in 1992.

CSX train crosses Forty-fifth Street, July 1989. Note the empty land in the back that is now the Midwest Central Business Park. (Photo courtesy of Mark Stanek) or homes under construction. The average home price at Briar Creek was in the $150–180,000 range. Focus Group of Merrillville developed Cobblestones in 1990 between "Mount Munster" and Main Street and sold over three hundred lots on 131 acres to buyers of $225,000 to $300,000 single-family homes and townhouses.

Northwest Homes developed Somerset in 1990 and filled it with 130 residences averaging twenty-five hundred to three thousand square feet each. Somerset's Parade of Homes in 1990 featured eight model homes priced between $270,000 and $334,000. Four thousand visitors willingly paid $4 to *look* at them. Many were from Illinois suburbs, attracted by good schools and "cheap" Indiana housing. "Improved" lots sold for $46,000. The average price of a home on a Somerset lot in 1990 was $250,000; some approached a half million. Demand for larger lots for even larger homes was strong. By 1992 Somerset was sold out, and lot prices zoomed on resale.

White Oak Estates, one of a few mixed town house-condo developments in town, was developed by ATG of Crown Point. ATG purchased 120 acres from the Zandstra family in an area bounded by Windfield, Somerset, and Briar Ridge. In 1993 ATG laid curving streets, dug ponds, and installed fountains between White Oak and Highland.

Two small parks were given to the town. White Oak Estates found plenty of eager buyers and builders; lots were transferred to new owners as fast as the little orange stakes could be driven into the ground.

ATG also asked the Town Plan Commission for permission to build an apartment complex in the White Oak development. The Commission refused, citing traffic and property values. ATG readily shifted to condos, and won approval for a 156-unit townhouse subdivision on fourteen acres at White Oak and Main Street. The "Townhomes at White Oak Estates" were designed by The Linden Group and built by Clark Builders, with funding from CFS.

Other flossy developments included Windfield, Meadows of St. George on White Oak south of Forty-fifth Street, and Twin Creek. Cambridge Court was a lower cost development on Fisher by ATG Corporation of nineteen two-story condo buildings.

The Somerset Subdivision was built west of White Oak and north of Main Street. This 1989 sign advertises the newly fashionable "extra wide lots."

Hartsfield Village, northwest Indiana's premier retirement facility containing apartments for independent living, assisted living, and skilled nursing.

One the last areas to be developed, West Lakes of Munster, was developed by Joe Williamson Associates, with lots for 448 upscale home sites south of Forty-fifth and west of Calumet Avenue. In its third stage of development in 2006, West Lake's small lakes and sites for large single-family homes attracted many from Illinois. Williamson gave the town a neighborhood park, now developed, and a twenty-acre site for West Lakes Park.

By 2000 Munster was almost "built-out." The north side, the oldest part of town, was a comfortable, woodsy pastiche of Cape Cods, bungalows, and ranches, with a few surviving farm homes from old Munster standing here and there along Ridge Road. Central Munster, which filled between 1960 and 1980, was a land of larger split-levels, ranches, more split-levels, and plenty of trees. Southern Munster, between Forty-fifth Street and Main Street, filled with palatial neo-Victorians, English manors with large lawns, "McMansions," and, something new in town, luxury townhouses and condos.

Commerce and Industry

By 1980 Munster was an attractive choice for larger businesses and light industries. The town genuinely welcomed *clean* businesses, and offered low tax rates, in comparison with Illinois. Commercial real estate sold for a fifth below the Chicago area average. Electrical rates from Northern Indiana Public Service Company (NIPSCO) were highly competitive, a low crime rate meant lower insurance rates, and tax abatements were always on the table. That combination worked very well.

Milford Haven west of Margo Lane in the new West Lake subdivision in the early twenty-first century.

Northwest Indiana Habitat for Humanity blitz build, August 2005. This house in Gary was built by members of Westminster Presbyterian and St. Thomas More Churches. Since its inception at Munster in 1986, the Northwest Indiana chapter has worked toward Habitat's worldwide goal of eliminating poverty housing. Habitat builds homes with the help of the new homeowners. (Westminster Presbyterian Church photos)

CHAPTER XII MODERN SUBURB 1980–2000 • 173

Commercial development also continued, although an old-fashioned brou-ha-ha emerged over a smaller operation, Clock Tower Mall, or, as its unhappy neighbors called it, "the "Jefferson Avenue Dump." Located on Calumet Avenue on the site of the defunct Munster Lanes, it was developed for smaller retail stores by George and Thomas Milne. In fact, the mall looked fine, but local residents thought it was a "mess" in back. The stormy issue disappeared after a fence was built, and the construction of a row of nice-looking town houses insulated the neighborhood from the mall.

Donald Powers' original Community Plaza project on Columbia south of the Hospital had faced opposition in 1973. Powers' original plan was for a Planned Unit Development (PUD) to include a retail complex, theatre, restaurant, and medical offices. In 1980 he proposed to replace the projected restaurant and theatre with medical office buildings, and sought a parking lot entrance on Columbia.

Local residents, who thought those issues had been settled, objected to the prospect of more traffic on Columbia, and provided all the usual objections involving property values and traffic. As so often happened, the Town Plan Commission was between the volleys. In the end a number of smallish and not unattractive medical buildings were constructed on the site, and life continued.

The Munster Industrial Park emerged when Kaiser Aluminum and partner Aetna Insurance purchased the site from Johnson and Seay of Chicago, hoping to build markets for metal buildings and sell insurance. Kaiser-Aetna was given a rezoning in 1974, and immediately began development. But a year later the park was sold to Transcontinental Properties, which renamed it the Midwest Central Business Park. Their new property occupied land west of Calumet on both sides of Forty-fifth Street. Transcontinental, with strong support from the town and generous tax abatements, gradually attracted a variety of office buildings, distribution centers, and light manufacturers.

CALUMET HARLEY DAVIDSON

A motorcycle store in Munster? Wow!

Owners Chuck and Cindy Kreisl purchased the Hammond Harley franchise in 1993, and moved to Calumet Avenue in Munster in April of 2002. They operate in a brand-new twenty-five-thousand-square-foot building with a showroom and a service department, and offer a full line of bikers' fashion apparel, parts, and accessories.

The Kreisls sell and service a complete line of Harleys, among them the popular "minimalist bikes," the Street Glide and the Street Bob, for $7000 to $21,000.

Customers come from Indiana and Illinois, and are typically males in their forties with a high school diploma and some college. But a growing number of women and professionals are also part of their customer base.

Ridge Road showing the town's oldest commercial building, the Klootwyk General Store.

At first, development was slow on the 585-acre site. Specialty hinge-maker Velko arrived in 1981. The Munster Economic Development Commission helped attract Miner Electronics Laboratories. Among other early move-ins was Star Case Packing, a manufacturer of custom instrument cases for traveling rock and roll bands, which employed seventy in 2005.

In 1983, with loans from the state, the SBA, and a local bank, Donald J. Bootee moved his Trakker Lighting Company to Munster from Tinley Park. Trakker was successful—perhaps too much so—and was sold to Lithonia Lighting, and moved away. General Electric Supply Company moved into a fifty-four-housand-square-foot building in 1988. Bowman Displays, a commercial photographer specializing in catalogue work, moved from South Holland.

From the Munster point of view, Rockwell Automation was an ideal tenant. Rockwell was "clean," quiet, and paid its forty-five employees an average wage of $28 per hour. An electronic products repair facility, Rockwell moved from Hammond into a new $1.6 million, forty-five-thousand-square-foot building in the Industrial Park. Architectural Accents

THREE FLOYDS BREWERY

Three Floyds opened in 1996 as a draft beer-only brewery on Calumet Avenue in Hammond, and moved to Indiana Parkway in Munster in 1999. The owners are Dr. Michael Floyd and his sons, Simon and Nick. There were eight employees in 2006. Brewmaster and sales director Jim Cibak had worked for Goose Island brewery.

The firm went public in 2005; those who invested are rewarded with a tasty dividend of one beer per day!

Their flagship brew is Alpha King Pale Ale. Robert the Bruce Scottish Ale, Pride and Joy Mild Ale, and other seasonal brews are also popular. In 2005 Three Floyds began offering upscale pub grub.

In 2006 Three Floyds was brewing fifty barrels and up to five hundred cases of bottled beer per week, and had more orders than it could fill. Much of the firm's output goes to Chicago liquor stores and pubs. There is a strong market for Three Floyds in the Northeast, especially New York.

Three Floyds enjoys a national reputation for exceptional brewing, and has won many prizes in national competition. Ratebrew.com ranks Three Floyds as the No. 2 microbrewery in the world!

Another Unnecessary Extravagance, for many years owned and managed by Shirl Pawlowski, was in the old Duffy's Castle building. Compare to photo in Chapter IX. (Shirl Pawlowski photo)

began as a hobby of Munster residents Michael and Nancy Harrigan. The two engineers originally made window frames in Hammond, ran out of space, moved to the industrial park in 1997, and expanded into custom woodwork.

Two major grocery companies, Whole Foods and Dawn Foods, built distribution centers in the Industrial Park. In 1999, with generous tax abatement, Dawn built a sixty-five-thousand-square-foot warehouse on Forty-fifth Street, and provided jobs for eighty employees. The town liked those tenants well enough, but decided that distribution centers attracted too many trucks for a quiet suburb. Slimfast leased space for a distribution center from Lake Business Center in 1991, missed a tax filing and entered into a long dispute with the county treasurer, finally resolved it, and moved on in 2000.

HAL MORRIS

William Harold "Hal" Morris III (born 1965) grew up in Munster, played in the Munster Little League, and attended Munster schools and the University of Michigan, where he was named All-Big Ten in 1986. His father, William, was a Munster pediatrician and a Little League coach.

Morris, a lefty, was drafted by the Yankees in 1986, and played on several other major league teams, but primarily for the Cincinnati Reds, where he hit .340 in his rookie season. He played outfield and first base, and was a designated hitter for the Yankees.

An All-Star player, Morris has been a candidate for the Baseball Hall of Fame.

"Hal Morris Day" in Munster is a big event for Little Leaguers. Hal meets with the kids and autographs baseballs. He assists the Munster Educational Foundation in fundraising projects.

He is one of three major leaguers in the family; his great-uncle played for the Washington Senators, and his brother Bob, for the Cubs.

After his playing career, Hal Morris earned an MBA at Stanford, and is currently working in venture capital projects. He is a Sagamore of the Wabash.

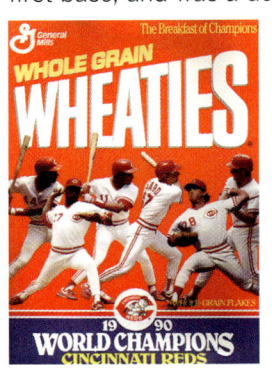

Wheaties Box with Hal Morris on the far right.

Hal Morris, son of William and Margaret Morris, on one of dozens of baseball cards with his picture. (Donated by his mother)

Top photo: Bowman Displays Digital Imaging Inc. on Progress Avenue in the Midwest Central Business Park.

By 1997 fifty lots had been sold; some were being held for investment purposes. Some decidedly nonindustrial organizations were built in the park, including Illiana Surgery Center and a second Hammond Clinic building.

The *Times* moved its plant and offices from Hammond to Munster in 1989. The paper was edited and printed thereafter in a new 135,000-square-foot building on Forty-fifth Street on new, state-of-the-art presses. Four hundred employees composed and printed the *Northwest Indiana Times* in several editions, now as a morning daily. The press run of the *Times* was between eighty and ninety thousand copies each day.

Lake Business Center, in the former Simmons plant, remained underutilized for years. LBC offered over a million square feet of business/industrial space, a hundred truck docks, and room for forty-two railcars, but found few takers. The aging plant was found wanting, and in 2006 plans were underway to demolish the entire structure and replace it with a retail center/office complex.

Schools

Despite the noisy confrontations of the preceding years, support for the schools remained strong. In 1984, after a too-lengthy debate, Munster voters endorsed an elected School Board. Lawrence Kocal and Linda Hess were the first elected members. Another hot issue: should School Board meetings be open to the public before votes were taken? Yes, was the decision, reached in 1990. On the generous side: in 1986 a town tax referendum asked for approval of a $600,000 boost in the school general fund for teachers' salaries, reduction of class sizes, and new equipment. It passed with a two-to-one margin.

Superintendent Wallace Underwood retired in 1990 after sixteen years of service. The operating budget then stood at $13.2 million. Underwood had directed a steady improvement in student performance, implemented advanced placement courses, raised graduation requirements, and oversaw almost continuous upgrading and remodeling of facilities. Wallace Underwood's now-mature school system held a remarkable number of local, regional, and national, recognitions for excellence. He was replaced by Edward Poole, who resigned less than a year later, and was followed by William Pfister.

Enrollments fluctuated. In 1980, 3,479 students were in attendance; in 1985 the number fell to 2,881, and to 2,823 in 1990. By 1995 it had recovered, to 3,233, and reached 3,782 in 2000. Excellence was visible: in the 1990s, nearly all graduates completed the SAT exam, and ventured into higher education, many with National Merit and other scholarships.

Office of the *Munster Times*, in Munster since 1989.

William Pfister has been superintendent of schools since 1992. (School Town of Munster photo)

The U.S. Department of Education rated Munster as one of few "National Blue Ribbon School Systems" in the country. Four of five Munster schools won a "Four Star" rating from Indiana Statewide Testing for Educational Progress (ISTEP). Munster was generally recognized as one of the top ten school systems in Indiana. The high school won a School of Excellence Award from *Redbook* magazine.

Construction and reconstruction continued. The original football field facilities were demolished and replaced in 1981. In 1996 the School Board commenced a two-year, $45 million (reduced from over $60 million by popular demand at some sixty public meetings) remodeling project. The elementary schools received a general overhaul.

The high school, last remodeled in 1980 after a fire, was given a new academic wing, three science labs, and a media center. The cafeteria became a food court. The middle school received $6.5-million addition with more classrooms, a field house, a phys ed facility, and a remodeled science lab.

Munster's parochial elementary schools thrived. St. Tom's was busier than ever. St. Paul's Lutheran parochial school arrived in 1981 when St. Paul's Church moved from Hammond. St. Paul's offered a full K–8 curriculum. By the end of the century, enrollment was over two hundred in double classes; another hundred were in preschool and day care programs. The great majority were St. Paul parishioners or from nearby Lutheran parishes.

The Munster Education Foundation (MEF) was a major nongovernmental asset, which involved parents, the town at-large, schools, students, and businesses. Fifth grade teacher Ed Woodrick, who died in 2002, was its first guiding light. Established in 1992 by parents and businesspeople, the Educational Foundation raised money through donations, membership drives, silent auctions, and wine tastings. It supported top-quality education, innovative teaching, enrichment programs, Indiana Birthday celebrations for fourth graders, Diversity Day at the high school, and Civil War Days in Community Park. MEF, with other donors, provided professional weather stations to the high school and Eads School.

The Center for Visual and Performing Arts

The Center for Visual and Performing Arts (CVPA) opened in 1988. A remarkable seventy-thousand-square-foot multipurpose facility, it housed two art galleries, a 370-seat theatre, classrooms, banquet and meeting rooms, and a variety of related spaces. Donald Powers' vision created the Center; John Mybeck and later Brad Ronco assisted him. The Center housed the Theatre at the Center, South Shore Arts, offices of the Northwest Indiana Symphony, MUN-CAB (the town cable access studio), the Munster Chamber of Commerce, and Villa Catering, which managed the banquet and meeting rooms and offered a popular Sunday brunch.

South Shore poster featuring the Center for Visual and Performing Arts was commissioned by the town and created by Fred Semmler in the year 2000.

South Shore Arts was formed in 1936 to encourage local artists. As the Hammond District Art Association, the group sponsored annual exhibitions in the E. C. Minas store in Downtown Hammond. One of the founders, Architect William J. Bachman, would later design the CVPA. The Art Association gradually broadened its membership, and in 1946 it became the Northern Indiana Art Patrons Association.

In 1969 it became the Northern Indiana Arts Association (NIAA), purchased a former church building in Downtown Hammond, and presented art exhibitions shows there and at the Hammond Public Library. When its membership base drifted southward, the Arts Association sold that site and moved to rented quarters on Calumet Avenue in Munster in 1982.

NIAA moved to the new Center in Munster in 1989. A major tenant, NIAA maintained the fifteen-thousand-square-foot Bachman Gallery, classrooms, and offices. The Arts

---

The Northwest Indiana Symphony Orchestra with Music Director Kirk Muspratt rehearses in the lower level at the Center for Visual and Performing Arts. (Photo courtesy of Larry Mickow Jr.)

The Northwest Indiana Symphony Chorus, with more than one hundred singers drawn from all over the Northwest Indiana and South Chicago area, rehearses with Dr. Nancy Menk at the CVPA. (Photo courtesy of Larry Mickow Jr.)

Association evolved into a three county-wide provider of art for adults and children's programs, with a strong emphasis on education, classes, and workshops. The NIAA opened branches in Hammond and Crown Point to serve its twelve hundred widely dispersed members. In 2006 NIAA became South Shore Arts, Inc. NIAA was also a regional partner of the Indiana Arts Commission.

The Northwest Indiana Symphony (NISO), which maintained offices in the Center, was founded in 1941 as the Gary Civic Symphony Orchestra; its first concert was on the evening of December 7. Over the years the orchestra performed at Seaman Hall, Memorial Auditorium, various high schools, and at IUN in Gary. The group assumed its current name in 1972. In 1981 NISO first performed at its current primary venue, Star Plaza in Merrillville. Six years later NISO established business and ticket sales offices in CVPA. The seventy-five-member orchestra played classical and popular music under the baton of Robert Vodnoy from 1982 to 1997, then under Conductor Tsung Yeh. Kirk Muspratt replaced him in 2000.

The Theatre at the Center (TATC) was established in 1991. Performances were given in a 450-seat thrust-stage theatre. Originally a non-Equity, three-weekend summer stock company, TATC gradually evolved into the Calumet Region's only professional theatre company. For its first full season, TATC staged five productions with Chicago actors, local talent, and a professional stage crew, musicians, and costume designers. Revivals of Broadway musicals, plays, and children's programs were featured. Martin Kappel was the founding art director, 1991–1992. Gary Giacomo managed a mixed Equity/non-Equity company between 1993 and 1998. Michael Weber served until 2005, and was followed by Chicago professional Bill Pullinsi. The nonprofit TATC was a year-round theatre company in 2006, supported by ticket sales, generous sponsors, and donations from the Friends of the Theatre group.

Captain Georg Von Trapp inspects his seven children in the 1995 production of *Sound of Music* at the Theatre at the Center. (Photo by Larry Brechner.)

Joseph and the Amazing Technicolor Dreamcoat ran to packed houses at Westminster Presbyterian Church in both 1994 and 1995. Directed by Chris Gloff, and staring Dan Vincent as Joseph, it was a benefit for the Samaritan Couseling Center. (*Times* photo by Geoffrey Black)

180 • MUNSTER, INDIANA: A CENTENNIAL HISTORY

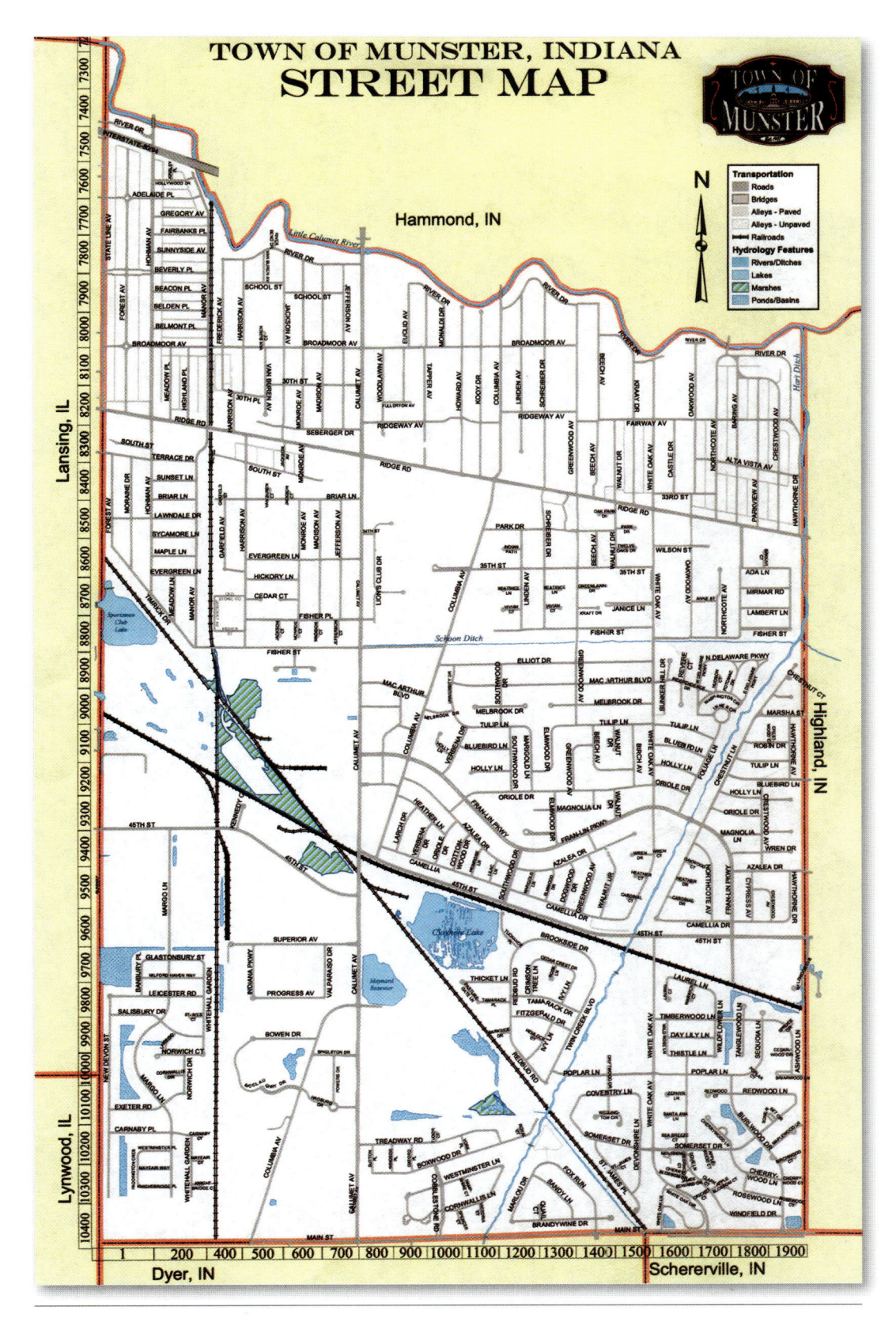

Munster Street Map, 2006.

CHAPTER XII MODERN SUBURB 1980–2000 • 181

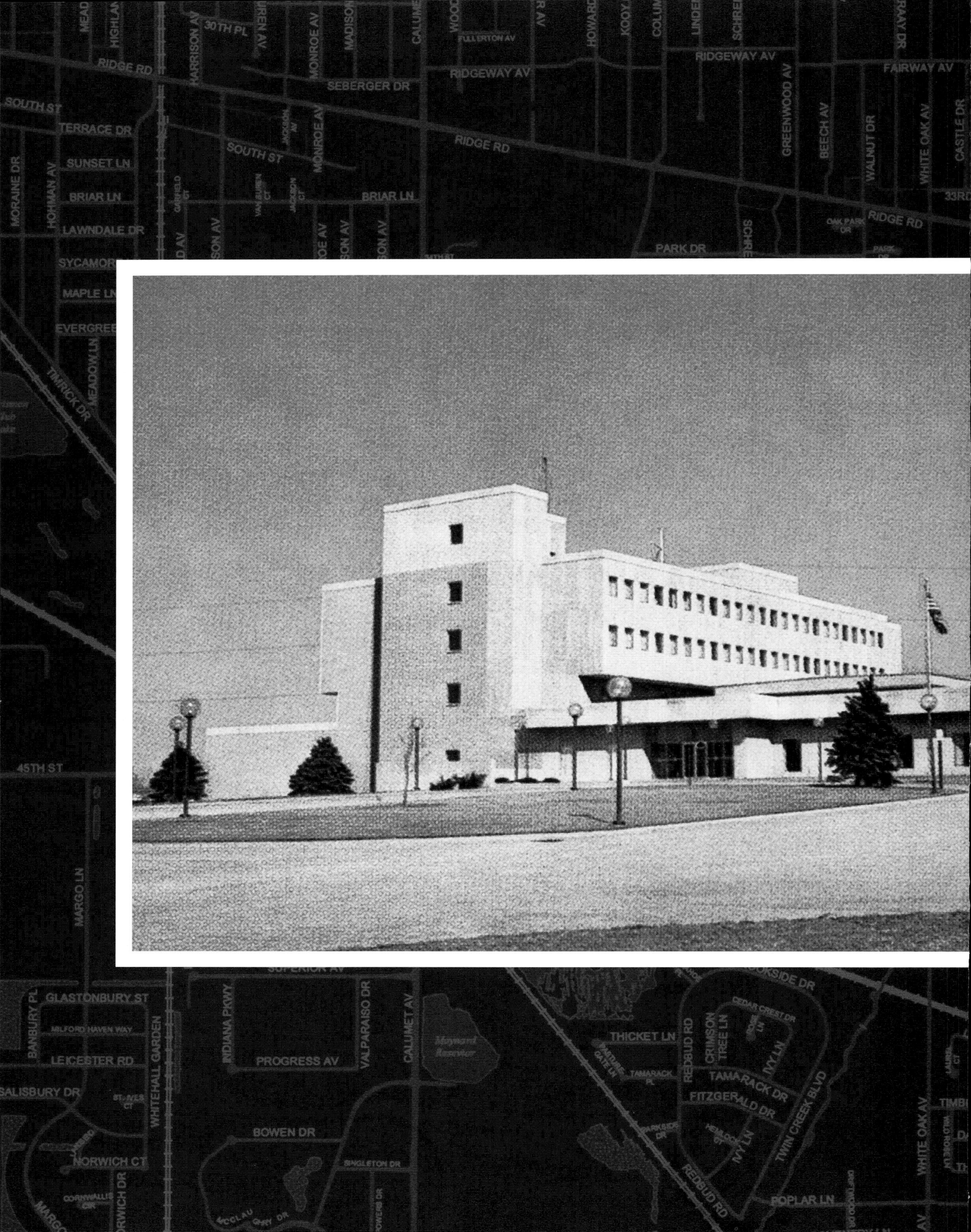

CHAPTER XIII

Munster Institutions

Community Hospital

From a one-doctor town, Munster evolved into a major regional medical center. Community Hospital is the jewel in its crown. Community was dedicated on a hot, hot August day in 1973; during the ceremony attendees' folding chairs slowly sank into the new asphalt parking lot. Community was nonprofit, nonsectarian, and would operate without public funds. On September, 11, 1973, as the first patient was admitted, Community had just over a hundred physicians on staff, a hundred beds, and 120 employees.

The $6.3-million hospital was the project of the Munster Medical Research Foundation, formed in 1964 by physicians at the Hammond Clinic, which had moved from Hammond to Munster in 1961. The hospital was supposed to be adjacent to the Hammond Clinic. Drs. Howard Brenner and Edward Alt were the original sparkplugs; Brenner was the Foundation's first president. In 1966 the Foundation asked Booz Allen Hamilton to generate a "Master Plan" for the new hospital. The Hammond architectural firm Bachman and Bertram was asked to map a proposal to win endorsements from the Hospital Planning Council of Metropolitan Chicago (HP-CMC) and the Lake County Medical Society.

Community Hospital, after years of work, truly a community effort. (Community Foundation photo)

In 1967 a new executive director, Edward P. Robinson, Munster's 1974 "Man-of-the-Year, had one task: *make it happen.* Prior to a formal fundraising drive, Mrs. Fannie Schlesinger, the widow of Dr. Jacob Schlesinger, presented a much-appreciated check for $50,000. Shortly afterward, HPCMC endorsed the new hospital.

Donald S. Powers and other local businessmen and developers donated land and cash to the project. Despite opposition from local and regional hospital accrediting agencies, centered on "overexpansion" of hospital facilities, the fundraising campaign began early in 1967. Edgar L. Peglow of E. C. Minas and Company chaired the fundraising drive, with the help of Joseph Burger and Vic Kirsch. All three made large donations. The Inland-Ryerson Foundation gave $100,000. Among the other corporate donors were Youngstown Steel, Northern Indiana Public Service Company (NIPSCO), American Oil, Simmons, and Mead Electric.

The Medical Foundation gave the Community Hospital Auxiliary the task of local fundraising. The two-hundred-member Auxiliary collected a half million dollars. For some years after 1967, the Auxiliary's annual Red Garter Night, a community-wide dinner-dance, attracted a thousand donors. The Red Garter Shoppe also provided steady support over the years.

A reorganization of the Medical Foundation made Harold Hagberg the president of the Foundation; Donald Powers later became the secretary. By mid-1969, the Foundation had collected $270,000, though much of that sum was conditional on actual groundbreaking (some donors relented when it appeared the entire project might founder). A "grass-roots," six-community-wide campaign tried to raise $3 million; a sale of tax-exempt bonds would supply the rest. By 1970 the Foundation held $1.5 million in cash and pledges.

Finding a home for the hospital was not easy. The original Hammond Clinic site was clearly too small, which mightily displeased Drs. Brenner and Alt. Moreover, future interaction between the Hammond Clinic, a for-profit entity, and the nonprofit Community Hospital seemed difficult. A second site between Broadmoor and Ridgeway at Tapper turned out to be too expensive. And the Town Board was bombarded with antihospital protests at public hearings on site rezoning, mostly from those living near the proposed hospital sites. But the Board also received a pro-hospital petition signed by twenty-six hundred. Munster clearly wanted a hospital—in someone else's backyard!

Disturbed over the Foundation's lack of consultation and, as always, sensitive to residents' protests, the Board refused to rezone the second site. Nearby towns now began angling for the hospital. The *Times* issued a "code blue" headline: "HOSPITAL

Edward P. Robinson, longtime executive director of the hospital. (Community Foundation photo)

First officers of the Community Hospital Auxiliary: Barbara Connor, president; Mary Beckman, vice-president; Margaret Bertagnolli, treasurer; Eleanor Peglow, recording secretary; and Mamie Jabaay, corresponding secretary. (From *Recipes Are for Sharing*, 1990)

DREAM DIES IN MUNSTER." But the Foundation, still struggling with funding, shifted to a much larger site facing Columbia Avenue between MacArthur Boulevard and Fisher. That idea won Town Board approval.

In 1971, with a $7.6 million loan and controversy aplenty, the Foundation asked Vic Kirsch to start infrastructure work and roll out the parking lots. Superior Construction then erected the hospital. Compromises had been necessary. Citing fire safety issues, the Town Board had limited the structure to seven stories, three fewer than planned. That ruling and a skimpy budget compelled the Foundation to slice the planned number of beds in half.

The new 104-bed hospital was an immediate success, in terms of both patient admissions and quality of services. In its first year of operation, every bed at Community Hospital was occupied for months on end. A few patients had to be turned away. For six years the hospital operated at 95 percent of capacity.

Even so, Community Hospital faced problems. Until 1976 it was outside of the Blue Cross–Blue Shield network, which denied its services to many and nearly starved the hospital to death. Money was scarce for years. Payrolls were hard to meet, and bond payments were occasionally late. Other hospitals and medical interests backing other new hospitals or satellite units of existing hospitals continued to snipe at Community.

In 1976 Mayor Richard G. Hatcher of Gary filed a discrimination suit against Community, and prompted an essentially political investigation of the hospital by Health, Education and Welfare (HEW) officials. This controversy cost a lot of money and needlessly delayed Community's expansion plans.

The $7-million South Pavilion became operational in 1979 and 1980. The new wing contained an Emergency Room, 136 more beds, and a 26-bed Surgical Unit. A new Obstetrical Unit became the busiest in the state, and by the later 1980s was delivering twenty-five hundred babies a year. Community was now a full-service facility.

In 1983 the hospital expanded its intensive care/coronary unit, and added a neonatal facility and laboratory facilities, at a cost of $2 million. A year later the hospital opened an Ambulatory Surgery and Outpatient Services Unit, a Nuclear Medicine Department, and installed a CT scanner, at a cost of $7 million. Between 1986 and 1988 the hospital

Munster Medical Research Foundation officers in 1967: Harold Hagberg, president; Judge James Richards, past president; Howard Brenner; and Russell Erickson, secretary. (Community Foundation photo)

Senator Birch Bayh speaks at the dedication ceremony. (Community Foundation photo)

CHAPTER VIII MUNSTER INSTITUTIONS • 185

opened two Cardiac Cath Labs, two Open Heart Surgical Suites, a six-bed Cardiovascular Unit, and an eighteen-bed Oncology Unit. In 1992 the hospital opened a $27-million, eighty-one-thousand-square-foot Oncology Center and a twenty-four-bed Intermediate Care Unit. It was no wonder that year after year Community was voted the No. 1 hospital in the Calumet Region.

Even more facilities were added as time passed. A Heart Center opened in 1996; 275 open-heart procedures were performed in its first year, and rose to more than one a day by 1999. In 1998, as Community's staff reached eighteen hundred, the $14-million, seventy-three-thousand-square-foot Fitness Pointe opened with two pools, an exercise center, a gymnasium, running track, health and wellness classes, a day spa, café, child-care facilities, and outpatient cardiac rehabilitation and physical therapy. Another $14 million jointly provided by Community and St. Margaret Mercy Hospitals underwrote Hartsfield Village,

---

Community Hospital with the South Pavilion, 1983. (Community Hospital Tenth Anniversary photo)

Munster Medical Research Foundation Board, 1989–1990. Front row: Harold Hagberg, Donald Powers, William Fitzpatrick, and Edward Robinson; second row: John Mybeck, George Kurteff, Helen Archer, Jeanne Driggs, George Watson, Ardith Anderson, Everett Ahlgrim, and Roen Speroff; third row: James Holcomb, George Compton, Raymond Monaldi, Joseph Morrow, John Trent, Albert Costello, Russell Snyder, Frankie Fesko, and Edward Meyer. Not present: Palmer Singleton, George Sutter, Robert Young, Albert Galante, George Rasch, Manuel Luna, and Thomas Frank. (Photo donated by John Trent)

a retirement community on Columbia. Hartsfield offered independent and assisted living in just over a hundred residential apartments, forty-two assisted living apartments, and a sixteen-bed Alzheimer's unit, plus nursing care, a chapel, a beauty salon, and a barbershop.

In 1998 Community, now a "multi-disciplinary use" hospital, opened a West Pavilion with an Oncology Center, a twenty-five-bed Rehabilitation Center, a twenty-nine-bed Transitional Care Unit, and a Retina Center for eye treatment and surgery. Soon after, a Medical Office Building opened with a Surgery Center on the first floor and Cardiovascular Services on the second. A 530-space, three-level parking garage was completed in 2001. Connected by walkway to the hospital and the Medical Office Building, it made coming and going much easier. And also in 2001, Community added the St. John Outpatient Center, a $15-million, sixty-nine-thousand-square-foot urgent care and outpatient services center for residents of central Lake County.

In November 2001, Community Foundation, Inc., acquired St. Catherine's Hospital in East Chicago and St. Mary's Medical Center in Hobart from Ancilla Systems, Inc. They were united with Community Hospital as Community Healthcare Systems. Reflecting that new base, the Community Foundation, Inc., became the Community Foundation of Northwest Indiana.

As Munster celebrated its centennial, Community Hospital (not to be confused with Community *Pet* Hospital on Calumet Avenue!) was a fully accredited, world-class medical center, with 361 beds, 575 physicians on staff, and twenty-one specialized service centers. The quality of services and medical staff ranked very high in national competition; HealthGrades placed Community in the top 5 percent of all American hospitals. Munster had become a fine place to get sick, and to recover!

DONALD S. POWERS

Donald Powers is chairman of the Board, president, and CEO of Community Foundation of Northwest Indiana, Inc., the parent corporation of Community Hospital. He has been secretary and president of the Community Hospital Board of Directors. He has been a member and president on the Purdue Board of Trustees, and serves on the boards of several major corporations.

A native of Kentucky, Donald Powers holds a bachelor's degree from Purdue University and honorary doctorates from Calumet College of St. Joseph and Purdue. He was a Navy fighter pilot in World War II and in the Korean War.

A man of many talents and a major asset to the community: insurance agent, developer, community builder, philanthropist, civic leader, prime mover in the creation of several major community institutions, most notably the hospital and the Center for the Visual and Performing Arts.

Powers is the recipient of many awards and recognitions, including Sagamore of the Wabash from two governors.

Hammond Clinic on North Calumet Avenue. (MHS photo)

There was much more to Munster's medical world. Munster had 350 doctor's offices in 2000. The Hammond Clinic, a sixty-bed hospital on Calumet Avenue, had arrived in Munster in 1961 as a "multi-specialty group practice," and became the largest HMO in Indiana. The Munster Med-Inn (1971), a 186-bed extended care facility with a staff of three hundred, was associated with the Hammond Clinic. In 1997, after its staff had doubled from fifty to ninety in five years, Hammond Clinic built a second site further south on Calumet Avenue, the Munster Primary Care facility. Several smaller clinics were essentially suites of physicians, like the older Broadmoor Medical Plaza on Hohman and the Dr. Eli Sherman Jones Clinic, which moved from Hammond in 1966. Twelve professionals practiced at Jones.

As the new century began, a surprising number of newer stand-alone clinics and specialty hospitals were part of Munster's medical ranks, among them: Heartland Memorial Hospital (known as Illiana Surgery from 1994 to 2005); the Calumet Surgery Center on Calumet Avenue, an acute care hospital since 2003; Cardiology Associates of Northwest Indiana; Midwest Clinic; Munster Medical Center at Forty-fifth and Calumet; a Heart-Lung Health Center; Patient Care Services; a Skin, Vein and Cosmetic Surgery Clinic; and several other large buildings packed with physicians of various kinds. Toothache? Visit any of forty-plus general dentists and specialists in town. Munster was a regional medical center that rivaled Chicago in many ways, and the parking was a darn sight better.

Public Safety

The Munster Town Marshal's Office was created on August 5, 1907, with a modest annual budget of $60. August Richter, who later served on the Town Board, was appointed the first town marshal, and, a year later, was given permission to buy a revolver. Richter was followed by Marshal Gerritt Jansen, who served until 1925. For decades the marshal's office was a typical, small-town, one-man operation. At first, day calls went to the Clerk's Office and were relayed to the marshal. Night calls went directly to the marshal's home. In 1916 Marshal Jansen's home became the town jail and Fire Department headquarters.

Crime was rare and petty for many years. In 1915 thieves raided Mr. Porter's chicken house and stole several geese from the Kirsch family. The Town Board once instructed the marshal to arrest anyone hauling dirt through town on Sundays. The marshal ordered Albert McKee to keep his saloon closed on Sundays and holidays. On a single busy day in August 1915, a motorcycle crashed through someone's yard and smashed a water trough and a tub and two cars collided at Stallbohm's Corner. In 1919 rising traffic problems forced the marshal to post warning signs: "NOTICE: KEEP MUFFLERS CLOSED & OBEY SPEED LAWS."

Jones Clinic at 110 Ridge Road moved to Munster in 1964.

Dr. Eli Sherman Jones, chief of surgery at St. Margaret Hospital in Hammond from 1950 to 1960, namesake of the clinic. (Photo donated by Ron Feldner)

Marshal Henry DeVries, who served from 1925 to 1932, was also the town water meter inspector. In 1925 he was issued a motorcycle and then a squad car. Marshal Edward Bennett, 1932–1946, was a downstate native, a former state trooper and Highland town marshal, and also the Munster Water Works superintendent, street commissioner, and meter inspector. The "unofficial mayor of Munster," Ed Bennett died in office of a heart attack at the age of fifty-three. Julius "Jake" DeMik served as acting marshal for a time after his death.

Charles Chapman served for a year, 1946–1947. Chapman organized a force of unpaid, volunteer deputy marshals for use in emergencies. Each was issued a pistol and a badge, but no police car. Chapman trained them on Monday nights at police school sessions in Town Hall. But in February 1947, Marshal Chapman was accidentally shot and killed by a visiting state trooper.

Deputy Clarence Siefken served as marshal for eight months in 1947, and was followed by Assistant Marshal William Retzloff, who served for nine months, 1947–1948. Unhappy with his salary, Retzloff resigned and returned to private employment, but rejoined the force four years later. Adam Funk served from 1948 to 1953. Funk had retired from the Hammond Police Force in 1945, and worked at Goldblatt's as a store detective. Funk guarded a peaceful community: in June 1948, except for dog bites and auto accidents, he reported no infractions of any kind!

Marshal Ed Bennett. (MHS photo)

Funeral procession for Town Marshal Charles Chapman. (MHS photo)

In 1953 the regular force was doubled to four, but only Funk and Assistant Marshal Robert Landon held full-time posts. At one point three paid positions were open, indicating a turnover problem. Twenty-three volunteers joined regular officers on patrol. In the early 1950s Munster employed one officer per 1,187 residents.

Funk, the "Christian Cop," devised modern solutions for youth problems. His Junior Deputy Marshals Association fought juvenile delinquency (BB guns were popular among young Red Ryders, and no streetlight was safe) with "wholesome entertainment," canteens, dances, picnics, and sports. An unofficial Juvenile Court passed on minor cases and gave "demerits" to the guilty. Funk tried to make Munster youth better citizens, but widespread vandalism in the newer subdivisions compelled him to resume enforcement of a 1930s curfew law. Marshal Funk resigned in 1953 for health reasons.

Munster's last town marshal (1953–1956) was Harold Pritchard. A deputy marshal since 1949, Pritchard also served a year as the town's first chief of police. An "activist" and a modernizer, when Pritchard left office Munster had four full-time officers and fifteen part-time deputies in service.

Perhaps he paid a price for his activism. In 1957 the Town Board "ousted" Pritchard and demoted him to the rank of first-class patrolman. Not all of the Board's reasons were revealed. Pritchard was warmly defended by many, including State Representative and Munster resident Walter Babincsak. Pritchard defended his record in an open meeting before the Town Board, but doubted he could change the outcome and declined to press for reinstatement.

Marshal Adam Funk and Deputy William Schmueser. (MHS photo)

Deputy Marshal Association, 1952, in front of Lanier School. Back row: Pritchard, Able, Schmueser, Schmidt, Lessentine, Pritz, VanWeiren, and Jurgens. Front row: DeMik, Shire, Helton, Funk, Schreiber, Moore, and Retzloff. The association was disbanded in 1961. (MPD photo)

The biggest administrative change in the force's history occurred in the winter of 1955–56, when Munster voters and the Town Board approved the formation of a modern police department. In January 1956, the Town Board established a metropolitan police system. The new Munster Police Department was supervised by an appointed, three-member Police Commission. Fingerprint and photo files were properly organized. A pension plan started with a $1,600 transfer from town general funds. In 1981 the Police and Fire Department Commissions were merged into a single Board of Safety.

For years the Town Marshal's Office depended on a telephone answering service, which relayed calls to Hammond Police Department Headquarters, which then forwarded calls by radio to Munster patrol cars. In 1956 Munster fired up its own transmitter for both Police and Fire Department calls, and hired radio operators (later called dispatchers). The Deputy Marshals Association had donated the transmitter to the town. Calls now went directly to the Marshal's Office at Town Hall, and actually reduced response time by fifteen minutes. Times do change: in 2006, dialing the 911 number produced an average call response time of two minutes.

Headquarters over the years were pretty basic. For thirty-four years the marshal hung his hat either in his home or, after 1921, in a small room on the first floor of Town Hall. In 1941 he was banished to the rear of the building. In 1968 the Town Board purchased the former town library and remodeled the one-floor-and-cellar building. That cost $21,000, mostly for four jail cells and a booking room in the former kiddies' reading area, and delayed the department's move until 1969.

By 1976, the department, with twenty-seven officers, seven civilian employees, a new and large radio transmitter, and nine crossing guards, was out of room. The ex-kitchen was a darkroom for developing "mug" shots. A mobile home was parked next to the building and eased things a bit. Finally, the department moved to excellent quarters in the new Municipal Complex. But continued departmental expansion and new technologies soon made even that space too small. In 2000, as part of a general remodeling, the police department received new computer systems with regional and national interfaces. Some jail cells were eliminated and the drunk tank was downsized.

The history of the department after the 1970s was one of continuous expansion in numbers, duties, and professionalism.

Harold Pritchard, deputy marshal and Munster's first chief of police. (MPD photo)

Munster Police Station on Ridge Road, 1968–1982. The former library had a second life serving the residents of the town. (Drawing by Barbara Meeker)

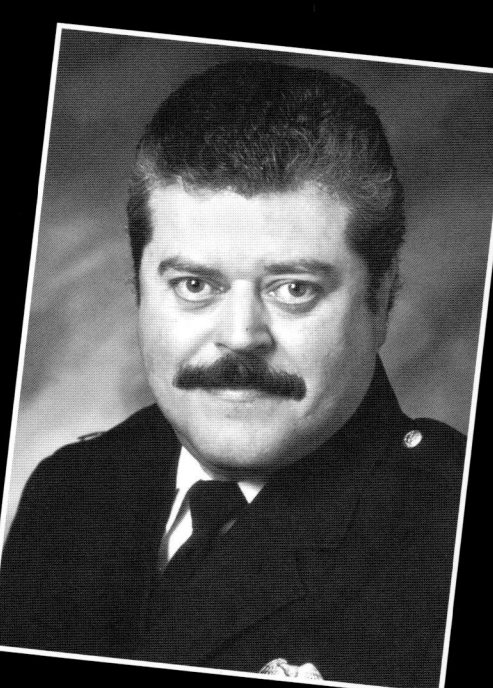

William Retzloff, police chief from 1957 to 1973. (MPD photo)

Louis Beratis, police chief from 1973 to 1983. (MPD photo)

Thomas Rhind, police chief from 1983 to 1987. (MPD photo)

Much of it centered on responses to rapid growth in population and the size of areas to be patrolled. Munster's town boundaries never changed after 1907, but in 1968 half the town was open farmland, in little need of police oversight. By 2006 there were only a few vacant lots left in town.

The chiefs under the Metropolitan Police System were: Pritchard, then William Retzloff, who served from 1957 to 1973. Louis Beratis served from 1973 to 1983, Thomas Rhind, from 1983 to 1987. His successor, William Sudbury, came from Oakland, Michigan, to join the force in 1987, and died suddenly in 2003. He was succeeded by Nick Panich, still the chief in 2006.

In the 1960s Munster crime patterns were typical of American suburbs. Home burglaries were a constant problem. Traffic violations, accidents, with an occasional fatality, DUIs, and vandalism consumed much administrative time and energy. With the expressway providing a quick getaway from Calumet Avenue, robberies of banks and other businesses were not uncommon.

The Indiana Traffic Team Survey found the Munster Police Department "outstanding," and called Munster as a town with a "healthy atmosphere," and a "safe and crime free city." One surprising crime: a "bank robbery" by a thirteen-year-old girl who somehow nabbed a bank deposit pouch containing $4,300. Her father paid for the crime after unwisely confiscating the loot.

In 1965 the Town Board established a Municipal "Cafeteria Court" at Town Hall, which freed violators from going to Dyer or Hammond. Parking violations were $2, while speeders were assessed $10 to $100, mostly for flying low through school zones. Clerk-Treasurer Leila Johnson thought most offenders were "the younger crowd" who somehow failed to see the three-foot-tall "19 MPH SCHOOL ZONE" signs in the middle of the street.

In the 1970s the number of traffic violations, DUIs, and vandalism cases rose steadily, reflecting population growth rather than rising crime rates. The crime *rate* actually remained low and steady, despite some increase in violent crimes.

In 1962 MPD employed ten uniformed officers and three female radio operators. By 1969 the number had grown to fifteen officers sharing five patrol cars, and five dispatchers. In 1974 the numbers were twenty-one and five dispatchers, twenty-seven in 1976, and so on at a steady rate, to forty in the next century. In 1979 the department hired its first female officer, Sherry A. Brown, a former Hammond Police Department records clerk. MPD was a very professional department, divided into two divisions, Uniform and Investigative (with four detectives). A modern Communications Center had local and national links.

Officer Sherry Brown, Munster's first female officer, served on the Police Department from 1979 to 2001. (MPD photo)

Dispatcher Jake Schoon and the Dispatch Room, which in 2006 has state-of-the-art equipment that allows police, fire, and ambulance personnel to respond to emergencies in record time. (MPD photo)

Officer Robert Grove was responding to a call on September 6, 1983, when was fatally hit by a car making a left turn. Corporal Grove had served with the Munster Police Department for ten years. (MPD photo)

Officer James Ghrist congratulates Jacqueline Silverman, a fifth grader at St. Thomas More School, who won an honorable mention in a statewide DARE poster contest. (MPD photo)

The Munster Police Explorers Post was started in 1997 with seven members and Officer Dan Ball as advisor. Post members are trained in many aspects of law enforcement and assist at many town events. Front row: Officer Tim Nosich, Kevin Watson, Jeff Reuter, Catherine Kirkpatrick, Ryan Drees, and Officer James Ghrist. Middle row: Advisor Jake Schoon, Matt Heintz, David Murks, Chris Sipes, and Adam Zitek. Back row: Officer Robert Leary, Carlos Alvarez, Eric Wallace, George Vauter, Bryan Buck, Mike McCarthy, Chad Holajter, and Sergeant Dan Ball. (MPD photo, summer 2006)

In the mid-1970s 90 percent of the force had some post–high school training. The Indiana Law Enforcement Academy and local universities and colleges provided advanced training. Half of the force attended classes in a federally sponsored program at St. Joseph's Calumet College, and earned certificates and degrees in law enforcement. By the 1990s all uniformed members of the force were graduates of the Indiana Law Enforcement Academy, most held bachelor's degrees, and some had master's degrees in law enforcement. A dozen cars patrolled Munster's streets and byways. It was not a good town for speeders.

The department also supported Neighborhood Watch and Officer Friendly, and managed the crossing guards. Officers and Fire Department volunteers conducted bicycle registrations and safety checks at the schools. The fifth grade anti-drug education program D.A.R.E. was established in 1988. The School Resource program stationed officers at the high school beginning in 1999.

Police Explorers Post No. 197 was organized in 1997 by Sergeant Daniel Ball. The post, which rather resembles Marshal Adam Funk's Junior Deputy Officers Association of the 1950s, offered involvement, education, training, and some fun to young people aged fourteen to twenty-one who were interested in careers in law enforcement. Sixteen members were active in 2005.

In 2006 Chief Nick Panich had almost forty uniformed and investigative officers on the force. Eleven dispatchers and office personnel and thirteen patrol cars completed the roster.

Munster Fire Department

Until 1925 a Ward 1-2-3-4 siren code told people about where to go in case of a fire. Every able-bodied person responded. Before the municipal water system was built in 1924, hand pumps or bucket brigades between the fire and ditches, cisterns, wells, or the Little Calumet were the primary means of fighting fires.

In 1925, twenty "young men of the town" organized a fire company. Leonard Brink was elected Munster's first fire chief. With donated and pooled money, the new Fire Department bought a two-wheeled hose cart with three hundred feet of hose. It went to fires behind a member's Model T Ford. Two years later the Fire Department bought its first fire engine, a pumper on a Dodge chassis, for $3,555.

The town marshal received fire calls, sounded the siren, and called the fire chief. The departmental alarm system was a telephone in the chief's home and a telephone tree to the members. The "vollies" served for many years without pay or even insurance until 1935. One of the founders at the age of sixteen, Cornelius Vander Vaart, a Hammond letter carrier, remained with the department for a half-century.

Chief Brink served from 1925 until 1930, and was succeeded by William Schmueser, who served until 1932, and again from 1937 to 1944. Peter C. Jabaay was chief from 1932 to 1937. "Corny" Vander Vaart served from 1944 to 1964. Myron C. Smith was chief from

Leonard Brink, fire chief 1925–30. (MFD photo)

William Schmueser, fire chief 1930–32, 1937–44. (MFD photo)

Peter C. Jabaay, fire chief 1932–37. (MFD photo)

Cornelius Vander Vaart, fire chief 1944–64. (MFD photo)

Myron Smith, fire chief 1964–82. (MFD photo)

Robert Nowaczyk, fire chief 1982–2004. (MFD photo)

196 • MUNSTER, INDIANA: A CENTENNIAL HISTORY

1964 to 1982, and Robert Nowaczyk, a member of the department since 1973, became Munster's first full-time fire chief in 1982. He died suddenly in office in November 2004, and was succeeded by Jim Knesek.

In 1960 the Town Board organized a three-man Fire Commission. William Jabaay, the grandson of Peter Jabaay, who had migrated from the Netherlands over a century earlier, was Munster's first fire commissioner. For years a route man for Borden Dairy in Hammond, Jabaay had helped organize the department in 1925, and was a long-term volunteer. After retiring from the department, Jabaay served for eight years on the Town Board.

Major conflagrations were rare. Except for the burning of most of grassy and undeveloped southern Munster in 1871, the first major fire occurred in January 1952, when the old Munster Church burned to the ground, despite the best efforts of four fire departments.

Early in 1960 the department rushed to the hundred-year-old home of seventy-five-year-old Albert Huizenga. His wooden home had stood for many years on Calumet Avenue before being moved to Main Street near Hart Ditch. The fire began while Huizenga was milking a cow in the barn. No hydrant was near, and the water in Hart Ditch was too low. Even with the assistance of a late-arriving tank truck, firemen were unable to save the old house.

On a very cold night in January 1961, the Lake Wholesalers Corporation, a building supply company, caught fire. Tom Petso, the building owner, had recently renovated the twenty-five-year-old former Munster Lumber Company building beside the Monon Railway tracks. Forty-five firemen from Munster, Lansing, and Highland fought the blaze, with little success. The fire finally burned out, leaving the remnants of the building encased in ice. Chief Vander Vaart was uncertain of the cause, but suspected a faulty furnace.

Munster Volunteer Fire Department, 1940s. (MHS photo)

In September 1994, a second fire in that area struck the Handy Andy Store, a home supply company in another former Munster Lumber Company building. Despite the efforts of men and equipment from nine communities, who fought it for five hours, it burned to the ground. No specific cause was found.

Over the years the department's equipment grew in size, sophistication, and number. In 1939 a $7,000 bond issue added a second pumper. As World War II drew near, the department operated two fire engines and a twenty-one-year-old equipment truck. In 1948, for a pricey $17,000, the department added a third pumper, with a forty-five-foot extension ladder. In 1952 a base station radio replaced the telephone system and the siren code. Radio monitors were soon installed in firemen's homes. In 1956 members were connected to the new transmitter at police headquarters. Volleys also responded to a loud whistle at town hall.

An emergency unit was added in 1956. Assigned to double duty as a secondary police car, it contained a two-way radio, two stretchers, and basic life-saving equipment. Now the department had two fire engines, a rescue unit, and an ambulance; but needed more and larger equipment because of population growth. Industries like the huge Simmons plant and other larger structures mandated serious changes in equipment, and in a few years the seven-story Community Hospital would require an aerial ladder truck. In 1957 the Indiana Fire Rating Bureau found Munster 23 percent deficient in equipment, and in 1961, the same agency reported a 45 percent deficiency. That was a matter of some importance, not only because of public safety, but because fire ratings dictated everyone's insurance costs.

In 1967 the department added a $36,500 pumper. In 1972 the department added Snorkel No. 1 or "Big Red," a $95,000 fire engine with a long arm that pumped a thousand gallons a minute. That brought the town's fire equipment inventory to four pumpers, including "Old Fox," a semi-antique 1938 Ahrens-Fox, and the new snorkel unit. As the new century dawned, the Munster Fire Department had two fire stations, six fire engines, a snorkel unit, an aerial reach truck, and a variety of secondary firefighting equipment.

Departmental budgets remained tiny until the later 1960s. In 1957 the total budget was $8,500, including $4,000 for radio service. The chief of the all-volunteer force was paid $100 per annum, the assistant chief, half that sum. In 1959, when the department responded to 234 calls, the budget was $8,499; five years later it had dropped to $8,401. Volunteers and the Auxiliary helped the department with the proceeds of card parties, entertainments, and open houses.

Munster's first real fire house was tacked on to the north wall of Town Hall in 1937. Three thousand dollars were raised by donations and a grant from the Indiana Tax Board.

Snorkel No. 1, "Big Red." (MFD photo)

The rather basic little block structure was built with labor supplied by the Works Progress Administration. In 1939 the building housed two engines. In 1949, because of additional equipment, the fire lads used donated funds and sweat equity to remodel the building. A substantial addition was completed in 1963, to house more equipment. In 1962 the department was assigned an office in Town Hall.

Fire Station No. 2 entered service in 1967 in a refurbished town garage on Fisher. As new subdivisions flowed southward it became more and more essential, but was clearly inadequate. In 1973 a new, four-bay Fire Station No. 2 was built at a cost of $165,000. It came with a hose-drying tower, offices, and a practice fire tower. Munster's third and handsomest fire house was a new Fire Station No. 1, a four-bay installation on the south end of the new Town Hall complex.

Even as late as 1950, the Fire Department was about the same size as when it was formed in 1925. The majority of the members were still of Dutch-American extraction well into the 1950s. By 1961 the roster had increased to twenty-seven, and to over forty in the 1970s. In 1929 the volunteers were paid $1 per duty hour. By 1957 volunteers were paid $2 per call; in 1961 the department paid members $3 an hour and included drill time on the pay schedule. Still paid-on-call in the new century, members, except for the full-time chief and a secretary, were paid $10.81 per hour.

In 1950 an Ambulance Committee collected $3,000 by canvassing the town. The new ambulance arrived in November 1950. Service was provided free to Munster residents for many years. In 1977 the department ended nonemergency service, and also raised the fee per call from $25 to $35. Fourteen men completed a standard course in emergency medical tech procedures and were given continuous in-service training.

But costs were escalating: a much-needed new ambulance with a full range of equipment cost $50,000. The department continued to provide ambulance service until 1999. The town then retired its two emergency vehicles and signed a service contract with private provider Co-Med. Co-Med went bankrupt in 2000, and was purchased by Daley's Ambulance Company's Superior Ambulance Service, which in turn became a property of Prompt Ambulance in 2004. The change to private services brought some administrative instability, but also faster response times, better-trained technicians, and more sophisticated equipment.

In the new century, Munster had a well-trained and well-equipped Volunteer Fire Department. In 2006 the staff consisted of a full-time chief, one deputy chief, three battalion chiefs, four captains, and around sixty members. They responded to four hundred emergency calls a year with an assortment of four fire engines, two snorkel units, a tower ladder, two reserve machines, and several smaller pieces of equipment.

The Post Office

Postal service in the village started in a corner of Jacob Munster's little grocery store in 1899. For ten years Munster sold stamps, and, with his daughters' help, stuffed mail in general delivery boxes. From 1909 to 1940, Munster had no Post Office. Mail was delivered to homes on "Rural Free Delivery Route 1, Hammond." Richard Huizenga of Highland delivered Munster's R.F.D. mail for twenty years.

In October 1940, the Hammond Post Office finally commenced home delivery to Munster. Munster had a "contract" Post Office for the first time "in many years" in 1941 after Phillip Schuringa, proprietor of the Munster Cash Grocery in the former Munster Store building, agreed to sell stamps, manage the General Delivery service, and tend to parcel post matters. Until then, most patrons did their postal business in Lansing or Highland. Herbert Postma, the town's lone letter carrier until 1946, traded stamps for pennies left in the mailboxes. Cornelius Vander Vaart next assumed that duty.

In 1948, after a year of rumors, the Hammond postmaster admitted that Munster was probably entitled to a Post Office, but, since townspeople did most of their postal business out of town, could not support one, and refused a petition for a Munster Post Office. A year later the *Times* called Munster the "NATION'S BIGGEST LITTLE TOWN WITHOUT POST OFFICE BUILDING," and charged townspeople with "indifference to or ignorance of practical postal business sense."

Sutter's Market on Ridge Road, then the site of another contract Post Office, sold stamps and money orders, and managed Parcel Post until 1948. Four Hammond-based letter carriers made home deliveries in Munster. Other contract sites over the years included App's Drug Store at the corner of Ridge and Hohman, and the O'Donnell Music Shop.

In 1951 the Munster Businessmen's Association petitioned the Post Office for a permanent building. The first "official" Munster Post Office opened two years later on Ridge Road in a small brick and block building leased from C. D. Schoon. Receipts for the first year were under $10,000.

The first respectable Munster Post Office, a spacious, four-thousand-square-foot building in Market Square, was dedicated on September 26, 1964, by Congressman Ray Madden, with every town official present. Still a branch of the Hammond Post Office, the Munster building then employed thirteen letter carriers on six routes. Chester Guse, the station superintendent since 1955, was buried on the same day.

The Munster Library

The first Munster Library was established in 1940 as a branch of the Gary Public Library in the kindergarten room of the Munster School. Federal funds from a statewide WPA project underwrote the project. Rising school enrollments soon crowded it out. The next "library" was a Gary Public Library trailer that was parked twice a week either on the school grounds or by the Monon Railway tracks. That arrangement worked badly enough to start a campaign for a permanent library building.

Poorly paid librarians came and went regularly over the next few years. Mrs. Elsie Crumpacker, the first librarian, was a WPA appointee. Her assistant was Miss Margaret McCloud of the Gary Public Library. "Mrs. Miller" served until February 1942, and was replaced by Doris Comstock. Mrs. Virginia Stodgell of Griffith and Mrs. Orion Ford were librarians in 1944. Library hours varied between afternoons and early evenings.

As a stopgap measure, the Community Library Board bought the former Wicker Park Estates sales room, a twenty-by-twenty-foot uninsulated frame building, and dragged it to the northeast corner of Ridge and Howard. The total cost of the building, shelving, one

---

Munster Post Office not far from the site of Jacob Munster's first post office. (MHS photo)

table, six chairs, a librarian's desk, a coal stove, and two thousand books was $4,000. Federal funds again helped. It was used for nine years after it opened in March 1944. In 1946 the little room—somehow—held several thousand volumes, and by 1950, five thousand.

Librarian Mrs. Clarence Keller, also known as "Grandma" Keller, was an "elderly widow." Mrs. Kellar, who once cheerfully told a reporter that she was still "looking for a man," was very good with children. Starting in 1946 she kept hours in the "obsolete," little building three afternoons and evenings a week. Grandma died in 1951 at eighty-three, and was missed by many. Her replacement, Mrs. Walter (Evelyn) Freese, survived winter drafts with a blanket and warm bricks under her desk, and served the Munster Library for twenty-five years.

A seven-year-long campaign for a new building opened in 1949, with support from the Town Board and the joint boards of the Gary Public Library and the Lake County Library. Wilhelmina Kaske provided an ideal library site in her will, as a memorial to her husband, Hugo F. Kaske, and her late granddaughter, Jan VanSteenburg. With the help of the Lions Club, Phil Ravenscroft, president of the Munster Library Association, directed the fundraising campaign. Two hundred Munster citizens and several local businessmen donated $8,600 to the fund. A second drive in 1953 netted another $1,300.

Bids came in far higher than estimated. Architect Ray S. Kastendieck of Gary designed the one-story and basement building, and construction began in the spring of 1952. The contractor built the exterior, and the interior was finished with donated materials by volunteer labor.

The new library—still part of the Gary system—was on the south side of Ridge Road, near the school. The main floor housed the books, which had been hand-carried to the new site by the Boy Scouts. The building was dedicated on August 8, 1953. The basement contained a public meeting room and a small kitchen; later the Children's Department was moved downstairs. A thousand residents, mostly school children, then held library cards.

But clearly a growing town needed a better library, and within ten years plans for a new building were underway. In 1958 the Munster Library joined the secession movement from the Gary Public Library into the Lake County Public Library (LCPL) system. The wisdom of remaining with the LCPL was soon questioned. The Chamber of Commerce and the Town Board were shocked by the size of the new system's countywide bond issue to build thirteen new libraries, and saw it as a stalking horse for ever-higher taxes. But in 1966 the town fathers and the LCPL finally reached agreement.

Turner and Turner designed the building, and construction began on a Calumet Avenue site in January 1967. On moving day, the collection was boxed by the Munster Women's Club and the Junior Women's Club, both long-term library supporters, and trucked to the new building. The library opened to the public on March 4, 1968.

Munster Public Library on Ridge Road. (MHS photo)

The new building was light years ahead of the little brick structure on Ridge Road. With sixty-three thousand square feet of floor space, it could shelve twenty-five thousand volumes. The library had air conditioning, carpeting, too-bright orange walls, and a parking lot. Furnishings for the community meeting room were donated by the Munster Junior Women's Club.

The new library was an instant success. Circulation increased rapidly. By 1980, when a nine-thousand-square-foot North Wing more than doubled the size of the original structure, the collection contained over forty thousand titles. That addition provided more shelving space, new service areas, meeting rooms, an area for a local history collection, an audiovisual area, and more parking spaces.

The library had remarkably few head librarians over the years. Charlotte Picha served from 1972 to 1989, and was succeeded by Linda Dunn, who remained active in 2006. By the early 1980s, six employees managed a collection of forty-two thousand volumes. Annual circulation was over one hundred thousand items.

Technology was the new order of the day: on-line access to the collection began in 1984, cable television access arrived in 1985, videos in 1986, and at about the same time, computer-aided reference searches went on-stream. The first CDs arrived in 1987. Phonograph records were retired in the 1990s. The library's new world of audio-visual media included personal computers with access to the Internet and databases (1997). Videos arrived in 1998, DVDs in 2000. More traditionally, the library added a Bestsellers Express collection and a paperback exchange in 2001.

Remodeling and updating made the library a less utilitarian-looking place. Better lighting helped, and the once so-trendy orange walls were repainted in 1995. In 1996 the building received new carpeting, and seating was reupholstered. By 2007 the Munster Public Library was a heavily used, widely respected, and mighty useful town institution.

A Town of Many Parks

The Munster Lions Club was the town's leading service group. The forty-one charter members of 1938 were a cross-section of town movers and shakers: Albert Bacon (the first club president), Russell F. McNutt, Ed F. Bennett, Francis M. Timm, Jr., Colin S. Howat, Henry Harder, Frank Warman, and others. Over the years club membership has averaged around one hundred.

The Lions sponsored a wide variety of civic events and projects, most of which were the responsibility of the town government a half-century later. For decades the Lions sponsored Scout Troop 33. In 1939 the club sponsored a Christmas Lighting Contest. In 1941 members worked on mosquito abatement and a townwide clean-up week.

Rotary sponsored a boys' basketball team, a girls' volleyball team, dances for teenagers, summer concerts by Martin Jabaay's Town Band, and home beautification projects. In 1942 the club sponsored a Halloween Party in the gym at the Munster School. In later years the club bought athletic equipment for the schools, supported musical organizations, underwrote trips abroad for language students, and funded QUEST, a middle-school drug education program.

Munster Public Library on Calumet Avenue, as it looked when it was new in 1968. (MHS photo)

The first of many Lions Club benefit events was a concert by the Calumet Industrial Glee Club of South Chicago in 1938. Car raffles and festivals raised $9,000. Beginning in 1948 the public tested its skills at target and trap shooting at the Lions Club Turkey Shoots (no one actually shot a turkey). Prizes were awarded in the form of packaged turkeys, ducks, and chickens. A rented tent housed refreshments, and, wonder of wonders, a television set was tuned to "all the big games." The Annual Steak Fry, later renamed the Steak and Chicken Grill, was a lasting and popular event. The Community Park Fall Festival began in 1951. The Horse Show galloped for ten years after 1954. In 1955 the Lions began their most durable annual event, the annual Pancake Breakfast. Profits went to the park and other civic projects.

The Lions Club's greatest contribution to the town was Community Park. The Lions Civic Improvement Committee was formed in 1948 with Al Bacon as chair. P. H. Mueller and Homer O. Hitt were active members. The park was planned to offer organized recreational programs, sports fields, playgrounds, perhaps a pond for fishing and swimming, a bandstand, tennis courts, picnic grounds, an ice skating rink, and even a Boy Scout camping area.

In 1949 the Lions bought fourteen acres of land beside Calumet Avenue from Vic Kirsch and the E. C. Minas Investment Trust. Their intention was to eventually donate the park to the town. In 1951 "Lions Acres," as it was first called, was transferred to the Munster Community Park Association, Inc. Association Board members were drawn from several civic organizations, although the Lions Club continued to sponsor many park events. Support came from donations and from townspeople who joined the Association for $2—later, $3—a year. In 1949 the Lions raised over $4,300 for a Community Park social center.

The Association gradually enlarged the park. A variety of events and membership fees raised $3,000 in 1957, $6,400 in 1968. Businessmen, Joe Burger among them, contributed cash, services, and materials. Productions of local playwright Lee Allen's plays raised more money for the park. By 1955 the Association had collected $24,000. The formal dedication took place on July 1, 1957, as part of the Munster Golden Anniversary Celebration, which, according to Town Board President William Jabaay, "would be quiet and tranquil in keeping with the climate of the town."

Lions Turkey Shoot. To raise money for local charities, particularly Community Park, the Munster Lions Club sponsored an annual Turkey Shoot. Participants here were Jack Keener, Irving Lindman, Ora Vergin, and Fred Anderson.

Scouts at the second annual Horse Show at Community Park, 1956. (MHS photo)

Eleanor Kennedy pitches for the Maroon Team in the Munster Girls Softball Instructional League. (Photo by her dad, Steven Kennedy)

Brad Sikora gets a single to start the Little League Indians game, July 1, 2006.

The Munster Pool, before the High School was built. In the foreground is the "baby pool," the large pool is in the background. (MHS photo)

Community Park was a great success. Over the years the "Lions Shelter," a warming house, and washrooms were added. In 1964 volunteers planted hundreds of seedling trees in the park. Beginning in 1966, the Chamber of Commerce sponsored Fourth of July Festivals in the park, with grand parades, dances, and fireworks. Four hundred Little Leaguers played baseball every summer on four diamonds.

In 1977, its work complete, the Community Park Association deeded Community Park to the town. Without a single tax dollar, a quarter century of civic-spirited cooperation had created a thirty-three-acre park and equipped it with baseball fields, tennis courts, a Scout shelter, a pavilion, a Social Center, and a variety of other facilities.

With a master plan in hand, in 1978 the Parks and Recreation Board issued a half-million-dollar bond issue to buy property on the east side of Community Park for better access, more parking, and for improvements in park facilities. Banquet and meeting facilities were added to the Social Center in 1980, and have well served a variety of senior citizens' and other activities. In 1994 a bond sale funded a $1.2-million general facelift of Community Park.

As Munster celebrated its centennial, Community Park housed seven baseball diamonds, four basketball courts, ten tennis courts, a skate park, a playground, concession stands, restrooms, and a shelter. Countless Little League, softball, and Babe Ruth Baseball games were played there every summer. Community was still Munster's largest fully developed park in 2006.

The Munster Pool at the south end of the park was also a popular spot. The Munster Women's Club planned the project in 1955 and donated startup funds. Volunteers in "Operation Cool Plunge" sent out mass mailings and knocked on doors. The Lions, Panhellenic, the Chamber of Commerce, and the Independence Park Association also made contributions.

The pool complex was built for around $100,000 on a site provided by O. C. Robbins. Thomas Cosgrove chaired a nonprofit Pool Corporation that issued bonds that covered much of the cost of construction. In October 1955 the first two bonds were sold to Miss Myrtle Munster and Mrs. Nellie Weeldon, daughters of Jacob Munster. Season memberships paid the bills.

Lions Club Shelter and Memorial Grove dedication on June 10, 1995. In recognition of its work in creating and supporting Community Park, Munster Parks and Recreation named the park's roadway in honor of the Munster Lions Club. (Munster Parks photo)

The Munster Pool opened in the summer of 1956, and soon found an abundance of members. Long-term Pool Manager and Coach Mike Niksic's swim teams for youths eight to seventeen years old were undefeated between 1956 and 1972. The Munster High School swim dynasty enjoyed a major head start from this community pool.

By 1990 the pool corporation had lost its nonprofit status, and was being hounded by the county for back taxes. Parks and Recreation assumed responsibility for the operation. In 2002 the aging 1956 pool was replaced, at a cost of $3.2 million. The new Munster Pool was bigger, with a three-lane lap pool, a diving well, a water slide, and a sand volleyball court. A thousand members signed up for its first season.

The town Parks and Recreation Department had been organized back in June 1966, principally as a public agency to seek grants to help close the landfill. But the Parks Board was also responsible for existing parks, and was charged with developing a master town parks plan. Rather than depend on volunteers, the Parks Board built a paid staff, to manage existing parks and supervise organized activities.

Several directors held office, and each contributed to the development of a remarkable park system. Allan Hughes was park director from 1976 to 1980, Richard Murray from 1980 to 1989. Kevin Briski, who came from Mishawaka, served from 1990 to 1998, and Charles Gardiner, from 1998 to 2005. Robert M. O'Shaughnessy assumed the post in 2005.

At first the Parks Board concentrated on buying land. In 1969 the Parks Board and the School Town jointly paid $50,000 for thirty-two acres on Columbia Avenue. Most of that purchase became the Middle School campus, but the Parks Board retained seven acres on Ridge Road. A $90,000 grant from the Youth Conservation Corps, a state-federal organization, was used to develop Bieker Woods Nature Preserve and establish a tree nursery. By 1973, five new parks were underway. In 1975 a $535,000 bond issue supported four major park projects. In 1979 the Parks Department moved into the former Munster Store, and remained there until the new Municipal Center was completed in 1982. The little store was torn down in 1986.

More parks were coming: in 1979 the town required developers to set aside parkland in each subdivision. Some became playgrounds, but a few were given walking trails and ball fields. In 1991 Parks and Recreation prepared a five-year plan for subdivision parks, and sought matching funds for their development. Improvements for Sunnyside, Frank Hammond, Ridgeway (now Grove), and Bluebird Parks cost $720,000.

Parks and Recreation built eight Neighborhood Parks in locations about town. Some, like Beech, Frank H. Hammond, and White Oak Parks (1996), contain soccer fields, baseball diamonds, and basketball and tennis courts. Others ranged from "tot lots" to a few acres. Circle Park in Independence Park was a basketball court. Five Playground Parks hosted platoons of moms, kiddies, strollers, and tricycles.

Three were classed as Natural/Historic Parks. The sites of two of those were sold to the town by Helen Kaske Bieker in 1986. Included on one were her home (on which she retained a life right) and a barn. She passed on two years later.

The drop slide at the new Munster Community Pool. (Munster Parks photo)

The Park Board had made a "wise investment" in a site noted for "its natural beauty, its historic value and its contribution to the open space plan of the community." Eventually dubbed Heritage Park, the buildings on the eastern site needed immediate stabilization. The 1909 Kaske House was structurally sound, but desperately needed a new roof, rewiring, and a general restoration.

A Bieker Property Committee, made up of Town Councilors, Park Board members, Heritage Commissioners, and Historical Society members, including Elaine Olson, Walter Helminski, James Gustat, and others, was charged with determining future uses of the Bieker properties. The committee elected to keep the woods "woodsy," rather than create a "dolled up" park. Among the other ideas discussed for the property was the creation of a historic village around a green.

Good things and one bad thing followed. The Kaske House was restored and, in 1998, placed on the National Historic Register. It became a museum of early Munster life, maintained by volunteers from the Munster Historical Society. In 1999 the Park Board built a handsome Gazebo for public gatherings, weddings, and summer concerts. A forty-foot-tall antique windmill from C. D. Schoon's Wheatfield farm was installed on the property.

On the bad side, in 2002 the barn—one of the last in town—was burned to the ground, probably by vandals. The Society's collection of antique farm tools, housed in the barn, was destroyed. In 2006 plans were afoot for a replacement of the barn and a reconstruction of the Brass Tavern; will stagecoaches once again clatter down the Ridge?

The western portion of the property became Bieker Woods Nature Preserve. Much of the site had once been open fields, and was overgrown with a mixture of second growth elms, maples, sycamores, locusts, oak, hickory, and invasive trees. One part was indeed native woods with old growth timber. The site, perhaps a tad charitably, was described by District Forester Steve E. Winicker as "a unique and interesting community of plants and animals which is unusual in an urban setting."

The Stallbohm Barn had stood for more than one hundred years when it burned to the ground in 2002. (1982 photo by Lance Trusty)

The Gazebo at Heritage Park has become a popular place for weddings, often with Clerk-Treasurer David Shafer presiding. (MHS photo)

CHAPTER VIII MUNSTER INSTITUTIONS • 207

The U.S. Department of the Interior provided $36,000 in 1980 for the development of Bieker Woods as a site for environmental education in the schools. A new work machine—two dozen teenagers—cleared the dead wood and excess shrubbery and planted native species. Trails were laid out and marked. Bieker Woods became a popular ecological center or "outdoor lab" and the focus of school science projects. An autumn Night Walk in the "haunted woods" attracted fans of ghosts, owls and other spooky things.

A third and smaller "historic" park faced the Kaske House across Ridge Road. The Munster Rotary Club was organized in 1960 with twenty members, elected James C. Johnson president, and soon joined into town affairs. Rotary actively supported a tree-planting program, Little League, equipment purchases for the Athletic Association, and other community projects. For the Bicentennial, in 1976 the Rotarians commissioned Hammond sculptor Fred Holly and Bill Ores to design and build iconic sculptures of an Indian, a settler, and a steelworker. They were made with Cor-Ten® steel donated by the Gary Works of US Steel, and mounted in Rotary Club Park.

The Parks Department also sponsored a wide range of trips, classes, sports leagues, a Summer Arts and Crafts Fair that began in 1981, and a Spring Arts and Crafts Fair after 1995, summer concerts, and a Blues, Jazz, and Fine Arts Festival. Sledding began in 1979 on "Mt. Trashmore" (more officially, Mt. Munster), a "made" hill towering some eighty feet above Calumet Avenue. In the summers many struggled through the popular Mt. Trashmore mountain bike competition.

Back in 1968 Parks and Recreation had developed a plan for a two hundred-plus-acre park, to include the still-active brickyard, the clayhole, a pond, and Mt. Trashmore. In 1975 the *Times* sniffily predicted that in twenty years "Munster residents will be cavorting all over a twenty-acre pile of garbage." Fair game: a park did seem an unlikely outcome for a sanitary landfill then in daily use by four towns. But the last cell was closed in July 2004, and after a major reclamation project, the area was dubbed Centennial Park and was scheduled to open in July 2007 at a cost of over $13 million.

The existing Lakewood Park was absorbed into the new park in 2005. Lakewood had opened in 2001 near the brickyard with a playground, soccer fields, and a pavilion. A sculpture walk, biking tails, and a manicured lake were planned for the near future. Other facilities planned for Centennial Park were—after many truckloads of fill and a lot of earthmoving—a nine-hole golf course, a clubhouse, a pro shop, a grill, a driving range, and a one-bay fire station. The park would be well lighted and was intended for year-round use. Co-sponsors of the new Centennial Park included the ever-ready Lions Club and the Munster Civic Foundation.

By 2006, Parks and Recreation was managing twenty-three parks with a $1.4-million annual budget drawn from programs, local taxes, state and federal grants, and the Civic Foundation.

The Community Veterans Memorial was dedicated on Sunday, June 1, 2003. (Kevin Nowaczyk photo)

Community Veterans Memorial, a triangular, nine-acre park at the intersection of Calumet, Columbia, and Superior Avenues, was a more serious place. The idea for the memorial originated among veterans in 1999, and was carried forward by Donald S. Powers and Edward P. Robinson. The project manager was former Town Councilman Don P. Johnson.

Seed money for the $4-million project was provided by the Community Hospital; development costs were absorbed by the Hospital, the Hospital Auxiliary, and American Legion Post 168. Grants and donations came from the Community Foundation, businesses, the U.S. Army, and many individuals. The Memorial was dedicated on June 1, 2003.

Local veterans served as thematic advisors. The Memorial depicted the contributions of those who served in America's twentieth-century wars. Architect Fred Kaplan drew up the overall plans; artists Omri and Julie Rotblatt-Amrany created the highly detailed, realistic, life-size bronzes; the landscaping was designed by Cindy Jo Berry, using indigenous plant material and structures that reflected actual battlefields. Explanatory texts were displayed on bronze plaques. Several military artifacts were either salvaged or recreated, including a remarkably realistic P-51 fighter plane tail section and a real Vietnam-era helicopter.

Perhaps a hundred thousand visitors walk its inspiring pathways annually. The Community Foundation contributed a pavilion, which was dedicated in 2006 and leased to the Memorial. Plans were made to build an endowment, and eventually Veterans' Memorial will join the town park system.

And a Town of Many Churches

In 2006, twenty-two churches and one monastery-church were active in Munster, ranging from the oldest, the "Munster Church," as the Christian Reformed Church on the corner of Ridge and Hohman was known, to a remarkable new "mega-church," the Family Christian Center on Forty-fifth Street. In between, Munster was home to a Catholic Parish, a variety of Protestant churches, a Korean Church, and one Ukrainian Church.

Edward Robinson tells of the history of the memorial project. (Kevin Nowaczyk photo)

After the dedication, visitors tour the memorial. (Kevin Nowaczyk photo)

The "Dutch" or First Christian Reformed Church was organized in 1870 by thirteen Dutch-American families. Until 1900 services were held in a rather plain wooden building. A much larger church was dedicated in 1900, and a parsonage in 1914.

Separations, called "swarming" by the churches involved, affected the congregation in the twentieth century. In 1908, prompted by the size of the congregation rather than theological issues, thirty-eight families departed, with good will on all sides, to organize a "daughter" Christian Reformed Church in Highland.

For decades language debates roiled the last Reformed church in the area to hold services in Dutch. Evening services were first conducted in English in 1914. In 1919 language issues compelled forty families to form the First Christian Reformed Church of Lansing. But the language question continued; for many years even the church records were written in "Dutchlish." The 1928–29 financial report referred to "Licht, Kerk and Chapel," and "Organisten." By then services were mostly in English, but the use of Dutch continued as late as 1954.

In 1928 the church young people donated a new organ. The congregation had expanded so much by the early 1930s that services were sometimes held in the Munster School. A major expansion of the building increased seating from four to six hundred in 1940. Two charter members of the church, Dingeman A. Jabaay and his sister, Mrs. John Broertjes, were then still active.

The most terrible event in the congregation's history occurred on January 3, 1952. Fire destroyed the wooden church, two years after a general remodeling. But after three years as guests in Lansing churches, on February 2, 1954, a new "simplified Gothic" church and a new parsonage were dedicated. By 1981 the Christian Reformed Church had over a thousand members. The congregation neared twelve hundred in 1990.

In 1945, Catholic Bishop John Francis Noll of Fort Wayne concluded that it was time to establish a Munster Parish. Father Robert B. Weis, a Hammond native and the assistant pastor in Griffith, was charged with the task. Father Weis found 150 willing Catholic families, a three-acre site on Calumet just south of Ridge Road was purchased, and the first St. Thomas More Church was quickly built by the men of the new parish. The first Mass was celebrated in that homely, asbestos-shingled box on February 25, 1946.

Munster Christian Reformed Church, the first church organized in the town.

Three years later a five-hundred-seat permanent church and a combined elementary school and convent for the teaching Sisters of St. Benedict, were dedicated. A parish activities building was completed in 1954. And in 1970, the current, modern-styled twelve-hundred-seat church was completed. The second church building was incorporated into the growing parochial school.

Father Weis was joined by an assistant pastor, the Reverend William J. Gieranowski, in 1951. Founding Father Weis was elevated to the rank of monsignor in 1984, retired a year later, and passed on in 1992. He was succeeded in 1985 by Monsignor Carl Mengeling, who was assisted by Fathers Joseph Angotti and Andrew Malarz. The church celebrated its fiftieth anniversary in 1995. In 2006 Fathers Michael Yadron and Michael Hoffman were the parish priests for over five thousand families.

The 1950s brought more churches to town. In 1950 after fighting with the Free Polish Army in World War II and forced stays in Siberia and Communist-dominated Poland, four Friars in the Order of Discalced (barefoot) Carmelites, led by Father Bernard Ciesielski, arrived in Hammond. Two years later the order purchased the former Mount Mercy Sanatorium on Ridge Road near White Oak, and built a sanctuary.

The Carmelites soon added a monastery, a church, a chapel, and ten grotto-shrines decorated with rare stones, sculptures, and murals. They planted trees, shrubs, gardens, and lawns. A new chapel was completed in 1991. The shrine commemorated Polish civilization and culture, and was a popular destination for pilgrims. The friars conducted services and tours. Thirteen priests and brothers were in residence in 2000, when the order celebrated its golden anniversary.

St. Thomas More Catholic Church on Calumet Avenue.

Other arrivals included the Munster Bible Church. The congregation was an independent and fundamentalist group of forty-seven families, organized by the American Sunday School Union in 1949. Congregation members built the church between 1949 and 1952. Ridge United Methodist Church was organized with fifty-eight members in 1955 as Munster Methodist Church. For five years the congregation met in the Independence Park Community Hall, Burns Funeral Home, and upstairs in Town Hall. In 1961 the congregation moved to a new church on a spacious site on Columbia Avenue at Park Drive. A Sanctuary was added in 1984.

Trinity Reformed Church was a daughter church of the First reformed Church of Lansing. Organized in 1956, the congregation moved to a handsome church on the corner of Ridge and Columbia a year later. By the 1980s 140 families were active in the congregation.

Even more churches arrived during the 1960s. With a congregation of a hundred families drawn from several towns, St. Nicholas of Myra Byzantine Slavonic Catholic Church was dedicated in 1963 at Broadmoor and Columbia. The church and parish social center were combined in one building. A Byzantine Rite Church, its roots had been planted in Hammond in 1922.

Ridge United Methodist Church on Columbia Avenue.

Trinity Reformed Church on Ridge Road, a daughter church of First Reformed Church in Lansing.

St. Nicholas of Myra Byzantine Slavonic Catholic Church on Columbia Avenue.

Westminster Presbyterian Church on Columbia about 1967. (MHS photo)

Munster First Church of the Nazarene moved from Maywood in 1965 into a contemporary-style, 288-seat church with fourteen Sunday school rooms and a nursery at the of White Oak and Fran-Lin. After merging with two Hammond churches, it became Fairmeadow Community Church of the Nazarene.

Westminster Presbyterian Church was organized in 1961 by eight families in the First Presbyterian Church of Hammond. An open meeting at Town Hall in 1961 attracted more members, and Westminster was formally organized a year later. Within a year the congregation had grown to more than two hundred members, and reached three hundred a year later.

Services were held over the next few years in various locations. A site at the corner of Elliott and Columbia was purchased, and a two-hundred-seat, modern-styled church was dedicated on Palm Sunday, 1965, with five hundred members present. Several wings were added over the years.

The First Church of God had been organized in 1935, and met in homes and storefronts in Hammond until a church was built on 173rd and Jackson in 1950. An expanded congregation led to sale of that edifice, and in 1968 the congregation moved to a new church on Ridgeway.

St. Josephat Ukranian Catholic Church also joined the roster in 1968. Affiliated with St. Nicholas Byzantine Rite Catholic Diocese in Chicago, St. Josephat Parish had been formed in 1958; the congregation met at first in a home, then a storefront, then in a church on Columbia Avenue in Hammond. A site at Ridge and White Oak in Munster was purchased in 1963, and a new church was dedicated in 1968.

The religious migrations slowed a bit in the 1970s. South Side Christian Church had originated in 1920 in a rented tent on the corner of 165th Street and Madison in Hammond. After a fire consumed most of the congregation's second Hammond church in 1974, the members decided to move to Munster, bought land, and dedicated a new church on Broadmoor in 1977.

St Paul's Evangelical Lutheran Church on Harrison Avenue is affiliated with the conservative Missouri Synod. The church began its ministry in 1888 in Hammond with a German-American congregation. The old church on Erie Street in Hammond was closed

Temple Beth-El on South Columbia Avenue.

in 1977, and St. Paul's moved into its mission chapel on Columbia in Munster. In 1980 the congregation moved to a new, contemporary-design church on Harrison and Briar Lane. The mission site was sold to the Salvation Army.

St. Paul's Episcopal Church, at Columbia and Park, was built in 1989 on a site purchased from Helen Bieker. Eighty-five families were active in the congregation. In 1996 the church added a spacious parish hall, the "Cloister in the Woods." By 2006 the congregation had grown to almost two hundred families.

Temple Beth-El was founded in 1911 as a Reform Congregation, and eventually occupied a building on Hohman at Mason Street in Hammond. In 1955 the congregation moved to a larger temple on Hohman, still in Hammond. The congregation moved into a modern-styled building on Columbia Avenue in 1999. Another Hammond temple, Congregation Beth-Israel, broke ground for a new temple on Calumet Avenue in 2005.

The Family Christian Center (FCC) on Forty-fifth Street was one of America's new megachurches. Founded in Hessville in 1953, in 1974 it moved to North Broad Street in Griffith, and in 1996 its four thousand members settled into to a brand-new Center on Forty-fifth Street in Munster. The Family Christian Center was readily identifiable by its seventy-foot cross on the front of the building, with a life-size Last Supper scene in its center.

The Reverends Dr. Stephan K. Munsey and Melodye Munsey led a "modern" church. Reverend Munsey was quoted as saying "If churches don't change, they will die." Reverend Munsey preached from a boat, with electronic access to the rumble of thunder and flash of lightning for emphasis during his sermons.

The Center was a busy place: some twenty thousand people from several communities visited on religious holidays and many attended a variety of events all week long. Visitors could study a "set" of Jerusalem with a real dirt road. A ten-thousand-seat Performing Arts Center with a two-hundred-by-one-hundred-foot stage offered seasonal productions, including an annual Passion Play. FCC was definitely part of a new scheme of religious things.

Family Christian Center on Forty-fifth Street.

RIDGE RD
30TH PL
FULLERTON AV
RIDGEWAY AV
FAIRWAY AV
SEBERGER DR
SOUTH ST
TERRACE DR
SUNSET LN
BRIAR LN
LAWNDALE DR
SYCAMORE LN
MAPLE LN
MORAINE DR
HOHMAN AV
HARRISON AV
MONROE AV
MADISON AV
HOWARD
GREENWOOD AV
BEECH AV
WALNUT DR
WHITE OAK AV
CASTLE DR
33RD
PARK DR
SCHREIBER
OAK PARK DR
TIMRICK DR
MEADOW LN
45TH ST
MARGO LN
GLASTONBURY ST
MUNSTER
CONSERVATORY
of
MUSIC
BALDWIN
PIANOS - ORGANS

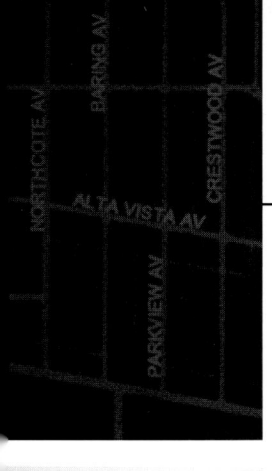

Bibliography

Chrzastowski, Michael J and Thompson, Todd A. 1992. "Late Wisconsin and Holocene coastal evolution of the southern shore of Lake Michigan." *Quaternary Coasts of the United States: Marine and Lacustrine Systems*, SEPM Special Publication No. 48 pp.397–413.

Division of Education, Purdue University. *Report on a Cooperative Study of School Building Needs of the Munster City Schools, Munster, Indiana*. West Lafayette: 1957.

Eenigenburg, Harry. *Early History of the Calumet Region*. N.p.: 1935.

Hansen, Diane. "Town of Munster, 1982–2003." Research paper, Purdue University Calumet: 2003.

Kaske, Wilhelmina Stallbohm. "Early Days in Munster," in Alice M. Demmon, Jesse Little, Philip M. McNay, and Arthur G. Taylor, eds., *History of Lake County* XI. Crown Point: Calumet Press, 1934.

League of Women Voters. *Munster: A Guide to Your Community*. Munster: 1976.

McDonough & Co. *Directory 1925–1927*. (For Munster, Highland, Griffith, Schererville, St. John, Dyer). Chicago: 1925.

Moore, Powell A. *The Calumet Region: Indiana's Last Frontier*. Reprinted, with an "Afterword" by Lance Trusty, "The Calumet Region, 1933–1977." Indianapolis: Indiana Historical Bureau, 1959, 1977.

Munster, the Centennial Committee. *Centennial of the First Christian Reformed Church, Munster, Indiana*. Munster: 1970.

Munster Christian Reformed Church. *Diamond Jubilee, 1870–1945*. Munster: 1945.

Munster League of Women Voters. *Community Housing Survey, Munster, Indiana*. Munster: 1970.

Munster Historical Society, comp. *Munster Community Organizations and Churches*. Munster: 1976.

Munster Junior Women's Club. *Munster, This is Our Town, 1857–1957*. Munster: 1957.

Northern Indiana Public Service Company. Northern Indiana "An Area of Challenging Opportunities." Hammond: 1977.

Norbert J. Nelson, et al. *The School Town of Munster: Looking Toward the Future, Munster, Indiana*. An Inter-University Study. Purdue University: West Lafayette, 1968.

Schoon, Kenneth J. *Calumet Beginnings: Ancient Shorelines and Settlements at the South End of Lake Michigan*. Bloomington: Indiana University Press, 2003.

Schoon, Kenneth J. and Schoon, Margaret S. *Portraits of a Ridge Family: The Jacob Schoons*. Munster; 1981.

Trusty, Lance. *Town on the Ridge: A History of Munster, Indiana*. Illustrations Collected and Prepared by Kenneth J. Schoon. Hammond: The Regional Studies Institute, Purdue University Calumet, 1982.

U.S. Works Progress Administration. "Final Report, Real Property Survey of Lake County, Indiana." Mimeographed, N.p., 1936.

NEWSPAPERS:
The Times (Lake County, Hammond, Northwest Indiana)
Sun-Journal. (Various editions)

Munster Conservatory of Music on Calumet Avenue. (Calumet Regional Archives photo)

30TH PL
RIDGE RD
HARRISON AV
MONROE AV
SEBERGER DR
RIDGEWAY AV
FULLERTON AV
HOWARD
RIDGEWAY AV
FAIRWAY AV
TERRACE DR
SOUTH ST
RIDGE RD
GREENWOOD AV
BEECH AV
WALNUT DR
WHITE OAK AV
CASTLE DR
SUNSET LN
BRIAR LN
BRIAR LN
33RD
HOHMAN AV
LAWNDALE DR
MONROE AV
OAK PARK DR
RIDGE RD
PARK DR
SYCAMORE LN
MAPLE LN
EVERGREE
MEADOW LN
TIMRICK DR
45TH ST
MARGO LN
MUNSTER PUBLIC SCHOOL
GLASTONBURY ST
BANBURY PL
LEICESTER RD
INDIANA PKWY
PROGRESS AV
VALPARAISO DR
CALUMET AV
THICKET LN
REDBUD RD
CRIMSON TREE LN
TAMARACK DR
FITZGERALD DR

Index

A

Able, Deputy Marshal, 190
Ace Hardware, 16
Adley, M., 147
Adley, R., 129
Aetna Industrial Park, 154
Ahlgrim, Everett, 186
Airport, 63, 95, 96, 163
Allen, Lee, 136, 203
Allen, Maurice, 89, 94
Al's Barber Shop, 90
Alt, Edward, 183, 184
Alvarez, Carlos, 194
Amber, Douglas, 160
Ambulance service, 199
American Brick Company, 79, 162, 163
American Legion, 117, 209
American Oil, 184
American Savings FSB, 138
Anderson, Ardith, 186
Anderson, Eric, 153, 166
Anderson, Fred, 203
Anderson, Grace, 100
Anderson, Vernon, 95
Andrews, Jake, 70
Angotti, Joseph, 211
Animal Control Commission, 153
Annexation, 61, 92, 94–95, 116
Another Unnecessary Extravagance, 175
Anton's Calumet Restaurant, 142
Apartments, 112, 144, 151, 161, 172
A&P Food Store, 138
App, J. P., 117
App's Drug Store, 117, 200
Archer, Helen, 186
Architectural Accents, 175–176
Aring, Egbert, 77
Armitage, Hazel, 87
Armstrong, Clarence, 87, 107
ATG Corporation, 172
Aurelius, Michael, 153

B

Babincsak, Walter, 190
Bachman, William J., 179
Bachman and Bertram, 114, 145, 183
Bacon, A. H., 107
Bacon, Al, 202, 203
Bacon, Jean, 100
Bailey, W., 129
Bailly, Joseph, 33
Bailly Homestead, 32, 33–34
Baker, G., 147
Baker, Yvonne, 100
Baker family, 93
Bakker, Jacob, 62, 77
Bakker family, 49
Ball, Daniel, 194, 195
Banner Foods, 140
Banta, Jane, 100
Baptist Church, 115
Bartlett, Tim, 19
Baskin-Robbins, 140
Baudino, R., 147
Bayh, Birch, 185
Becker, Ida, 89
Beckman, Mary, 184
Beckman, T., 147
Beech Park, 206
Behling Gil and Son, 19
Belden Place, 113

Bellows, Randy, 129
Belman, Creighton, 82
Belman, W. C., 82
Belmont Avenue, 105
Belshaw, M. E., 106
Benedictine Sisters, 114–115
Benes, Marty, 79
Ben Franklin, 138
Bennett, E. N., 96
Bennett, Ed, 104, 107, 189, 202
Benoit, Norma, 153
Bensemmer, Robert, 106
Beratis, Louis, 192, 193
Berg, Bernard L., 100
Berghian, Pat, 129
Berry, Cindy Jo, 209
Bertagnolli, Margaret, 184
Betz, Frank, 95
Bicentennial celebration, 154–155, 207
Bieker, Helen Kaske, 40, 41, 163, 206, 215
Bieker, Lawrence, 40, 41
Bieker Property Committee, 207
Bieker Woods, 206, 207–208
Bike path, 169
Blake, M., 129
Blink, Jacob, 14
Blocker, Mark, 159
Bluebird Park, 206
Blues, Jazz, and Arts Festival, 14, 170
Bock Hardware, 90
Boender, B., 147
Boender, Chester, 102, 103, 105
Boender, Cornelius, 102, 103, 105
Boender, Douglas, 102, 103, 105, 130
Boender, Henry, 124
Boender, Martin, 88, 89
Boender Open Air Market, 97
Bogusz, J., 147
Bogusz, M., 147
Bohling Florists, 140
Bohn family, 49
Bolls, S., 147
Bolt, Henry, 76
Boonstra, Roger, 106
Bootee, Donald J., 175
Bouwkamp, Miss, 75
Bowman, Antonie, 44, 48
Bowman, Jannigje, 44
Bowman, Neeltje, 44
Bowman Displays, 175, 176
Boy Scouts, 108, 109, 201
Boy Scout Troop 33, 84, 87, 110, 120, 202
Branch, John, 77
Brant, William J., 128
Brass, Allan H., 36, 47
Brass, Cecilia, 36
Brass, Julia Watkins, 36
Brass, Oliver, 36
Brass Tavern, 29, 36–39, 65, 75, 207
Brauer, Hugh, 168
Brenner, Howard, 183, 184, 185
Briar Creek, 170, 172
Brick plant, 49, 77–79, 93, 121, 137, 162, 163
Brink, Leonard, 195
Brinson, Al, 160
Briski, Kevin, 206
Broadmoor Avenue viaduct, 167
Broadmoor Medical Plaza, 188
Broadmoor subdivision, 82
Broertjes, John, 49, 104
Broertjes, Mrs. John, 55, 210

Broertjes family, 49
Brogan, D., 129
Brown, Harry S., 61
Brown, Helen, 20, 166, 167
Brown, Sherry A., 193
Brundige, Beulah, 76
Buck, Bryan, 194
Buehler, J., 136, 147
Bulte, Peter, 81
Bultema, Harold, 102, 103, 105
Bultje, Martin, 78
Bunnell, John, 136, 137, 142, 153
Bunnell's Grocery, 112
Burger, Joseph, 129, 138–140, 184, 203
Burger, Mrs. Joseph, 138
Burger King, 140, 162
Burger's Grocery Store, 134, 135, 139, 141, 162
  cemetery beneath, 121
Burke, Leo J., 130
Burke's Furniture Store, 138
Burns Ditch, 24
Business, 15–16, 60, 61, 173–174
  1800s, 49
  early 1900s, 77–79
  between the wars, 89
  1950s, 121–124
  1960s, 138–142
  1970s, 162
Bus service, 66
Butkus, B., 147

C

Cable access, 178
Cady Marsh, 24, 53, 57
Cafe Elise, 16
Cain, M., 147
Caldwell, M. A., 88
Calumet Avenue, 13, 66, 132, 137, 162, 169
  at railroad tracks, 13, 83
Calumet Harley Davidson, 174
Calumet National Bank, 122, 123
Calumet Shopping Center, 15, 142, 169
Calumet Surgery Center, 188
Cambridge Court, 172
Camellia Drive, 161
Camp Wicker, 83
Cardiology Associates of Northwest Indiana, 188
Carey, Robert, 79, 162
Carmelite Monastery, 21, 211
Carpetland, 140
Carter, Carol, 100
Carter, Louise, 71
Cashman, Robert, 86
Cashman, William, 86
Castle Estates, 126, 161
Caviness, Violet E., 107
Cellular telephone towers, 168
Cemeteries, 57, 67, 84, 121
Centennial celebration, 11–12, 153
Centennial Park, 13, 208
Center for Visual and Performing Arts, 18, 178–180
Centier Bank, 16
Chamber of Commerce, 16, 18, 97, 99–100, 117, 170, 178, 205
Chapman, Charles, 189
Charlie's Ale House, 16
Chase Manor, 126
Chelich, Matt, 159

Munster Public School, later renamed Lanier Elementary School. (MHS photo)

About the Authors

LANCE TRUSTY IS PROFESSOR EMERITUS OF AMERICAN HISTORY AT PURDUE UNIVERSITY Calumet. He is a native of Hampton, Virginia, and holds an A.B. degree from the College of William and Mary and an A.M. and Ph.D. from Boston University. His specialties are antebellum American history and Calumet Regional history.

He has taught at Boston University, The Ohio State University, and, from 1964 to 2004, at Purdue University Calumet. At Purdue he served as department head and director of the Regional Studies Institute. He holds two distinguished teacher awards. He helped develop and taught a course on How to Study in College, which has been given in colleges and universities across America.

Professor Trusty has written several books and articles on American history and Calumet Regional history. He is currently recovering from researching and writing the present work.

Kenneth J. Schoon is a professor of science education and teaches methods of teaching science at Indiana University Northwest. He has an A.B. in geology and an M.S. in secondary education both from Indiana University and a Ph.D. in curriculum and instruction from Loyola University of Chicago. Since January of 1999 he has served the School of Education as associate dean.

In 1990, after twenty-two years of teaching middle and high school science, Dr. Schoon joined IUN's Urban Teacher Education Program (UTEP). In 1999 he was invited to join the Indiana University Faculty Colloquium on Excellence in Teaching (FACET).

Dr. Schoon's research interests center around local studies and misconceptions in science. He serves as the state membership director of Indiana Science Olympiad, a national middle and high school science competition, and works with the regional tournament at IUN. He is president of the Board of Indiana Dunes Environmental Learning Center at Camp Good Fellow. In Munster, he is a longtime member of the Munster Historical Society, the Munster Lions Club, the Munster Board of Parks and Recreation, and chairs the Centennial Committee.

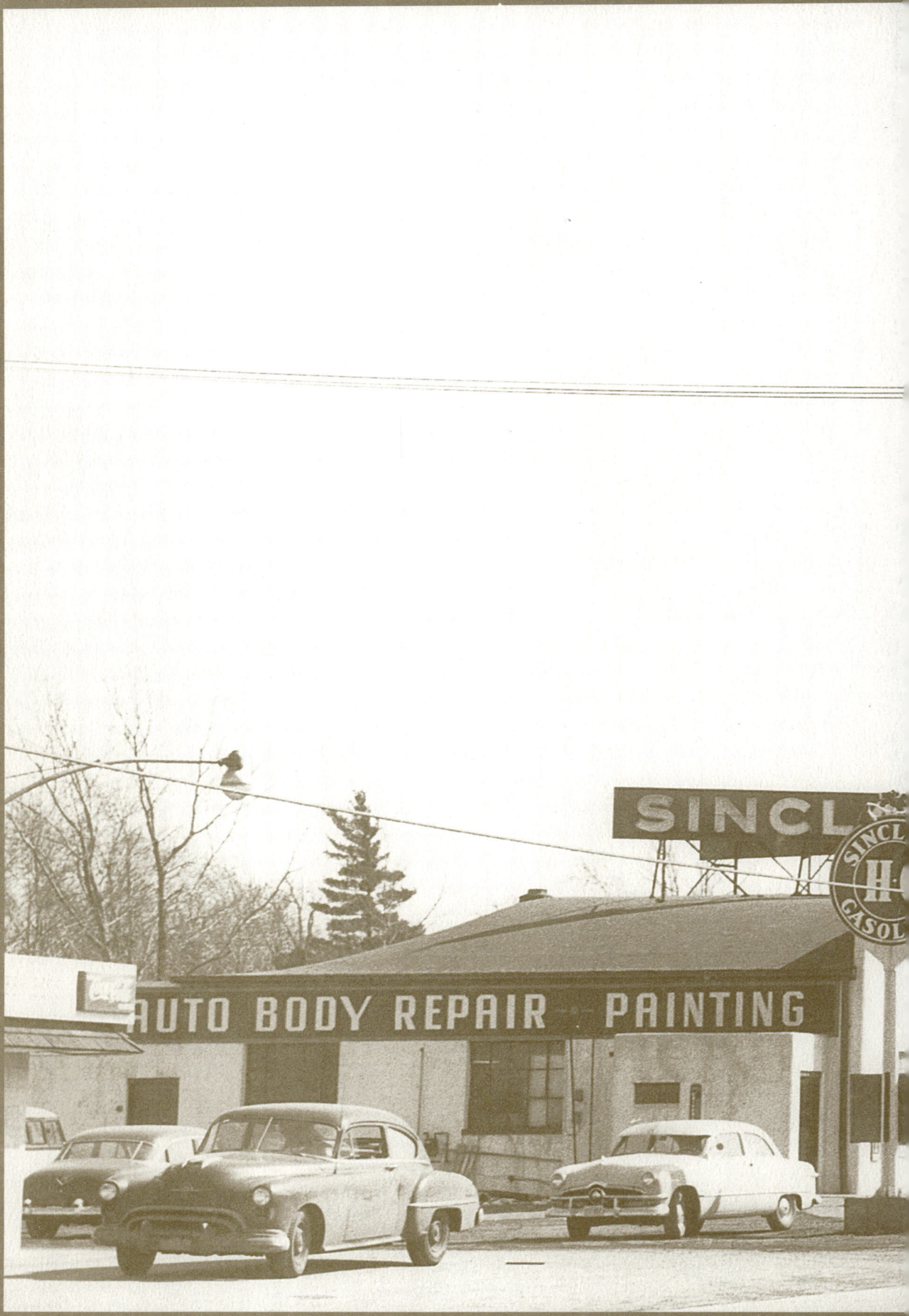
SINCL
AUTO BODY REPAIR PAINTING